Learning VMware Workstation Pro for Windows: Volume 2

Implementing and Managing VMware's Desktop Hypervisor Solution

Peter von Oven

Apress®

Learning VMware Workstation Pro for Windows: Volume 2: Implementing and Managing VMware's Desktop Hypervisor Solution

Peter von Oven
FAIRFORD, UK

ISBN-13 (pbk): 979-8-8688-0863-0 ISBN-13 (electronic): 979-8-8688-0864-7
https://doi.org/10.1007/979-8-8688-0864-7

Managing Director, Apress Media LLC: Welmoed Spahr
Acquisitions Editor: Aditee Mirashi
Development Editor: James Markham
Coordinating Editor: Kripa Joseph

Cover designed by eStudioCalamar

Cover image by Unsplash (www.unsplash.com)

Distributed to the book trade worldwide by Apress Media, LLC, 1 New York Plaza, New York, NY 10004, U.S.A. Phone 1-800-SPRINGER, fax (201) 348-4505, e-mail orders-ny@springer-sbm.com, or visit www.springeronline.com. Apress Media, LLC is a California LLC and the sole member (owner) is Springer Science + Business Media Finance Inc (SSBM Finance Inc). SSBM Finance Inc is a **Delaware** corporation.

For information on translations, please e-mail booktranslations@springernature.com; for reprint, paperback, or audio rights, please e-mail bookpermissions@springernature.com.

Apress titles may be purchased in bulk for academic, corporate, or promotional use. eBook versions and licenses are also available for most titles. For more information, reference our Print and eBook Bulk Sales web page at http://www.apress.com/bulk-sales.

Any source code or other supplementary material referenced by the author in this book is available to readers on GitHub (https://github.com/Apress). For more detailed information, please visit https://www.apress.com/gp/services/source-code.

If disposing of this product, please recycle the paper

As always, this book is dedicated to my family who have again supported me along the way while I have been busy writing.

Table of Contents

About the Author

Peter von Oven is an experienced technical consultant working closely with customers, partners, and vendors in designing technology solutions to meet business needs and deliver outcomes. During his career, Peter has presented at key IT events such as VMworld, IP EXPO, and various VMUG and CCUG events across the UK. He has also worked in senior presales roles and presales management roles for Fujitsu, HP, Citrix, and VMware and has been awarded VMware vExpert for the last ten years in a row, vExpert EUC for the last three consecutive years, vExpert Desktop Hypervisor, and more. He recently became part of the new Omnissa Tech Insiders program.

In 2016, Peter founded his own company specializing in application delivery. Today, he works with partners and vendors helping drive and deliver innovative technology solutions. He is also an avid author, having now written 19 books and made numerous videos about VMware end-user computing solutions. In his spare time, Peter volunteers as a STEM Ambassador, working with schools and colleges, helping the next generation develop the skills and confidence in building careers in technology. He is also a serving Royal Air Force Reservist, recently becoming a commissioned officer working with the Air Cadet organization.

Introduction

The VMware Workstation Pro solution is a type 2 desktop hypervisor solution that enables you to run virtual machines, containers, and Kubernetes clusters on your local PC or laptop. It provides the ideal solution for building and testing virtual machines locally before moving them into production.

This second book will focus on some of the more advanced features of VMware Workstation Pro.

Throughout this book, we will work proactively with the Workstation Pro solution to enable you to build and manage virtual machines and containers locally, using step-by-step instructions with real-life screenshots to demonstrate each key feature and how it works.

We start with a high-level overview of how VMware Workstation Pro works with running containers starting with a brief overview of how containers differ from virtual machines. Then, we will look at how to set up and configure VMware Workstation Pro for running containers and then take a deep dive into the **vctl** command that is used for managing container environments.

Following on from managing and working with containers, we will look at the **vmware** command for running Workstation Pro from the command line of the host machine.

In the next couple of chapters, we will look at the **vmrun** command, a command line utility available in Workstation Pro that allows you to control virtual machines and automate guest operating system actions on virtual machines, and then the Workstation Pro API.

After we have taken a look at support and troubleshooting tips, we will take a look at VMware Workstation Player, a cut down version of Workstation that is primarily used for running preconfigured virtual machines.

In the previous *Workstation Pro* book, Volume 1, we installed Windows-based operating systems as well as a completed vSphere cluster. In this second part, we are going to install a Linux-based virtual machine as well as an alternative hypervisor (Proxmox in this example).

The penultimate chapter will build on the installation of Workstation Pro that we covered in Volume 1, but in this second part, we will look at how to perform an unattended installation.

Finally, since Volume 1 of the book was published last year (2023), we are going to discuss all the new updates and features that have been launched since that book was published.

CHAPTER 1

Working with Containers

In this first chapter, although this book focuses on VMware Workstation Pro as the desktop hypervisor for hosting virtual machines, we are also going to look at one of the newer features that was introduced in Workstation Pro 16, and that is the ability to manage containers.

The ability to run containers in Workstation Pro started with the project Nautilus back in January 2020. Project Nautilus was a tech preview feature included in VMware Fusion, the Apple Mac version of Workstation Pro. It then became available in Workstation Pro version 16 controlled and managed by using the new vctl command line utility.

Before we start to get into the specific details of running containers, we are first going to take a step back and describe what a container actually is and how it differs from a virtual machine.

What Is a Container?

A question that often gets asked is "So how does a container differ from a virtual machine or hypervisor-based solution?" and why are we discussing this in a book that is all about a desktop hypervisor?

P. von Oven, *Learning VMware Workstation Pro for Windows: Volume 2*,
https://doi.org/10.1007/979-8-8688-0864-7_1

In this section, we are going to briefly compare containers and virtual machines just to serve as a reminder to what we originally discussed in the first book and to set the scene for this chapter.

As we have previously discussed, a virtual machine runs a full-blown guest operating system instance that shares the physical resources of the host machine on which it runs. It is a guest on the host's hardware. In the case of this book, Workstation Pro provides the hypervisor layer on top of an existing operating system, referred to as a type 2 hypervisor.

In contrast, a container is an environment that runs an application that is not dependent on a guest operating system. Instead, it isolates just the application by bundling (or containerizing) the application's code together with the related configuration files and libraries and with the dependencies that the application requires for it to run.

The diagram in Figure 1-1 shows the comparison between a hypervisor-based VM solution and a containerized environment.

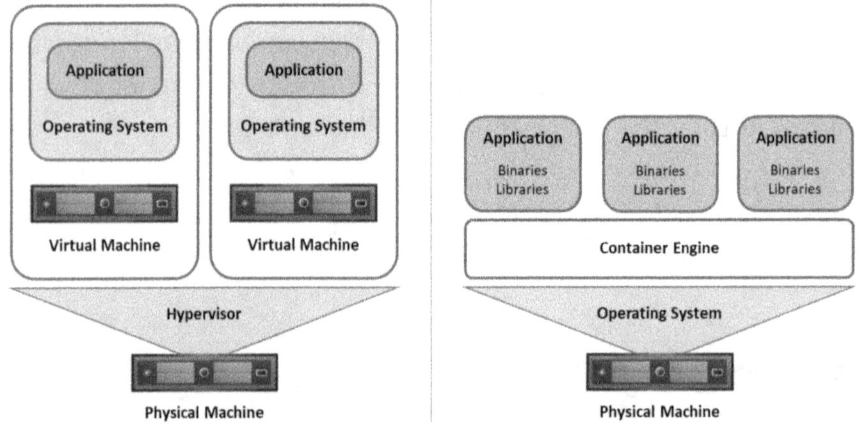

Figure 1-1. *Comparison Between a Hypervisor and a Container*

This bundling is where the container name originates from. If you think about moving house and using a shipping container into which you place all your belongings, by doing this, it makes it easy to move everything around in one hit. It is the same for applications. In this analogy, substitute your household belongings for the application runtimes, config files, and libraries and there you have your containerized apps, ready to run across environments.

Containers provide a straightforward way to build, test, deploy, and redeploy applications on multiple environments either from a developer's local machine to an on-premises data center or to the cloud.

The most common examples of container engines are Docker and Kubernetes.

VMware Workstation Pro enables you to manage containers as well as virtual machines. With containers the **vctl** command, integrated into Workstation Pro, provides you with the ability to create, run, and manage containers from the command line and is the subject of this first chapter.

Getting Started with the vctl Command

Now we have brought you up to speed with what a container is and how it works; in this next section, we are going to get started with running containers in VMware Workstation Pro.

To run Kubernetes clusters and manage containers using Workstation Pro, the **vctl** command is used.

What Is the vctl Command

You can use the vctl command line utility in Workstation Pro to manage containers. In addition, the vctl command provides support for KIND (Kubernetes IN Docker) so that KIND can use vctl containers as nodes to run local Kubernetes clusters.

The vctl is a command line utility that is already bundled inside the Workstation Pro application and is supported only on host machines that are running Windows 10 1809 or later. If you are running Workstation

Pro on hosts that are running either a Linux-based operating system or Windows operating system version prior to Windows 10 1809, then these versions do not support the vctl command line, and therefore, it cannot be used.

We have just highlighted the fact that the required executable files are already included and bundled within in the Workstation Pro application, so the question is what they are and where would you find them.

To answer the latter part, you will find the files located in the C:\Program Files (x86)\VMware\VMware Workstation folder by default. If you choose to install Workstation Pro in a different folder location, then you will find them in the folder you created.

Next is what these files are called and what functionality do they provide. The three executables of the vctl command line utility are described below:

- **containerd.exe** – This is a runtime daemon that runs in the background on the host machine. The containerd daemon must be started first before you can run any container-related operation. To start it, you use the vctl system start command, and to stop it, use the vctl system stop command. We will cover these commands later in this chapter.
- **containerd-shim-crx-v2.exe** – When a new container is started, a new containerd-shim-crx-v2 process is launched and acts as an adapter between the container in the CRX virtual machine and the containerd daemon.
- **bin/vctl.exe** – Is a command line utility that runs in the foreground and relays the user input to the containerd daemon.

Before you start running any of these commands, there are a couple of prerequisites you need to be aware of as we will discuss in the next section.

vctl Command Prerequisites

Although the vctl command is included with Workstation Pro and is available to run without the need to install any additional software or Workstation Pro features and is available from the standard command prompt windows or form a Windows PowerShell window, there are a few prerequisites you need to meet first as described below:

- VMware recommends that you use a modern solid-state drive (SSD) as system disk in the host machine to provide the required performance.
- The host operating system must be Window 10 1809 or later.
- Before using the vctl command to run any operation on a container image or container, the container runtime must be started first.

The container runtime doesn't start automatically when the Workstation Pro application launches and does not stop automatically when you exit and close the Workstation Pro application. You must manually start and stop the vctl command which we will cover in the next section.

You can check as to whether the container runtime is running by following the steps described:

1. On the host machine that is running Workstation Pro, open a command prompt or a PowerShell session.
2. At the command prompt, type the following command: **`vctl system info`** and press Enter.

3. You will see the following screenshot with the red box highlighting the status of the container runtime which in this example shows that it is not currently running (stopped) as shown in Figure 1-2.

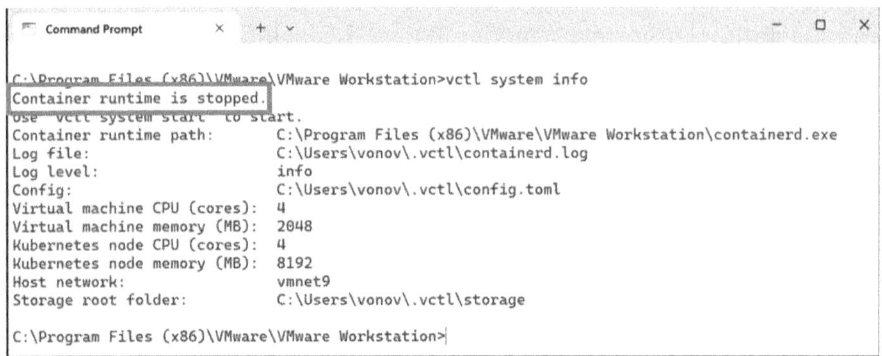
```
C:\Program Files (x86)\VMware\VMware Workstation>vctl system info
Container runtime is stopped.
Use 'vctl system start' to start.
Container runtime path:       C:\Program Files (x86)\VMware\VMware Workstation\containerd.exe
Log file:                     C:\Users\vonov\.vctl\containerd.log
Log level:                    info
Config:                       C:\Users\vonov\.vctl\config.toml
Virtual machine CPU (cores):  4
Virtual machine memory (MB):  2048
Kubernetes node CPU (cores):  4
Kubernetes node memory (MB):  8192
Host network:                 vmnet9
Storage root folder:          C:\Users\vonov\.vctl\storage

C:\Program Files (x86)\VMware\VMware Workstation>
```

Figure 1-2. *Checking the Status of the Container Runtime*

4. If the container status showed as running, then you would be able to continue and manage the running containers using the vctl commands.

Having said all that, the first time you start the container runtime, a few more steps are required, which are automated, that basically download the virtual machine that acts as the container runtime for managing the Kubernetes nodes as well as the nodes themselves.

Setting Up and Managing a Container Runtime

Running the vctl command for the first time will download the required files and set up the container runtime environment before automatically starting it.

To do this, follow the steps described:

1. On the host machine that is running Workstation Pro, open a command prompt or a PowerShell session.

2. At the command prompt, type the following command: **`vctl system start`** and press Enter.

3. You will see the following as shown in Figure 1-3.

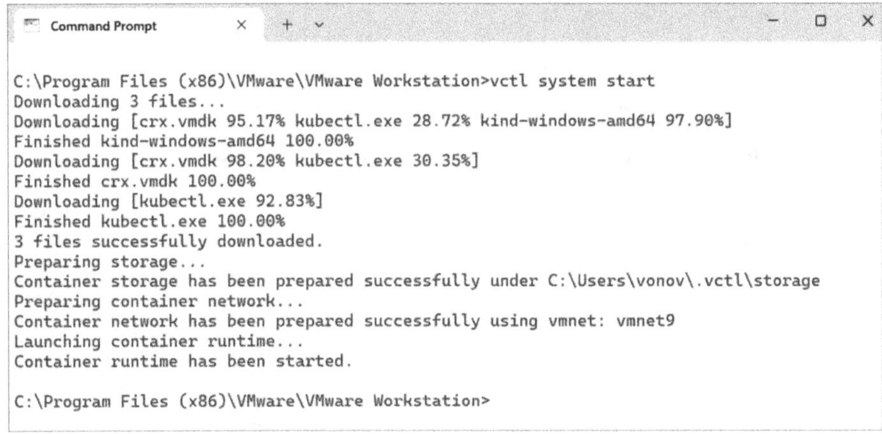

Command Prompt
C:\Program Files (x86)\VMware\VMware Workstation>vctl system start
Downloading 3 files...
Downloading [crx.vmdk 95.17% kubectl.exe 28.72% kind-windows-amd64 97.90%]
Finished kind-windows-amd64 100.00%
Downloading [crx.vmdk 98.20% kubectl.exe 30.35%]
Finished crx.vmdk 100.00%
Downloading [kubectl.exe 92.83%]
Finished kubectl.exe 100.00%
3 files successfully downloaded.
Preparing storage...
Container storage has been prepared successfully under C:\Users\vonov\.vctl\storage
Preparing container network...
Container network has been prepared successfully using vmnet: vmnet9
Launching container runtime...
Container runtime has been started.
C:\Program Files (x86)\VMware\VMware Workstation>

Figure 1-3. *Starting the Container Runtime*

4. You will see that three files are downloaded:

   - **kind-windows-amd64** – Kubernetes IN Docker, local clusters for testing Kubernetes, is a tool for running local Kubernetes clusters using Docker container nodes. kind was primarily designed for testing Kubernetes itself.

   - **crx.vmdk** – This is the virtual disk for the CRX (Container Runtime Executive) virtual machine appliance used for the container host environment and is user for kind.

- **kubectl.exe** – kubectl is a command line tool that is used to run commands against Kubernetes clusters. It does this by authenticating with the master node of the cluster and then making API calls to perform the management actions.

5. These three files are saved in a folder called **bin** which in turn is created in a folder called **.vctl**. The folders are created the first time you run the vctl command.

   The folders will all be created under the currently logged in user. In this example, the username of the currently logged in user is vonov, and so you will find the folders in the ***c:\users\vonov*** folder as shown in Figure 1-4.

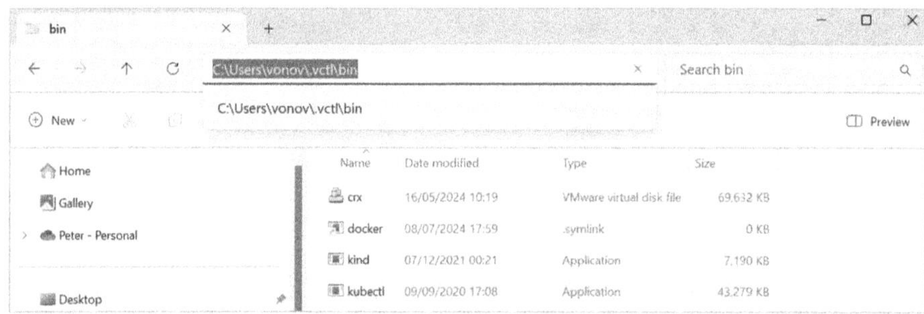

***Figure 1-4.** Downloaded Container Files*

There are two other files that we are going to take a closer look at. Both files can be found in the **.vctl** folder. One file relates to the configuration of the Kubernetes node, and the other file relates to the CRX virtual machine appliance.

If you navigate to the **c:\users\\<username>\\.vctl** folder, as shown in Figure 1-5, then you will see the files in question highlighted in red.

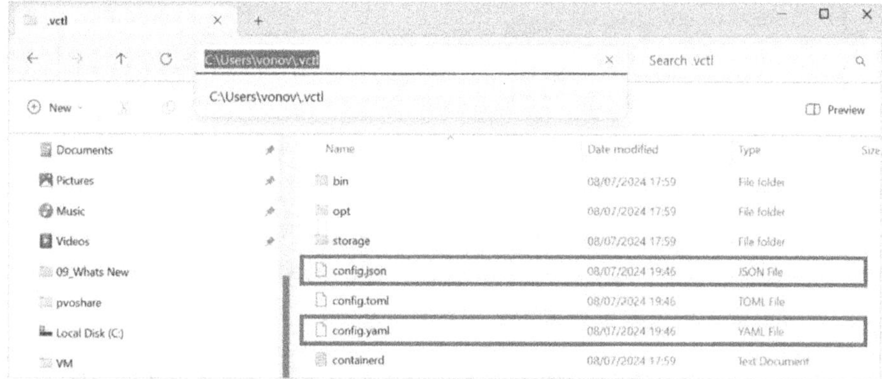

Figure 1-5. *Container Configuration Files*

If you open the **config.json** file using something like Notepad, you will see the following detail shown in Figure 1-6.

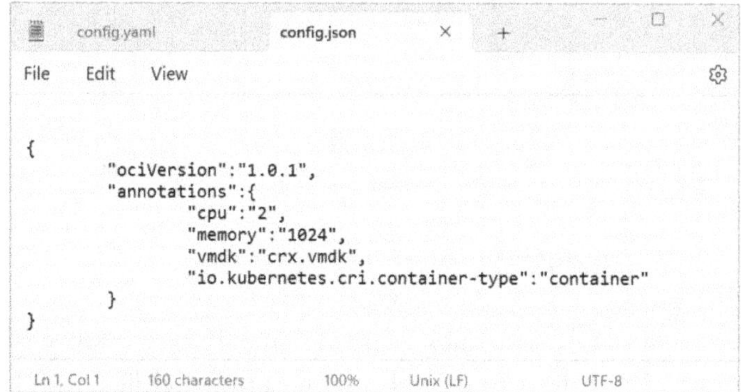

Figure 1-6. *config.json File*

As you can see from the config.json file, this virtual machine is configured with two CPUs and 1GB memory and uses a virtual disk file called crx.vmdk. But the question is, what is this virtual machine and why is it required when we are talking about running containers?

The name of the virtual disk file gives this away. CRX, as we have highlighted before, stands for Container Runtime Executive for ESXi. It is a virtual machine, as you can see from the configuration details, that is highly optimized to run a Linux kernel that in turn is highly optimized to enable you to run containers.

With the container runtime running, you will see the virtual machine and the Kubernetes node by running the **vtcl system info** command at the command prompt. This is shown in Figure 1-7.

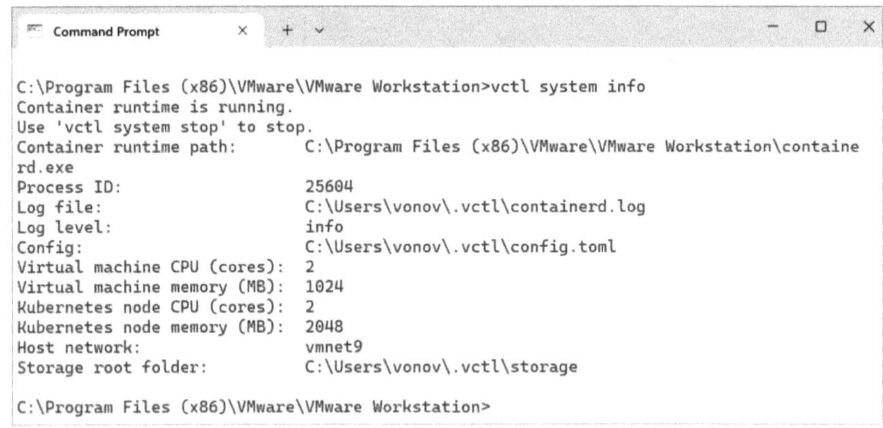

Figure 1-7. *System Information and Status*

On the subject of the container runtime, it will have been started as part of the vtcl system start command and once the files have been downloaded. The next time it starts, then it will just start without the need to download anything.

As the container service is now running, that means that vctl-based KIND is now also ready. This means that kind will run local Kubernetes clusters by using vctl containers as nodes and all Docker commands have been aliased to use vctl so that Docker commands performed in the currently opened window will be executed through vctl.

We previously showed the configuration of the virtual machine and Kubernetes node in terms of CPU and memory, but you will also see that a new virtual network for containers, **vmnet9**, has been created. To show this, if you launch Workstation Pro and then open the **Virtual Network Editor**, you will see the new network as shown in Figure 1-8.

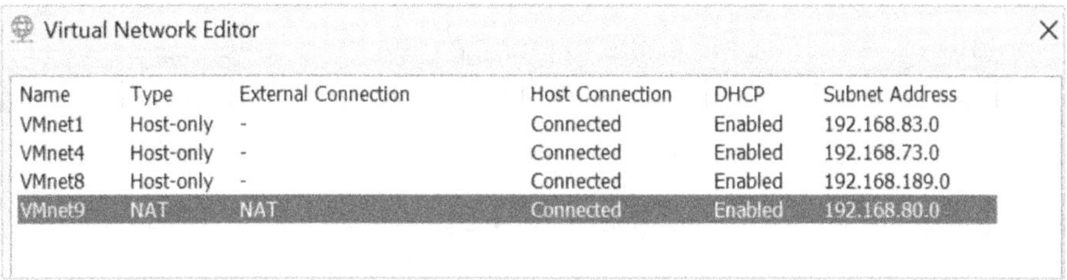

Virtual Network Editor

Name	Type	External Connection	Host Connection	DHCP	Subnet Address
VMnet1	Host-only	-	Connected	Enabled	192.168.83.0
VMnet4	Host-only	-	Connected	Enabled	192.168.73.0
VMnet8	Host-only	-	Connected	Enabled	192.168.189.0
VMnet9	NAT	NAT	Connected	Enabled	192.168.80.0

Figure 1-8. *New vmnet9 Network Created*

In the previous examples, we have just stuck with the default configuration values for CPU and memory for the virtual machine and the Kubernetes node, as well as the container storage volume size. In the next section, we are going to look at how to change or update the configuration.

Updating the CRX VM and Kubernetes Node Configuration

When it comes to the configuration of the virtual machine and the Kubernetes node, so far, we have stuck with the default configuration. However, depending on what you are planning on running, then there may be the need to change the configuration to add more memory or CPU resource.

These changes can be made when you start the container service, reconfiguring the default CPU and memory sizes available to the virtual machine and the Kubernetes node. First, let's look at increasing the resources on the virtual machine that hosts the Kubernetes node.

The command to do this would look something like the following:

```
vctl system config --vm-cpus <CPU QTY> --vm-mem <MEMORY SIZE>
```

When running the command, replace **<CPU QTY>** with the number of CPUs you want to configure in the virtual machine, and then replace the **<MEMORY SIZE>** with the new memory size for the virtual machine.

In this example, we are going to change the virtual machine configuration to have four CPUs and 2GB of memory. The command to make that configuration change would look like the following:

```
vctl system config --vm-cpus 4 --vm-mem 2048
```

If you then run the **`vctl system info`** command, then you will see the following as shown in Figure 1-9.

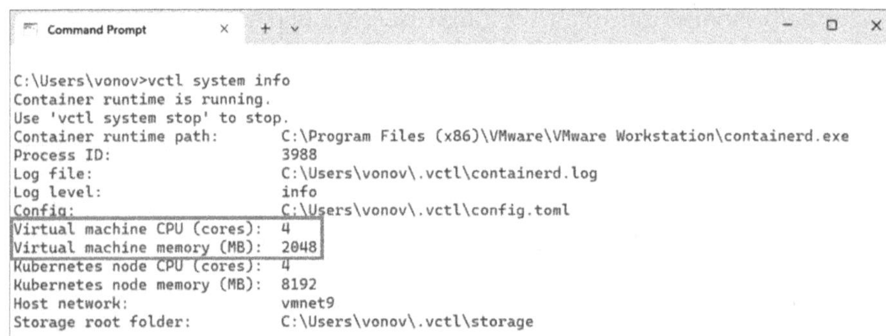

***Figure 1-9.** Updated Virtual Machine Configuration*

Now, let's look at increasing the resources for the Kubernetes node.

This command is almost identical to the previous command, but now we replace **vm** with **k8s**. Therefore, the command would look something like the following:

```
vctl system config --k8s-cpus <CPU QTY> --k8s-mem <MEMORY SIZE>
```

As with the previous command, replace **<CPU QTY>** with the new number of CPUs you want to configure in the Kubernetes node, and then replace the **<MEMORY SIZE>** with the new memory size for the Kubernetes node.

In this example, we are going to change the Kubernetes node configuration to have four CPUs and 8GB of memory. The command to make that configuration change would look like the following:

```
vctl system config --k8s-cpus 4 --k8s-mem 8192
```

If you then run the vctl system info command, then you will see the following as shown in Figure 1-10.

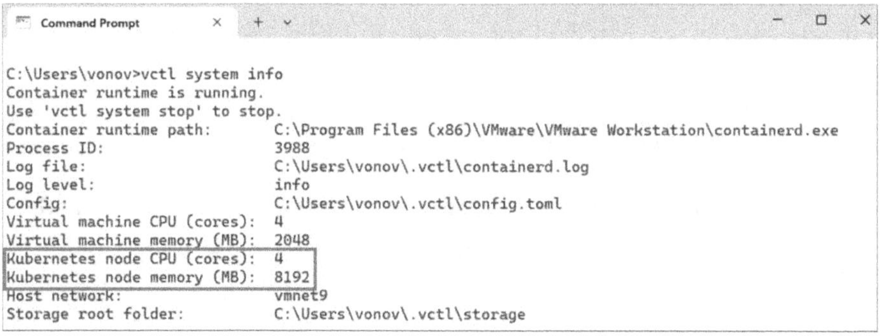

```
C:\Users\vonov>vctl system info
Container runtime is running.
Use 'vctl system stop' to stop.
Container runtime path:       C:\Program Files (x86)\VMware\VMware Workstation\containerd.exe
Process ID:                   3988
Log file:                     C:\Users\vonov\.vctl\containerd.log
Log level:                    info
Config:                       C:\Users\vonov\.vctl\config.toml
Virtual machine CPU (cores):  4
Virtual machine memory (MB):  2048
Kubernetes node CPU (cores):  4
Kubernetes node memory (MB):  8192
Host network:                 vmnet9
Storage root folder:          C:\Users\vonov\.vctl\storage
```

Figure 1-10. *Updated Kubernetes Node Configuration*

As you have updated the configuration of both the virtual machine and the Kubernetes node, then the corresponding configuration files will also have been updated, therefore making these changes persistent.

If you open the **config.yaml** and the **config.json** files, then you will see this updated configuration within the respective configuration files.

Now that we have downloaded the required files and configured and started the container service, we can now turn our attention to the commands that can be used in building and managing containers.

vctl Commands

We have already looked at some of the vctl commands in the previous section. Those commands were used to configure the CRX virtual machine and the Kubernetes node.

The next set of commands we are going to cover is for building, controlling, and managing the containers themselves. We will cover these commands in the following sections.

The build Command

The build command enables you to build a container image from a Dockerfile. To run the build command, you would use the following syntax:

```
vctl build <COMMAND_OPTIONS> <PATH>
```

When running the command, replace the **<COMMAND_OPTIONS>** field with the build option you require, which we will discuss next, and replace the **<PATH>** field with the path to the Dockerfile from which you want to build your image.

build Command Options

The build command has several options that can be specified when running the command that allows you to configure how the container image is built. The command options are as follows:

> **`--builder-mem <string>`** - Configures a limit for the amount of memory that is available to the container. You can enter MB or GB). By default, the container is built with 4GB (4g). Replace the **<string>** field in the command with the amount of memory you want to configure.

-c, --credential <string> - Enables you to specify the path to the file that is used to store the private registry authentication credentials. Replace the **<string>** field in the command with the path.

-f, --file <string> - Enables you to configure the path to the target Dockerfile that the container will be built from. By default, the path is set to PATH\Dockerfile. Replace the **<string>** field in the command with the name of the Dockerfile.

-h, --help - Displays the help screen. In this case, by using the build command, the help shown will be specific to the build command.

--kind-load - Enables you to load the container image to a local kind cluster.

--no-local-cache - Configures the container to not use local storage as cache for the base image.

-t, --tag <string> - Enables you to specify the name of the container image that gets built. Replace the **<string>** field in the command with the tag you want to use.

With each of the command options described above, where you see the **<string>** field requires you to input a string value such as entering a name or the amount of memory.

Next, we are going to look at the completion command.

The completion Command

With the completion command, you can output the shell completion code for reporting on whether the shell loading has completed successfully. You have the choice of the shell that you output the completion code to with the command supporting Bash, Zsh, Fish, and PowerShell.

As a prerequisite for this command to work, you will need to have your chosen shell application installed and the completions feature enabled where appropriate. In the next sections, we are going to look at the syntax for each of the supported shell options.

Bash

If you want to output the completion code to Bash, then you would run the completion command for each session using the following syntax:

```
vctl completion bash > /usr/local/etc/bash_completion.d/vctl
```

Zsh

If you want to output the completion code to Zsh, then you would run the completion command for each Zsh shell session using the following syntax:

```
vctl completion zsh > "${fpath[1]}/_vctl"
```

Note For this command to take effect, then you will need to start a new shell.

Fish

If you want to output the completion code to Fish, then there are two options. The first option is to output the completion code to the current shell. To do this, you would use the following syntax:

```
vctl completion fish | source
```

The second option is to load the completion code for each session. The command syntax for this option is as follows:

```
vctl completion fish > ~/.config/fish/completions/vctl.fish
```

Finally, we are going to look at the PowerShell option.

PowerShell

Finally, there is the option to output the completion code to PowerShell.

Again, there are two options with the completion command when used with PowerShell. The first option executes the completion command once using the following command syntax:

```
PS> vctl completion powershell | Out-String | Invoke-Expression
```

The other option is to load completions for every new session, using the following command syntax:

```
PS> vctl completion powershell > vctl.ps1
```

In the next section, we are going to look at the **create** command.

The create Command

With the **create** command, you can create a new container from an existing container image.

To run the build command, you would use the following syntax:

```
vctl create <OPTIONS> <IMAGE> <COMMAND> <ARGUMENTS>
```

When running the command, replace the <**OPTIONS**> field with the build options you require, which we will discuss next. Then replace the <**IMAGE**> field with the path to the image file from which you want to create a new container image from. Then you can add commands in the <**COMMAND**> field and any arguments for those commands in the <**ARGUMENTS**> field.

create Command Options

The create command has several options that can be specified when running the command that allows you to configure how the container image it creates. The command options are as follows:

- **`--entrypoint <string>`** - Enables you to override the default entry point of the container image
- **`-e, --env <strings>`** - Enables you to set environment variables in the container
- **`--hostname <string>`** - Enables you to set a hostname for the container
- **`-i, --interactive`** - Enables you to keep the STDIN (standard input) open even if not attached
- **`-l, --label <strings>`** - Enables you to configure additional labels on the container
- **`-n, --name <string>`** - Enables you to assign a name to the container
- **`-r, --privileged`** - Enables you to run the container with extended privileges

- **-p, --publish <strings>** - Allows you to bind host machines network ports to the container network ports

  When using the **--publish** option, you need to make sure that the vctl utility doesn't have a subnet or a link feature to connect multiple containers to a subnet.

  To enable the communication between containers, you will need to start the container with the **--publish** command option. Adding this command will bind the container port to the host machine port so that the container is accessible on the network from outside of the host machine.

  For example, **-p 8080:8080** would bind port 8080 on the host machine to port 8080 on the container.

- **-t, --tty** - Allows you to allocate a terminal session for the container

- **-v, --volume <strings>** - Enables you to bind folders on the host machine to folders in the container

  When you use the **--volume** command option, you need to ensure that you specify paths to the folder level rather than a specific file as the **--volume** command does not support path to files.

  You also need to make sure that you use the absolute path as relative paths are not supported.

  Mounting named volumes is not supported, and so you can only mount anonymous volumes.

  For example: **--volume %userprofile%\Documents\container:/opt/pvo pvo**

- **-w, --workdir <string>** - Enables you to configure the working directory of the new process

As an example, we have simply created a new Nginx container image using the **vctl create nginx** command with no additional command options.

If you list the container images that are available, you will see that this new container is listed as nginx-330d.

As a second example, we created another container image, again using the Nginx container image, but in this example, we have specified a name using the following command: **vctl create --name pvonginx nginx.**

If you again list the available container images, you will see that the pvonginx is now listed as well. Both containers use the original Nginx container image. This is shown in Figure 1-11.

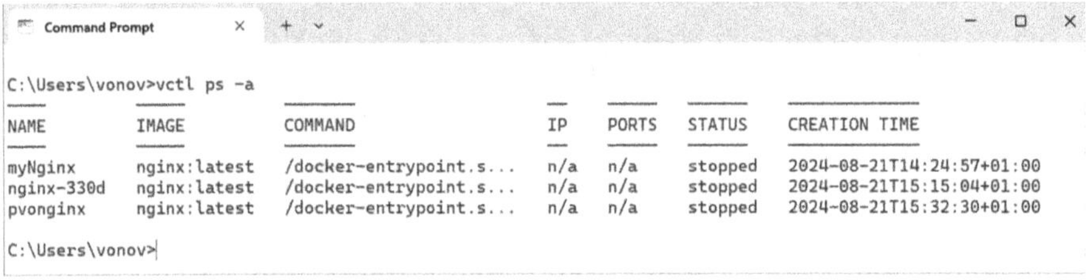

```
C:\Users\vonov>vctl ps -a
NAME        IMAGE          COMMAND                  IP    PORTS   STATUS    CREATION TIME
myNginx     nginx:latest   /docker-entrypoint.s...  n/a   n/a     stopped   2024-08-21T14:24:57+01:00
nginx-330d  nginx:latest   /docker-entrypoint.s...  n/a   n/a     stopped   2024-08-21T15:15:04+01:00
pvonginx    nginx:latest   /docker-entrypoint.s...  n/a   n/a     stopped   2024-08-21T15:32:30+01:00

C:\Users\vonov>
```

Figure 1-11. *Newly Created Container Images*

We will cover the command that we have just used for displaying container images later in this chapter.

Next, we are going to look at the describe command.

The describe Command

The describe command is used to show the details of a container. To run the build command, you would use the following syntax:

vctl describe <CONTAINER_ID>

When running the command, replace the **<CONTAINER_ID>** field with the name of the container you want to display the details for.

In the example screenshot shown in Figure 1-12, we have used the describe command to display the details for a container called ngnix-8a26. The command used is as follows:

```
vctl describe ngnix-8a26
```

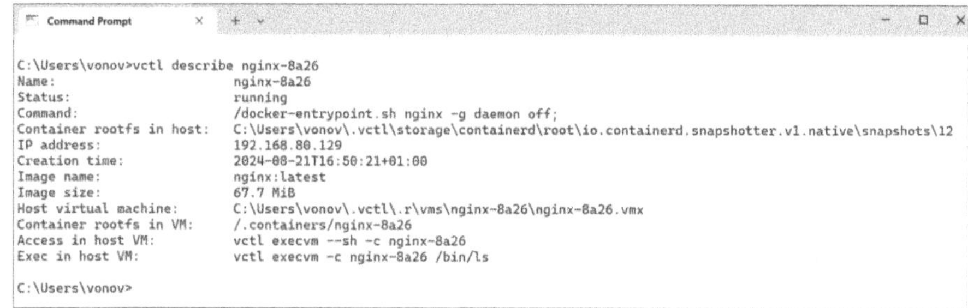

Figure 1-12. *Container Details Using the describe Command*

As you can see, the output shows useful details such as the IP address, image size, the image name, and how to access it from the host machine which we will cover with the exec command in the next section.

The exec Command

With the exec command, you can run a command inside a container. The container on which you want to run the command is specified as part of the command line.

To run the exec command, you would use the following syntax:

```
vctl exec <OPTIONS> <CONTAINER_ID> <COMMAND>
<COMMAND_ARGUMENTS>
```

When running the exec command, replace the **<OPTIONS>** field with the options you require, which we will discuss in the next section. Then, in the **<CONTAINER_ID>** field, enter the name of the container you want to run the command on.

Next is the actual command you want to run on the container in the **<COMMAND>** field, and if that command has any additional arguments or options, add these in the **<COMMAND_ARGUMENTS>** field.

exec Command Options

The exec command has several options that can be specified when running the command that allows you to configure how the command is run. The command options are as follows:

- **-d, --detach** – Enables you to run the command in background
- **-h, --help** – Displays the help screen for the exec command
- **-i, --interactive** – Allows the STDIN to remain open even if not attached
- **-t, --tty** – Enables you to allocate a terminal for the container

To show this, as an example, we are going to execute the top command in a container. In this example, this container is called PVOContainer. We are also going to run this command in the background, i.e., not attached to the current terminal.

In this example, the command would look something like the following:

```
vctl exec --detach PVOContainer top
```

Next, we are going to look at a similar command; however, this time, the command will execute on the virtual machine that is hosting the container.

The execvm Command

With the execvm command, you can run a command inside the virtual machine that is hosting the container. The virtual machine on which you want to run the command can be specified as part of the command line by adding the full path to the .vmx configuration file of the virtual machine.

Alternatively, you can use the --container options to identify the virtual machine which is hosting the specified container.

To run the exec command, you would use the following syntax:

```
vctl execvm <OPTIONS> (VMX|-c=<CONTAINER_ID>) <COMMAND>
<COMMAND_ARGUMENTS>
```

When running the exec command, replace the **<OPTIONS>** field with one of the options listed in the next section. Next replace the VMX field with the full path to the .vmx file of the virtual machine that is hosting the container or replace the **<CONTAINER_ID>** field with the name of the container.

Finally, add the actual command you want to run on the virtual machine in the **<COMMAND>** field, and if that command has any additional arguments or options, add these in the **<COMMAND_ARGUMENTS>** field.

execvm Command Options

The execvm command has several options that can be specified when running the command that allows you to configure how the command is run. The command options are as follows:

- **`-c, --container <string>`** - This allows you to use container as the identifier of the virtual machine that is hosting it
- **`-h, --help`** - Displays the help screen for the execvm command
- **`-s, --sh`** - Opens a shell session into the virtual machine specified or identified by the container that is hosted on it

To show an example of this command, we are going to launch a shell on the virtual machine that is hosting the container called nginx-8a26.

The command to do this would look like the following:

```
vctl execvm --sh -c nginx-8a26
```

Figure 1-13 shows the output of this command where you can see that a shell session has been opened to the virtual machine hosting the nginx-8a26 container and we have run a simple **ls** command on that virtual machine.

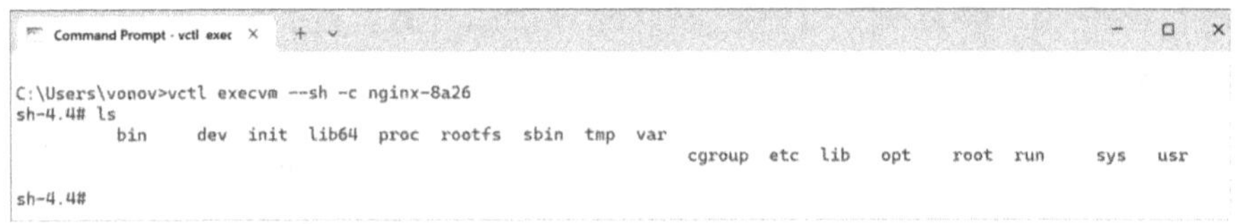

Figure 1-13. *execvm Command*

Next, we are going to look at the help command.

The help Command

If you need a prompt or assistance with any of the vctl commands and the various command options that are available, then there is a command line help screen available directly from the command line.

There are two levels to the help screen. The first is at the top level and lists all of the commands that are available.

Next you can get help on a specific command. This gives you the next level of help and displays all the specific command options and command syntax for the command that you have specified. For example, you could get more detailed help on the build command that would detail the various options for this command.

To access the help, there are three different commands, each one providing exactly the same help screens. The commands are as follows and are entered at the command prompt:

- vctl
- vctl -h
- vctl --help

If you type one of those to access help, then you will see the screenshot as shown in Figure 1-14 which shows the top-level help screen detailing all the command available when using the vctl command.

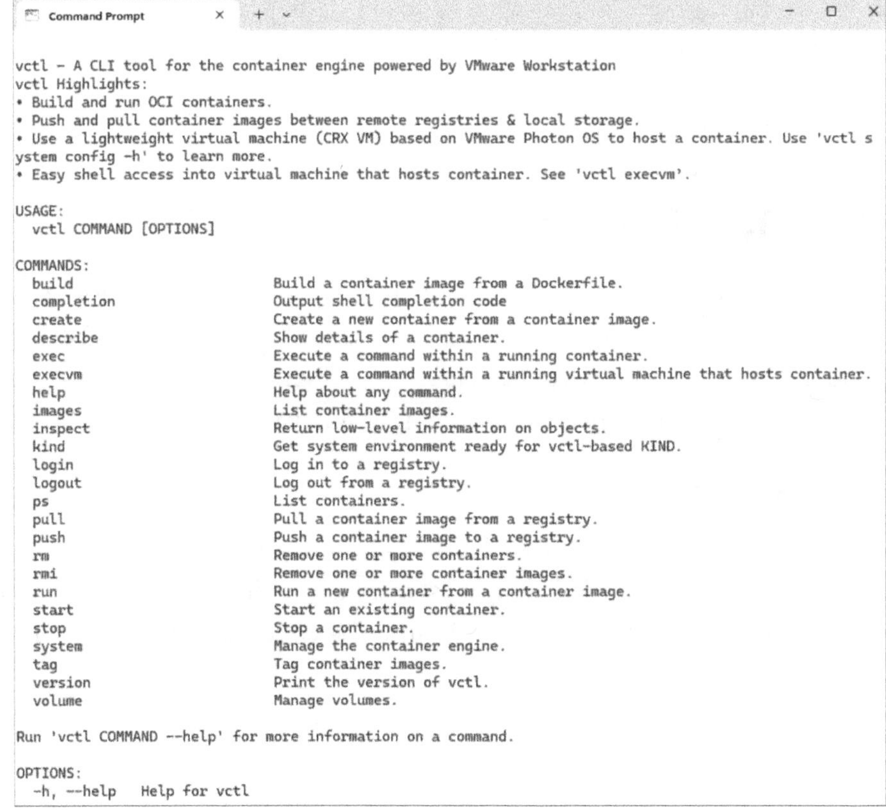

```
vctl - A CLI tool for the container engine powered by VMware Workstation
vctl Highlights:
• Build and run OCI containers.
• Push and pull container images between remote registries & local storage.
• Use a lightweight virtual machine (CRX VM) based on VMware Photon OS to host a container. Use 'vctl s
ystem config -h' to learn more.
• Easy shell access into virtual machine that hosts container. See 'vctl execvm'.

USAGE:
  vctl COMMAND [OPTIONS]

COMMANDS:
  build                        Build a container image from a Dockerfile.
  completion                   Output shell completion code
  create                       Create a new container from a container image.
  describe                     Show details of a container.
  exec                         Execute a command within a running container.
  execvm                       Execute a command within a running virtual machine that hosts container.
  help                         Help about any command.
  images                       List container images.
  inspect                      Return low-level information on objects.
  kind                         Get system environment ready for vctl-based KIND.
  login                        Log in to a registry.
  logout                       Log out from a registry.
  ps                           List containers.
  pull                         Pull a container image from a registry.
  push                         Push a container image to a registry.
  rm                           Remove one or more containers.
  rmi                          Remove one or more container images.
  run                          Run a new container from a container image.
  start                        Start an existing container.
  stop                         Stop a container.
  system                       Manage the container engine.
  tag                          Tag container images.
  version                      Print the version of vctl.
  volume                       Manage volumes.

Run 'vctl COMMAND --help' for more information on a command.

OPTIONS:
  -h, --help    Help for vctl
```

Figure 1-14. *Top-Level help Screen*

As we highlighted previously, you can ask for help on a specific command. In the example in Figure 1-15, the command **vctl tag --help** has been used to show the options available when running the tag command.

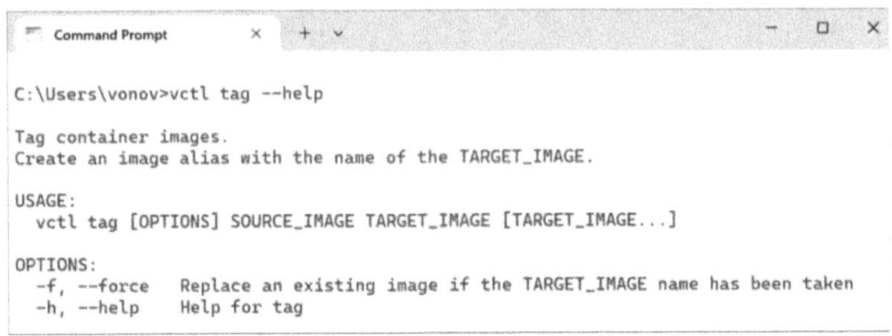

Figure 1-15. *help Screen for a Specific Command*

Next is the images command.

The images Command

If you want to list the container images currently available on the host machine, then you can run the images command. This command displays the details of one or more of the available container images available.

The command to display the images is as follows:

```
vctl images <OPTIONS> <IMAGE>
```

You can run the command without any options or any named container image which will display a list of **all** the available container images. The command for that would simply be **vctl images** as shown in Figure 1-16.

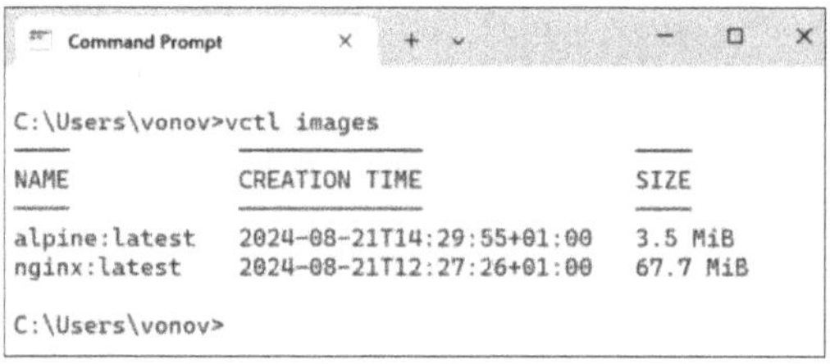

```
Command Prompt

C:\Users\vonov>vctl images
NAME            CREATION TIME                SIZE
alpine:latest   2024-08-21T14:29:55+01:00    3.5 MiB
nginx:latest    2024-08-21T12:27:26+01:00    67.7 MiB

C:\Users\vonov>
```

***Figure 1-16.** List of All Available Container Images*

If you wanted the details of a specific container, then the command would look like the following: **`vctl images nginx:latest`**.

images Command Options

There is just a single command option, excluding the help page. This option **`-d`** will display the available container image information complete with details of the digest.

The command to do this would look like the following: **`vctl images -d`**. It is shown in Figure 1-17.

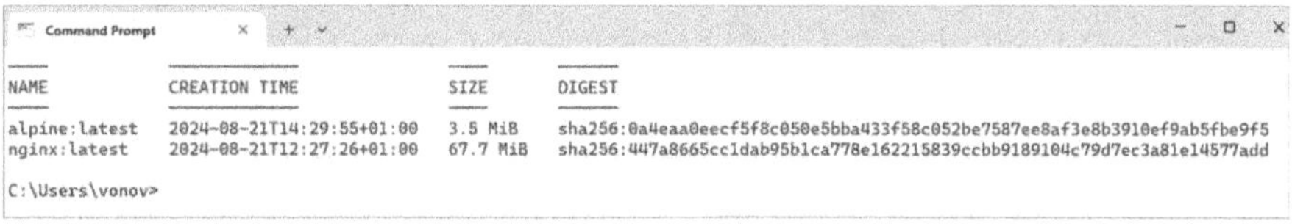

```
Command Prompt

NAME            CREATION TIME               SIZE       DIGEST
alpine:latest   2024-08-21T14:29:55+01:00   3.5 MiB    sha256:0a4eaa0eecf5f8c050e5bba433f58c052be7587ee8af3e8b3910ef9ab5fbe9f5
nginx:latest    2024-08-21T12:27:26+01:00   67.7 MiB   sha256:447a8665cc1dab95b1ca778e162215839ccbb9189104c79d7ec3a81e14577add

C:\Users\vonov>
```

***Figure 1-17.** List of All Available Container Images with Digest*

If you want to just display the digest and details of a specific container image, then you should add the name of the container image at the end of the command.

The command would look something like the following: **`vctl images -d nginx:latest`**.

Next, we are going to look at the inspect command.

The inspect Command

If you want to look at low-level detail of a container, then you can use the inspect command.

The command to inspect a container is as follows:

```
vctl inspect <CONTAINER_ID>
```

When running the command, replace the **<CONTAINER_ID>** field with the name of the container that you want to perform the low-level inspection on.

In Figure 1-18, we have run the inspect command on the container called nginx-8a26 using the command **`vctl inspect nginx-8a26`**.

```
Command Prompt

C:\Users\vonov>vctl inspect nginx-8a26
{
    "ID": "nginx-8a26",
    "Labels": {
        "io.containerd.image.config.stop-signal": "SIGQUIT"
    },
    "Image": "index.docker.io/library/nginx:latest",
    "Runtime": {
        "Name": "io.containerd.crx.v2",
        "Options": null
    },
    "SnapshotKey": "nginx-8a26",
    "Snapshotter": "native",
    "CreatedAt": "2024-08-21T15:50:21.6059498Z",
    "UpdatedAt": "2024-08-21T15:50:25.0876595Z",
    "Extensions": null,
    "Spec": {
        "ociVersion": "1.0.1",
        "process": {
            "terminal": true,
            "user": {
                "uid": 0,
                "gid": 0
            },
            "args": [
                "/docker-entrypoint.sh",
                "nginx",
                "-g",
                "daemon off;"
            ],
            "env": [
                "PATH=/usr/local/sbin:/usr/local/bin:/usr/sbin:/usr/bin:/sbin:/bin",
                "NGINX_VERSION=1.27.1",
                "NJS_VERSION=0.8.5",
                "NJS_RELEASE=1~bookworm",
                "PKG_RELEASE=1~bookworm",
                "DYNPKG_RELEASE=2~bookworm",
                "TERM=xterm"
            ],
            "cwd": "/",
            "capabilities": {
                "bounding": [
                    "CAP_CHOWN",
                    "CAP_DAC_OVERRIDE",
                    "CAP_FSETID",
                    "CAP_FOWNER",
                    "CAP_MKNOD",
```

Figure 1-18. *Output from a Low-Level Conatiner Inspection*

Next, we are going to look at the kind command.

The kind Command

The kind command is used to prepare the system environment for using the vctl command. This uses the vctl command as the provider for kind instead of Docker.

There are no real kind commands to run as such as everything is downloaded and prepared the first time you run the vctl system start command. If you refer to the beginning of this chapter, this is described in the setting up and managing a container runtime section.

With kind installed, then all Docker commands will be aliased to vctl in a new terminal.

Next, we are going to look at the login command.

The login Command

If you want to login to a registry to enable you to download and upload images, then the login command can be used.

The command to login to a registry is as follows:

```
vctl login <OPTIONS> <SERVER_NAME>
```

When running the command, replace the **<OPTIONS>** field with the required options which we will cover in the next sections, and then in the **<SERVER_NAME>** field, enter the details of the server you want to connect to. If you leave the server field blank, then by default, you will be logging in to Docker Hub.

login Command Options

There are a few command options that can be used with the login command. These command options are detailed below:

- **`--http`** - Allows you to use plain http to connect to a remote registry. If you don't use this option, then https is the default option.

- **-p, --password <string>** – Allows you to enter the password that is used to authenticate with the remote registry. Replace the **<string>** field with the password.
- **--password-stdin** – Will read the password from stdin.
- **--skip-ssl-check** – Configures the login to skip the ssl certificate validation.
- **-u, --username <string>** – Allows you to enter the username you want to login with in order to connect remote registry. Replace the **<string>** field with the username.

As an example of this command, we are going to login, using http (insecure), to a site called myregistry.com using the username of pvo and the password of password123.

The command to do this would look something like the following:

```
vctl login --http --username PVO --password password123
myregistry.com:5000
```

Next, we are going to look at how to log out of the server you have just logged in to.

The logout Command

In the previous section, we logged in to a registry; so in this section, we are going to log out of that registry.

The command to login to a registry is as follows:

```
vctl logout <SERVER_NAME>
```

When running the command, replace the **<SERVER_NAME>** field with the name of the server that you connected to. As with before, if you do not specify a server, then the default is Docker Hub.

The ps Command

If you want to list the containers that exist on the host machine, then you can use the ps command. Depending on the selected option, you can either show all containers or just those that are currently running.

The command to login to a registry is as follows:

```
vctl ps <OPTIONS> <CONTAINER_ID>
```

When running the command, replace the **<OPTIONS>** field with the required options which we will cover in the next sections, and then in the **<CONTAINER_ID>** field, enter the details of the container you want to list.

You can run the ps command without any options or specifically named containers. Doing this just shows the containers that are currently running.

The command to do this would be simply **`vctl ps`**.

Figure 1-19 shows the output of running the ps command without any command options or containers specified.

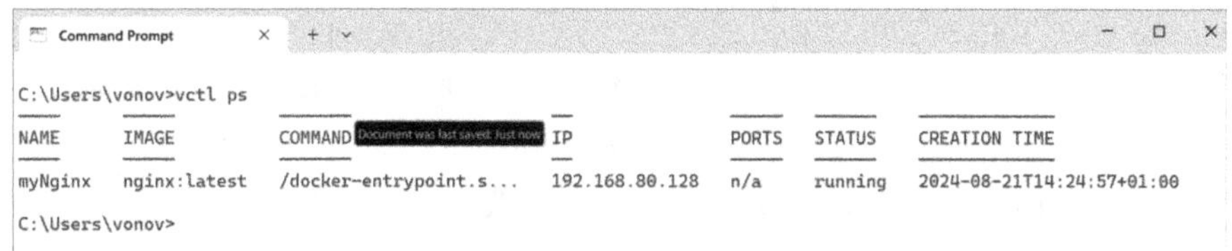

Figure 1-19. *List of Running Containers*

As you can see, there is just the myNginx container currently running. In the next section, we are going to look at the commands that can be used with the ps command.

ps Command Options

There are a couple of command options that can be used with the ps command that allow you to display different levels of information.

These options are as follows:

- **-l, --label <strings>** - Allows you to filter the list of containers by their labels. Replace the **<strings>** field in the command with the label you want to filter by.
- **-a, --all** - Lists all the containers that are resident on the host machine as shown in Figure 1-20.

```
Command Prompt

NAME         IMAGE          COMMAND                      IP               PORTS   STATUS    CREATION TIME
myNginx      nginx:latest   /docker-entrypoint.s...      n/a              n/a     stopped   2024-08-21T14:24:57+01:00
nginx-330d   nginx:latest   /docker-entrypoint.s...      n/a              n/a     stopped   2024-08-21T15:15:04+01:00
nginx-8a26   nginx:latest   /docker-entrypoint.s...      192.168.80.129   n/a     running   2024-08-21T16:50:21+01:00
pvonginx     nginx:latest   /docker-entrypoint.s...      n/a              n/a     stopped   2024-08-21T15:32:30+01:00

C:\Users\vonov>
```

Figure 1-20. *List of All Containers*

Next, we are going to look at the pull command.

The pull Command

The pull command is used to pull or download a container image from a registry or remote location and save it on the local host machine.

The command to login to a registry is as follows:

- **vctl pull <OPTIONS> <IMAGE>**

When running the command, replace the **<OPTIONS>** field with the required options which we will cover in the next section, and then in the **<IMAGE>** field, enter the details of the image you want to download.

By default, images will be pulled and downloaded from Docker Hub if you do not specify a registry, and the latest version will be downloaded by default if you do not specify a tag.

---

pull Command Options

There are a few command options that can be used with the pull command that allow you to configure the download.

These options are as follows:

- **--http** - Allows you to use plain http to connect to a remote registry. If you don't use this option, then https is the default option.
- **-p, --password <string>** - Allows you to enter the password that is used to authenticate with the remote registry. Replace the **<string>** field with the password. If you leave the --password field empty, then you will be prompted to enter your password manually.
- **--password-stdin** - Will read the password from stdin.
- **--skip-ssl-check** - Configures the login to skip the ssl certificate validation.
- **-u, --username <string>** - Allows you to enter the username you want to login with in order to connect remote registry. Replace the **<string>** field with the username.

As an example, we have downloaded the latest Nginx container image by using the following command:

```
vctl pull nginx
```

Figure 1-21 shows the image being downloaded.

```
Command Prompt

C:\Users\vonov>vctl pull nginx
INFO Pulling from index.docker.io/library/nginx:latest
────                                                                                  ──────  ────────
REF                                                                                   STATUS  PROGRESS
────                                                                                  ──────  ────────
index-sha256:447a8665cc1dab95b1ca778e162215839ccbb9189104c79d7ec3a81e14577add          Done    100% (10272/10272)
manifest-sha256:5f0574409b3add89581b96c68afe9e9c7b284651c3a974b6e8bac46bf95e6b7f       Done    100% (2295/2295)
layer-sha256:23fa5a7b99a685258885918c468ded042b95b5a7c56cee758a689f4f7e5971e0          Done    100% (1398/1398)
layer-sha256:2a0cb278fd9f7737ef5ddc52b4198821dd02e87ed204f74d7e491016b96ebe7f          Done    100% (41875782/41875782)
config-sha256:5ef79149e0ec84a7a9f9284c3f91aa3c20608f8391f5445eabe92ef07dbda03c         Done    100% (7486/7486)
layer-sha256:e4fff0779e6ddd22366469f08626c3ab1884b5cbe1719b26da238c95f247b305          Done    100% (29126232/29126232)
layer-sha256:03de31afb03573e0fa679d6777ba3267c2b8ec087cbc0efa46524c1de08f43ec          Done    100% (956/956)
layer-sha256:7045d6c32ae2d3dc002f33beb0c1cdd7f69b2663a9720117ac9b82ec28865e30          Done    100% (627/627)
layer-sha256:0f17be8dcff2e2c27ee6a33c1bacc582e71f76f855c2d69d510f2a93df897303          Done    100% (394/394)
layer-sha256:14b7e5e8f3946da0f9120dab3b0e05ef24a5ca874ba484327db8b3308a92b532          Done    100% (1210/1210)
INFO Unpacking nginx:latest...
INFO done
```

Figure 1-21. *Pulling the Latest Nginx Container Image*

As another example, if you wanted to download a container image called pvo:latest from a remote registry called pvonamespace which needs authentication using a username of pvo and a password of Password123, then the command would look something like the following:

```
vctl pull -u pvo --password Password123 pvonamespace/pvo:latest
```

In the next section, we are going to look at the reverse of the pull command and look at how you push a container image to a registry.

The push Command

The push command is used to push or upload a container image or prebuilt container image from the local host machine to a registry or remote location.

The command to login to a registry is as follows:

```
vctl push <OPTIONS> <IMAGE> <REMOTE_URL>
```

When running the command, replace the **<OPTIONS>** field with the required options which we will cover in the next section, and then in the **<IMAGE>** field, enter the details of the image you want to push or upload.

Finally, in the **<REMOTE_URL>** field, enter the url of the remote registry you want to push or upload to.

If you do not specify a remote url that the URL will be inferred from name of the image and if you do not specify a registry, then Docker Hub will be used as the default registry the image is uploaded to.

Next, we are going to look at the command options that can be used with the push command.

push Command Options

There are a couple of command options that can be used with the push command that allow you to configure how the image is uploaded.

These options are as follows:

- **--http** - Allows you to use plain http to connect to a remote registry. If you don't use this option, then https is the default option.
- **-p, --password <string>** - Allows you to enter the password that is used to authenticate with the remote registry. Replace the **<string>** field with the password. If you leave the --password field empty, then you will be prompted to enter your password manually.
- **--password-stdin** - Will read the password from stdin.
- **--skip-ssl-check** - Configures the login to skip the ssl certificate validation.
- **-u, --username <string>** - Allows you to enter the username you want to login with in order to connect remote registry. Replace the **<string>** field with the username.

As an example, if you wanted to push a container image called pvo:latest from the local host machine to a remote registry called pvonamespace which needs authentication using a username of pvo and a password of Password123, then the command would look something like the following:

- **`vctl push -u pvo --password Password123 pvonamespace/pvo:latest`**

In the next section, we are going to look at the rm command for removing containers from the host machine.

The rm Command

If you want to remove a container, then you would use the rm command. This command allows you to remove all containers or to remove a specific container by specifying the container name.

The command to do this is as follows:

```
vctl rm <OPTIONS> <CONTAINER>
```

When running the command, replace the **<OPTIONS>** field with the required options which we will cover in the next section, and then in the **<CONTAINER>** field, enter the name of the container that you want to remove.

rm Command Options

There are a few command options that can be used with the rm command that allows you to configure how containers are removed.

These options are as follows:

- **`-a, --all`** – Allows you to delete all containers
- **`-f, --force`** – Will force the removal of a container regardless of its status
- **`-v, --volume`** – Allows you to remove any anonymous volumes that are used by the container

As an example, we are going to remove the container called pvonginx. The command to do this is as follows:

```
vctl rm pvonginx
```

Figure 1-22 shows the output of running the command, the result being that the container has now been removed.

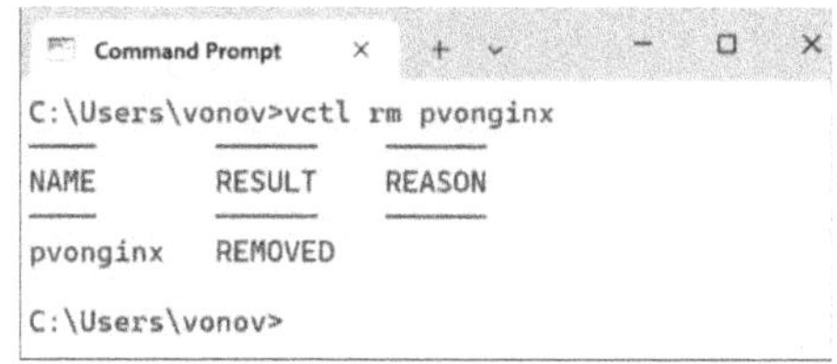

Figure 1-22. *Removing a Container*

Next, we are going to look at how to remove a container image.

The rmi Command

In the previous section, we looked at how to remove a container. In this section, we are going to look at how to remove the container image.

If you want to remove a container image, then you should use the rmi command. This command allows you to remove all container images or to remove a specific container image by specifying the name of that container image.

The command to do this is as follows:

```
vctl rmi <OPTIONS> <CONTAINER_IMAGE>
```

When running the command, replace the **<OPTIONS>** field with the required options which we will cover in the next section, and then in the **<CONTAINER_IMAGE>** field, enter the name of the container image that you want to remove.

rmi Command Options

There are a few command options that can be used with the rmi command that allows you to configure how container images are removed.

These options are as follows:

- **-a, --all** - Allows you to delete all container images
- **-f, --force** - Will force the removal of a container image regardless of its status

As an example, we are going to remove the container image called alpine:latest. The command to do this is as follows:

```
vctl rmi alpine:latest
```

Figure 1-23 shows the output of running the command, the result being that the container image has now been removed.

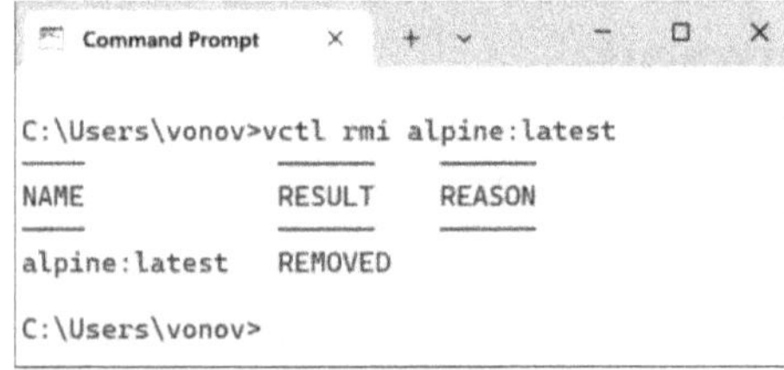

Figure 1-23. *Removing a Container Image*

Next, we are going to look at the run command.

The run Command

With the run command, you can create and run a new container from an existing container image.

When you run a new container, it runs in a separate virtual machine which is created using the same name as the container. This virtual machine will start up when the container starts and shuts down and is removed when you stop the container.

When you run the new container, then you also have the option of configuring the amount of memory and CPU resources that are available to the container. By default, it will be configured with two CPUs and 512MB of memory. We will cover how to reconfigure these resources when we discuss the run command options.

However, it is worth noting that a container running in a virtual machine will share the memory with its hosting virtual machine. For example, if you have a virtual machine configured with 1024MB memory, then the maximum memory that is available to the container will be 512MB.

As part of running the new container, you can specify additional commands along with any command arguments. However, it is worth noting that if you don't add any commands, then the default command from the image will be executed.

The syntax for the run command is as follows:

```
vctl run <OPTIONS> <CONTAINER_IMAGE> <COMMAND> <ARGUMENTS>
```

When running the command, replace the **<OPTIONS>** field with the required options which we will cover in the next section, and then in the **<CONTAINER_IMAGE>** field, enter the name of the container image that you want to use to run the new container from.

Then optionally, in the **<COMMAND>** field, enter any commands you want to run along with any command arguments in the **<ARGUMENTS>** field.

run Command Options

There are a few command options that can be used with the run command that allows you to configure how to run the container.

These options are as follows:

- **-c, --cpus** - Enables you to configure the number of CPU cores for the container. If you don't configure this option, then the default of two CPUs will be configured.
- **-d, --detach** - Configures the container to run in background.
- **--entrypoint <string>** - If configured, this setting overrides the default entrypoint of the container image. Replace the <string> field with the entrypoint you want to use.
- **-e, --env <strings>** - Enables you to configure environment variables to set in the container. Replace the <strings> field with the environment variables you want to configure.
- **--hostname <string>** - Enables you to configure a hostname for the container. Replace the <string> field with the hostname you want to use.
- **-i, --interactive** - Enables the STDIN to remain open even if not attached.
- **--keepVM** - Configures the host virtual machine to continue running even after the container is stopped. When using the --keepVM command, you will need to use the vmrun stop VMX command to manually stop the host virtual machine before using the container again.
- **-l, --label <strings>** - Allows you to set additional labels for the container. Replace the <string> field with the label you want to set.

- **-m, --memory <string>** - Configures a memory limit that is available to the container. If you don't configure this command option, then the default memory size of 512MB will be used. Replace the <string> field with the memory limit size for the container.
- **-n, --name <string>** - Enables you to configure a name for the container. Replace the <string> field with the name you want to use for the container.
- **-r, --privileged** - Runs the container with elevated privileges.
- **-p, --publish <strings>** - Binds the network ports on the host machine to network ports on the container. Replace the <string> field with the port numbers.
- **--rm** - Automatically removes the container when it exits.
- **-t, --tty** - Allocates a terminal for the container.
- **-v, --volume <strings>** - Enables you to bind host folders to container folders.
- **-w, --workdir <string>** - Working directory of the new process. Replace the <string> field with the name of the working directory you want to use.

As an example, we are going to run a new container and call it myNgnix. We are going to run it detached and also allocate a terminal for this container.

The command to do this is as follows:

```
vctl run -n myNginx -t -d nginx
```

Figure 1-24 shows the output from running this command.

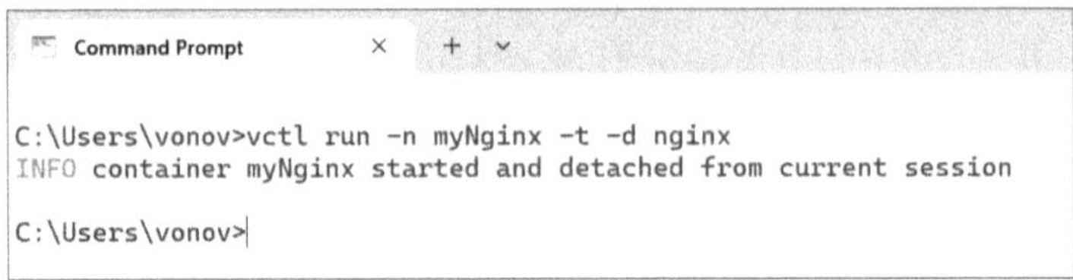

Figure 1-24. *Running a Container*

As you can see, the container called my Nginx is now started and is running detached from the current session.

To test whether the container is actually running and working as expected, we are going to connect to the web page for the nginx web server. The IP address can be found when you inspect and look at the container details.

As you can see in Figure 1-25, we have successfully opened a browser and navigated to the IP address and have landed on the nginx web server home page.

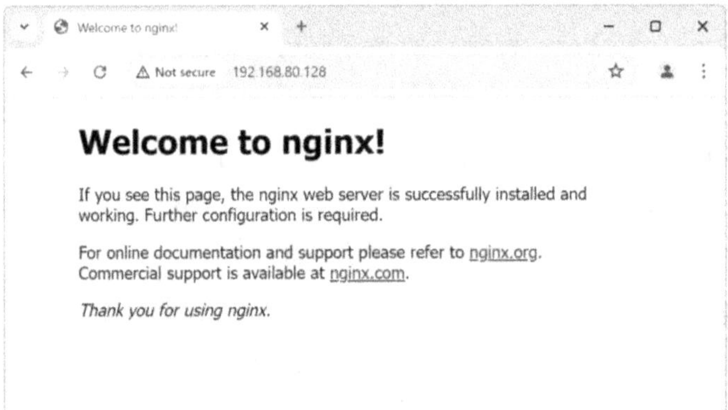

Figure 1-25. *Nginx Web Server Container Successfully Running*

In the next section, we are going to look at the start command.

The start Command

The start command is very similar to the run command; however, this time rather than create the container, it is used to start an existing container or one that has been stopped.

When you start a container, it runs in a separate virtual machine which is created using the same name as the container. This virtual machine will start up when the container starts and shuts down and is removed when you stop the container.

When you start the container, you also have the option of changing the configuration of the amount of memory and CPU resources that are available to the container. By default, it will be configured with two CPUs and 512MB of memory. We will cover how to reconfigure these resources when we discuss the run command options.

However, it is still worth noting that a container running in a virtual machine will share the memory with its hosting virtual machine. For example, if you have a virtual machine configured with 1024MB memory, then the maximum memory that is available to the container will be 512MB.

The syntax for the start command is as follows:

```
vctl start <OPTIONS> <CONTAINER>
```

When running the command, replace the **<OPTIONS>** field with the required options which we will cover in the next section, and then in the **<CONTAINER>** field, enter the name of the container that you want to start.

start Command Options

There are a few command options that can be used with the run command that allows you to configure how to run the container.

These options are as follows:

- **-c, --cpus** - Enables you to configure the number of CPU cores for the container. If you don't configure this option, then the default of two CPUs will be configured.
- **-d, --detach** - Configures the container to run in background.
- **--keepVM** - Configures the host virtual machine to continue running even after the container is stopped. When using the --keepVM command, you will need to use the vmrun stop VMX command to manually stop the host virtual machine before using the container again.
- **-m, --memory <string>** - Configures a memory limit that is available to the container. If you don't configure this command option, then the default memory size of 512MB will be used. Replace the <string> field with the memory limit size for the container.

As a quick example, we are going to simply start the container called nginx-8a26. The command that was run to do this is as follows:

```
vctl start nginx-8a26
```

Figure 1-26 shows the output from running the command and the container now successfully started.

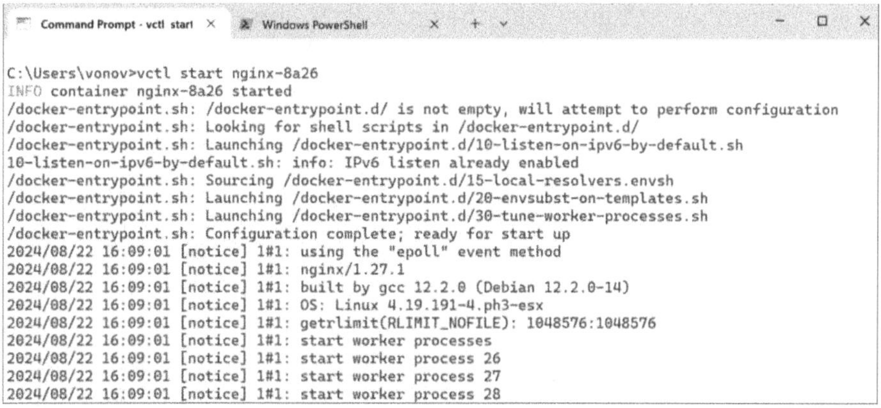

```
Command Prompt - vctl start    Windows PowerShell

C:\Users\vonov>vctl start nginx-8a26
INFO container nginx-8a26 started
/docker-entrypoint.sh: /docker-entrypoint.d/ is not empty, will attempt to perform configuration
/docker-entrypoint.sh: Looking for shell scripts in /docker-entrypoint.d/
/docker-entrypoint.sh: Launching /docker-entrypoint.d/10-listen-on-ipv6-by-default.sh
10-listen-on-ipv6-by-default.sh: info: IPv6 listen already enabled
/docker-entrypoint.sh: Sourcing /docker-entrypoint.d/15-local-resolvers.envsh
/docker-entrypoint.sh: Launching /docker-entrypoint.d/20-envsubst-on-templates.sh
/docker-entrypoint.sh: Launching /docker-entrypoint.d/30-tune-worker-processes.sh
/docker-entrypoint.sh: Configuration complete; ready for start up
2024/08/22 16:09:01 [notice] 1#1: using the "epoll" event method
2024/08/22 16:09:01 [notice] 1#1: nginx/1.27.1
2024/08/22 16:09:01 [notice] 1#1: built by gcc 12.2.0 (Debian 12.2.0-14)
2024/08/22 16:09:01 [notice] 1#1: OS: Linux 4.19.191-4.ph3-esx
2024/08/22 16:09:01 [notice] 1#1: getrlimit(RLIMIT_NOFILE): 1048576:1048576
2024/08/22 16:09:01 [notice] 1#1: start worker processes
2024/08/22 16:09:01 [notice] 1#1: start worker process 26
2024/08/22 16:09:01 [notice] 1#1: start worker process 27
2024/08/22 16:09:01 [notice] 1#1: start worker process 28
```

Figure 1-26. *Starting the nginx-8a26 Container*

Next, we are going to look at how to stop a currently running container.

The stop Command

In the previous section, we looked at how to start an existing or already stopped container. In this section, we are going to look at how to stop a running container.

The command to stop a container is as follows:

```
vctl stop <CONTAINER>
```

Unlike some of the other commands we have discussed, the stop command has no command options, and so when running the command, simply replace the **<CONTAINER>** field with the name of the container that you want to stop.

As an example, we are going to stop the container called nginx-8a26. The command to do this is as follows:

- **`vctl stop nginx-8a26`**

As you can see in Figure 1-27, the nginx-8a26 container has successfully been stopped.

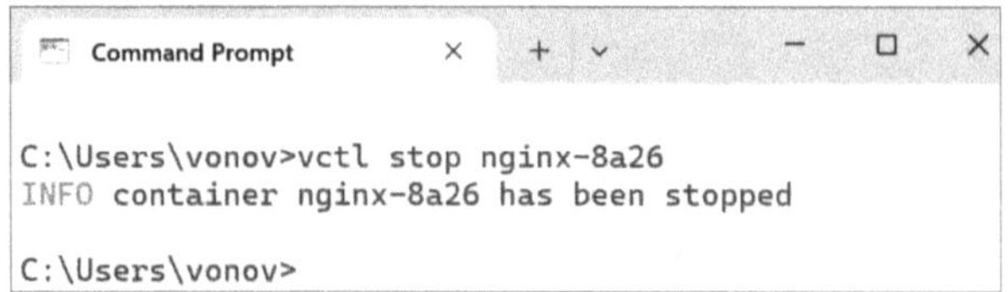

Figure 1-27. *Starting the nginx-8a26 Container*

The next command we are going to look at is the system command.

The system Command

With the system command, you can manage the container engine as well as the system environment.

The system command syntax is as follows:

```
vctl system <COMMAND> <OPTIONS>
```

When running the command, replace the **<COMMAND>** field with the required commands which we will cover in the next section, and then in the **<OPTIONS>** field, enter any command options you want to add.

system Commands

With the system command, you can run the following commands:

- **config** - Enables you to config and initialize the system environment for the container engine. This was detailed at the beginning of the chapter in the setting up and managing a container runtime section.
- **info** - Displays the container engine information as shown in Figure 1-28.

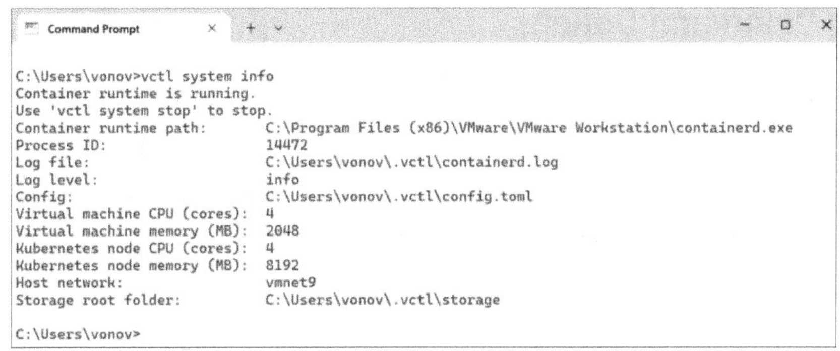

Figure 1-28. *Output from Running the System Info Command*

- **start** - Starts the container engine. We have covered this previously in the start command section of this chapter.
- **stop** - Stops a running container engine. We have covered this previously in the stop command section of this chapter.

The next command we are going to look at is the tag command.

The tag Command

The tag command is used to create an image alias that uses the name of the target image.

The system command syntax is as follows:

vctl tag <OPTIONS> <SOURCE_IMAGE> <TARGET_IMAGE>

When running the command, replace the **<OPTIONS>** field with the required command options which we will cover in the next section.

Then in the **<SOURCE_IMAGE>** field, enter the details of the source image, and then in the **<TARGET_IMAGE>** field, enter the name you want to create as the alias.

tag Command Options

There is just a single command option when running the tag command. This is as follows:

- **-f, --force** – Replaces an existing image even if the TARGET_IMAGE name has already been taken

Next, we are going to look at the version command.

The version Command

If you want to know what version of vctl you are running, then you can find this out by running the version command.

The version command syntax is as follows:

```
vctl version
```

Running the command will show the following as shown in Figure 1-29.

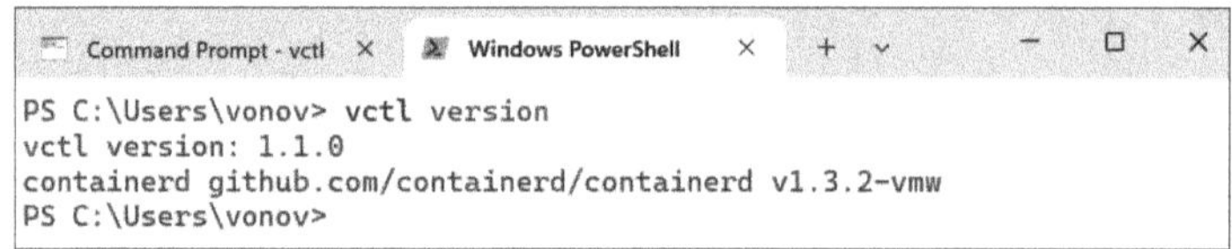

Figure 1-29. *vctl version Command*

The final command we are going to look at is the volume command.

The volume Command

The volume command is used to manage storage volumes on the host machine and currently only supports the volume prune option.

The volume command syntax is as follows:

```
vctl volume <COMMAND>
```

When running the volume command, replace the **<COMMAND>** field with the command you want to run. As the volume command currently only supports the prune command that removes all unused local volumes, then there is just the one command which would look like the command below:

```
vctl volume prune
```

Before any local volumes, you will see the following warning message shown in Figure 1-30.

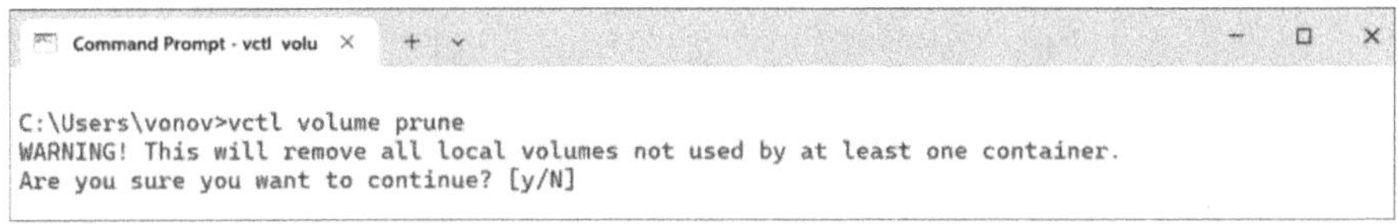

Figure 1-30. *vctl volume prune Command*

Type **y** to continue with the removal process or **n** to cancel and return to the command prompt.

We have now completed the overview of the vctl command and its various options and use cases.

Summary

In this chapter, we have taken a comprehensive look at working with containers in Workstation Pro.

We started the chapter by reminding you what the differences are between a virtual machine and a container.

Next, we got started by deploying a container environment ready for use, looking at how to manage and change the configuration of the components that make up the environment.

Throughout the rest of the chapter, we took a detailed look at all the commands that are available in Workstation Pro to work with and manage containers, explaining each command, its different options, and in some cases looking at real-life examples with actual screenshots.

In the next chapter, we are going to look at the **`vmware`** command, a command that is used for starting or launching the Workstation Pro application and enabling you to add startup options and parameters such as automatically launching a virtual machine.

CHAPTER 2

Using the vmware Command

In this second chapter, we are going to look at the **vmware** command. This is a command line that is used for starting or launching the Workstation Pro application and enabling you to add startup options and parameters such as automatically launching a virtual machine.

The use case for this command is to create Windows shortcuts on the host machine, perhaps on the desktop, that defines how Workstation Pro runs.

It is worth noting that this command does not control virtual machines, This is the vmrun command that provides this functionality and will be covered in Chapter 3.

In the next section, we are going to look at what the syntax of the vmware command looks like.

P. von Oven, *Learning VMware Workstation Pro for Windows: Volume 2*,
https://doi.org/10.1007/979-8-8688-0864-7_2

vmware Command Syntax

The **vmware** command is found in the default folder along with the other commands that we will cover in the coming chapters. It is the most important command as it is the executable that is used to launch the Workstation Pro application in the first place. vmware.exe to give it its full name is Workstation Pro if you like.

The folder and path of where you will find the command, if you have used the default installation path, are as follows:

C:\Program Files (x86)\VMware\VMware Workstation\vmware.exe

When you run the command, you would add any command options after the vmware.exe command, followed by the path to the folder of where the configuration file (.vmx) of the virtual machine you are targeting is stored.

For example, you might want to use the command option to power up the virtual machine called windows.vmx which would be the path you would specify.

The default command syntax would look something like this:

```
vmware.exe -<COMMAND_OPTION> <PATH_TO_VM>
```

As already highlighted, you then have several options that can be specified to be used with the vmware command.

If you use the vmware.exe command without any command options, then it will just simply launch the Workstation Pro application as would happen if you just double-clicked the desktop icon for example.

In the next section, we are going to show each of those options along with the example output where applicable.

Command Options

In this section, we are going to look at the different options available when running the vmware command.

Show Program Version

The first command option displays the details of the Workstation Pro application. It's the same as clicking Help and About VMware Workstation from within the application.

To run this command, follow the steps described:

1. Open a command prompt.
2. Navigate to the **C:\Program Files (x86)\VMware\VMware Workstation** folder or ensure this location is added to the path.
3. At the command prompt, type **`vmware -v`** and press Enter.
4. You will then see, after a small delay while the command executes, the About VMware Workstation Pro 17 window appears that provides details about the Workstation Pro version and build number, licensing information, and details about the host machine.

   This is shown in Figure 2-1.

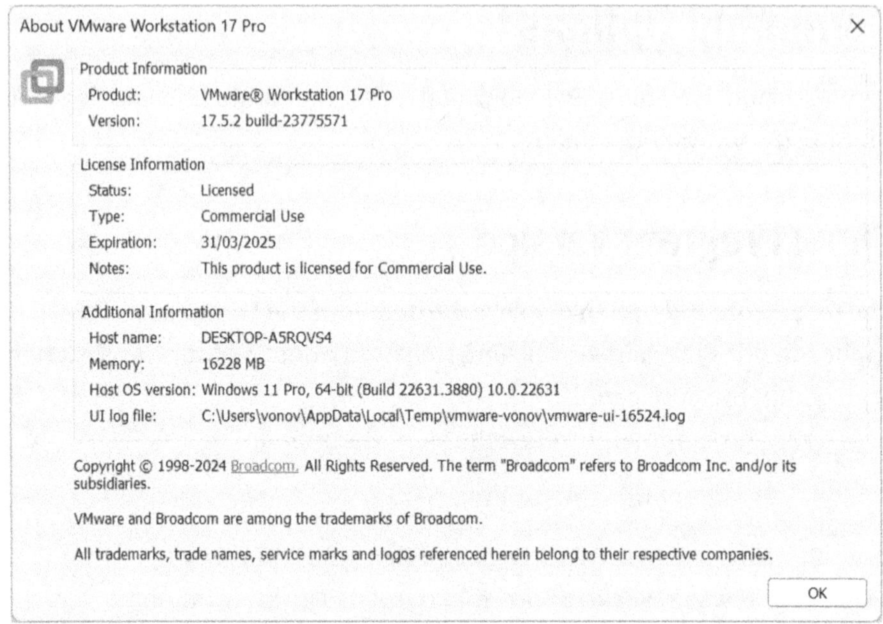

Figure 2-1. *About VMware Workstation 17 Pro Screen*

5. Click the **OK** button to close the window.

The next command option we are going to look at enables you to power on a virtual machine as VMware Workstation is launched.

Powering on a Virtual Machine

With this next command, you launch Workstation Pro and automatically power on a virtual machine. The virtual machine you want to power on is specified in the command line.

The command syntax is as follows:

```
vmware.exe -x <path_to_VM >
```

In this command, the **-x** is the command option required for powering on a virtual machine when Workstation Pro launches.

You then need to replace the **<path_to_vm>** field with the path to the configuration file (.vmx) for the virtual machine that you want to power on.

As an example of this command, we are going to power on a virtual machine called Win10 that has its .vmx file stored in the C:\VM folder.

To run this command, follow the steps described:

1. Open a command prompt.
2. Navigate to the **C:\Program Files (x86)\VMware\VMware Workstation** folder.
3. **At the command prompt, type `vmware.exe -x C:\VM\Win10.vmx`** and then press Enter.
4. Workstation Pro will launch, and then you will see that the specified virtual machine tab is the only tab in focus and that the virtual machine will have powered on as shown in Figure 2-2.

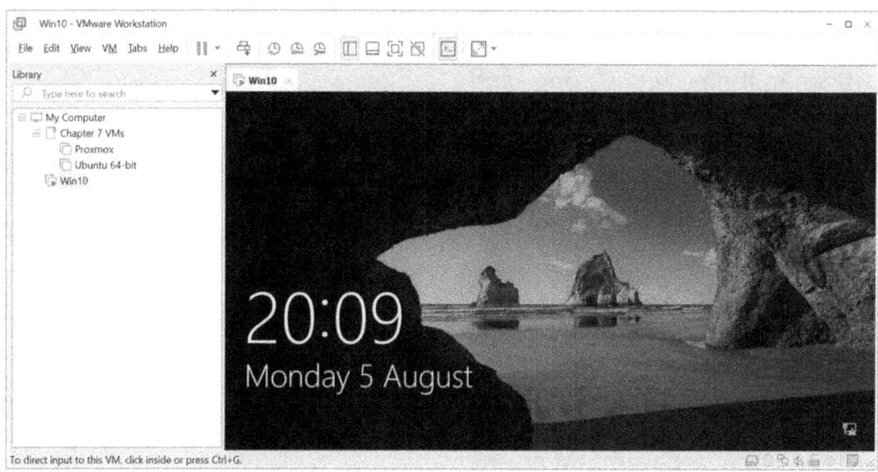

***Figure 2-2.** Virtual Machine Automatically Powered On*

Next, we are going to look at powering on a virtual machine again, but this time in full screen mode.

Note that it will take a few seconds or so for Workstation Pro to launch and the virtual machine to power on and be ready for you to be able to login to it and use it.

Powering on a Virtual Machine in Full Screen

With this next command, you launch Workstation Pro and automatically power on a virtual machine in full screen. The virtual machine you want to power on is specified in the command line.

The command syntax is as follows:

```
vmware.exe -X <path_to_VM >
```

In this command, the **-X** is the command option required for powering on a virtual machine in full screen mode when Workstation Pro launches.

Just to point out that this is an uppercase **X** rather than the lowercase **x** used in the previous command.

You then need to replace the **<path_to_vm>** field with the path to the configuration file (.vmx) for the virtual machine that you want to power on.

As an example of this command, we are going to again power on the virtual machine called Win10 that has its .vmx file stored in the C:\VM folder.

To run this command, follow the steps described:

1. Open a command prompt.
2. Navigate to the **C:\Program Files (x86)\VMware\VMware Workstation** folder.
3. At the command prompt, type `vmware.exe -X C:\VM\Win10.vmx` and then press Enter.

4. Workstation Pro will launch, and then you will see that the specified virtual machine, in this case the Windows 10 example virtual machine, will power on in full screen mode as shown in Figure 2-3.

Figure 2-3. *Virtual Machine Automatically Powered on in Full Screen Mode*

Next, we are going to look at how to launch Workstation Pro and start a virtual machine in a paused power state.

Start Virtual Machine in Paused Mode

With this next command, you can launch Workstation Pro and automatically set the power state of a virtual machine to paused or suspended mode. The virtual machine you want to power on is specified in the command line.

The command syntax is as follows:

```
vmware.exe -p <path_to_VM >
```

In this command, the **-p** is the command option required for starting a virtual machine in paused or suspended mode when Workstation Pro launches.

You then need to replace the **<path_to_vm>** field with the path to the configuration file (.vmx) for the virtual machine that you want to power on.

As an example of this command, we are going to launch Workstation Pro and start the example virtual machine in suspended mode. This example virtual machine is called Win10 that has its .vmx file stored in the C:\VM folder.

To run this command, follow the steps described:

1. Open a command prompt.
2. Navigate to the **C:\Program Files (x86)\VMware\VMware Workstation** folder.
3. At the command prompt, type **`vmware.exe -X C:\VM\Win10.vmx`** and then press Enter.
4. Workstation Pro will launch, and then you will see that the specified virtual machine, in this case the Windows 10 example virtual machine, will show as being in paused or suspended mode as show in Figure 2-4.

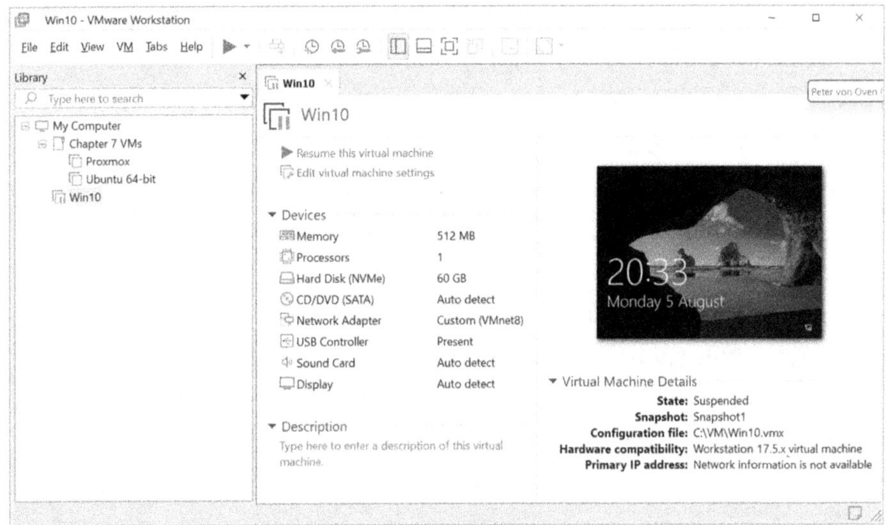

Figure 2-4. *Virtual Machine Automatically Started in Paused Mode*

Next, we are going to look at how to launch Workstation Pro and start a virtual machine, and then when you power off the virtual machine, Workstation Pro will exit.

Close a Virtual Machine on Power Off

With this next command, you can launch Workstation Pro and automatically power on a virtual machine, and then when you power off the virtual machine, the virtual machine tab will close if there are other virtual machines running or the Workstation Pro application will close if this is the only virtual machine that is running.

The virtual machine you want to close on power off is specified in the command line.

The command syntax is as follows:

```
vmware.exe -x -q <path_to_VM >
```

In this command, the **-x** is also used to specify the powering on of the virtual machine. Without having a virtual machine powered on first, then Workstation Pro won't know you want to quit the application when that virtual machine is powered off.

The **-q** command option is then to quit the Workstation Pro application that when the specified virtual machine is powered off then to quit the application.

You then need to replace the **<path_to_vm>** field with the path to the configuration file (.vmx) for the virtual machine that you want to firstly power on and then to trigger the exiting of the Workstation Pro application.

As an example of this command, we are going to launch Workstation Pro and start the example virtual machine in suspended mode. This example virtual machine is called Win10 that has its .vmx file stored in the C:\VM folder.

To run this command, follow the steps described:

1. Open a command prompt.
2. Navigate to the **C:\Program Files (x86)\VMware\VMware Workstation** folder.
3. At the command prompt, type **`vmware.exe -x -q C:\VM\Win10.vmx`** and then press Enter.
4. Workstation Pro will launch, and then you will see that the specified virtual machine, in this case the Windows 10 example virtual machine, will power on.
5. When you power off the Windows 10 example virtual machine, then you will see that Workstation Pro will close and exit.

You could also use the command option with the -X (uppercase) for powering on the virtual machine in full screen mode and then add the -q command option to quit Workstation Pro or close the virtual machine tab when the virtual machine is powered off.

The next command we are going to look at allows you to set a variable for the virtual machine as it is powered on.

Set a Virtual Machine Variable

With this next command, you can launch Workstation Pro, automatically power on a virtual machine, and then set a variable for the virtual machine. Variables are defined as those settings you will find in the .vmx configuration file that define the configuration of the virtual machine.

The virtual machine you want to set the variable for is specified in the command line.

The command syntax is as follows:

```
vmware.exe -x -s <variable> <path_to_VM >
```

In this command, the **-x** is also used to specify the powering on of the virtual machine. Without having a virtual machine powered on first, then Workstation Pro won't know not only which virtual machine to power on but more importantly which virtual machine you want to set the variable for.

Next, the **-s** command option is used to set the variable which is followed by the actual variable you want to set in the **<variable>** field.

Finally, you need to replace the **<path_to_vm>** field with the path to the configuration file (.vmx) for the virtual machine that you want to firstly power on and then to trigger the exiting of the Workstation Pro application.

As an example of this command, we are going to launch Workstation Pro and start the example virtual machine and change the variable name that sets the virtual machine name in the library view of Workstation Pro. We are going to change this to Win10_CH02.

This example virtual machine is called Win10 that has its .vmx file stored in the C:\VM folder.

To run this command, follow the steps described:

1. Open a command prompt.
2. Navigate to the **C:\Program Files (x86)\VMware\VMware Workstation** folder.
3. At the command prompt, type **`vmware -x -s displayName=Win10_CH02 c:\VM\Win10.vmx`** and then press Enter.
4. Workstation Pro will launch, and then you will see that the specified virtual machine, in this case the Windows 10 example virtual machine, will power on.
5. You will also see that the name in the library view now shows the virtual machine name as Win10_CH02 as shown in Figure 2-5.

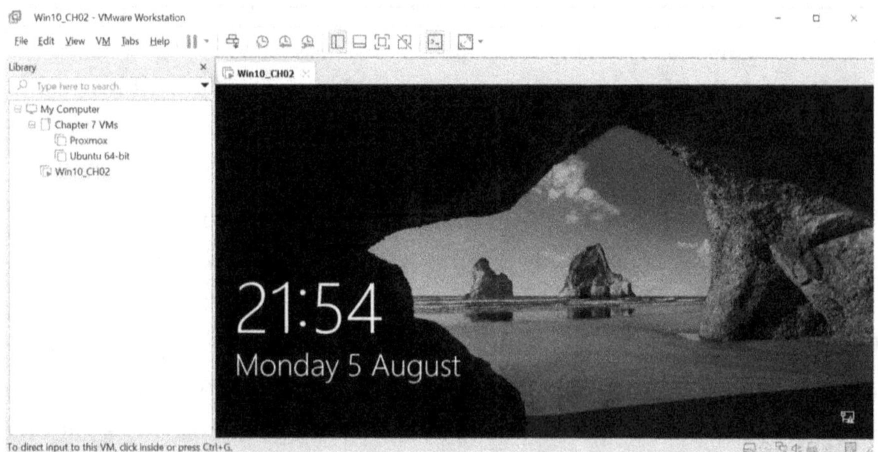

***Figure 2-5.** Virtual Machine Updated Name in the Library View*

As with previous commands and using more than one command option, you could also use this command with the -X (uppercase) command option for powering on the virtual machine in full screen mode.

When you power off the virtual machine, it will reset back to what is recorded in the .vmx file. The changes do not persist. So, the next time the virtual machine is powered on, it will display the original name, i.e., the name specified in the .vmx file.

Next, we are going to look at a command that enables you to open a new window in Workstation Pro.

Open a New Window

With this next command, you can open an additional Workstation Pro window or, to be more precise, launch another running copy of the app so that you have the Workstation App running multiple times.

Maybe this is to open another virtual machine or to just open another Workstation Pro session.

The command syntax is as follows:

```
vmware.exe -n
```

In this command, the **-n** is also used to open another Workstation Pro session or another copy of the application.

For example, if you already have a Workstation Pro session already running, using this command as shown above will open another Workstation Pro session that can be used independently to the other(s).

To run this command, follow the steps described:

1. Open a command prompt.
2. Navigate to the **C:\Program Files (x86)\VMware\VMware Workstation** folder.

3. At the command prompt, type **vmware -n** and then press Enter.

4. Workstation Pro will launch, and then you will see, as no virtual machine has been specified in the command line, that the Home tab is displayed as shown in Figure 2-6.

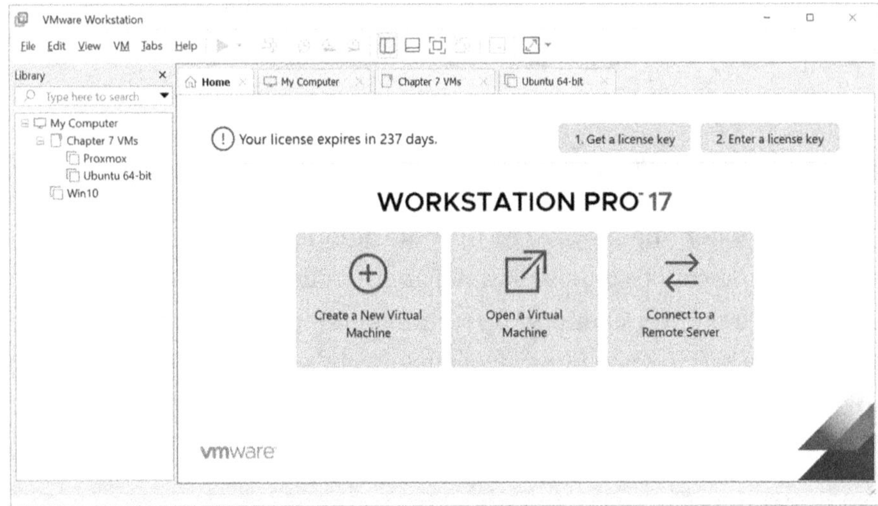

***Figure 2-6.** New Workstation Pro Window Opened*

We've just said that the Home tab is in focus as no virtual machine was specified in the command line, so what happens if you specify a virtual machine and what does that look like.

If we run the command again, this time, we will specify a virtual machine. In this example, we will use the Windows 10 example virtual machine again.

The command to do this will look like the following:

```
vmware -n C:\VM\Win10.vmx
```

As we have specified the -n command option, then a new Workstation Pro window will open, and now that a virtual machine has been specified in the command line, then you will see that the tab in focus is that of the virtual machine.

In this case, the Windows 10 example machine is shown in Figure 2-7.

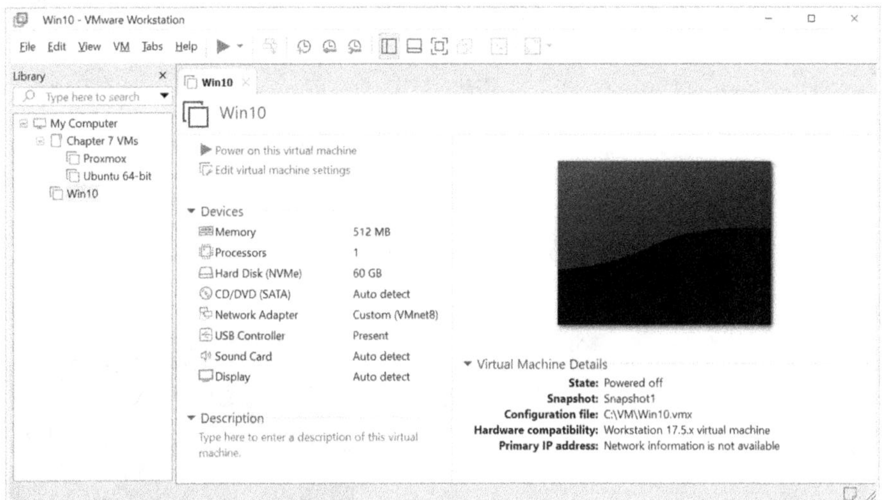

***Figure 2-7.** New Workstation Pro Window Opened for a Specific Virtual Machine*

You can build on this command by opening a new window, and instead of just targeting a specific virtual machine to be in focus, i.e., the virtual machines tab being in focus, you could also power on the virtual machine in that new window.

If we run the command to open a new window again (-n) but this time, as well as specifying a virtual machine, in this example we will use the Windows 10 example virtual machine again, we will also add the -x command option to power on that virtual machine.

The command to do this will look like the following:

```
vmware -n -x C:\VM\Win10.vmx
```

You will see another Workstation Pro window open, and in that window, the Windows 10 example virtual machine will power on.

In Figure 2-8, you will see an example where on the left the initial Workstation Pro app has been launched and is running and then on the right-hand side you can see a second instance of Workstation Pro running, and in this instance, you will see the Windows 10 virtual machine powered on and running.

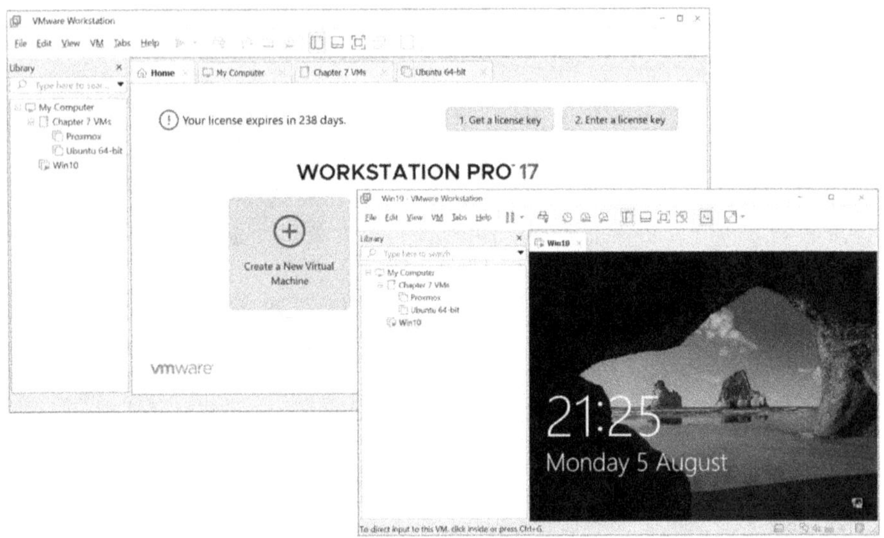

Figure 2-8. *New Workstation Pro Window Opened Running a Virtual Machine*

As we've shown previously, you could replace the -x (lowercase) with -X (uppercase) and open another Workstation Pro instance and power on the virtual machine in full screen mode.

It is also worth pointing out, given we are adding multiple command options, that if you added the -q command option to the command, then this would close that additional Workstation Pro instance when you power off the virtual machine that is running in it.

The next command we are going to look at is a second option for starting a virtual machine in full screen mode.

Launch in Full Screen Mode

We have already looked at the **-X** command option to open a virtual machine in full screen mode; however, there is also a second option for launching Workstation Pro and virtual machines in full screen mode, and in this section, we are going to look at a few examples of using this command.

The command syntax is as follows:

```
vmware.exe -f <path_to_VM >
```

In the first example of this command, we are simply going to run the vmware command with just the -f command option and no other command options, following the steps described:

To run this command, follow the steps described:

1. Open a command prompt.
2. Navigate to the **C:\Program Files (x86)\VMware\VMware Workstation** folder.
3. At the command prompt, type **`vmware -f`** and then press Enter.
4. Workstation Pro will launch in full screen, displaying the home screen as shown in Figure 2-9.

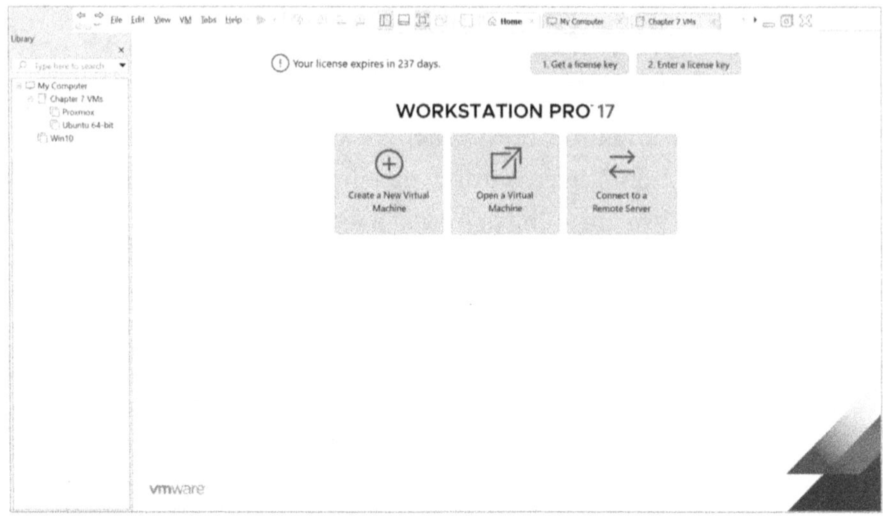

***Figure 2-9.** Workstation Pro Launched in Full Screen*

We can now take this example a step further and now to specify a specific virtual machine within the command line.

In this example, we are going to use the Windows 10 virtual machine used previously. This example virtual machine is called Win10 that has its .vmx file stored in the C:\VM folder.

To run this command, follow the steps described:

1. Open a command prompt.

2. Navigate to the **C:\Program Files (x86)\VMware\VMware Workstation** folder.

3. At the command prompt, type **`vmware -f C:\VM\Win10.vmx`** and then press Enter.

4. Workstation Pro will now launch in full screen, but as a specific virtual machine has been specified in the command line then as you will see in Figure 2-10, this virtual machine called Win 10 is in focus and the only virtual machine tab that is open.

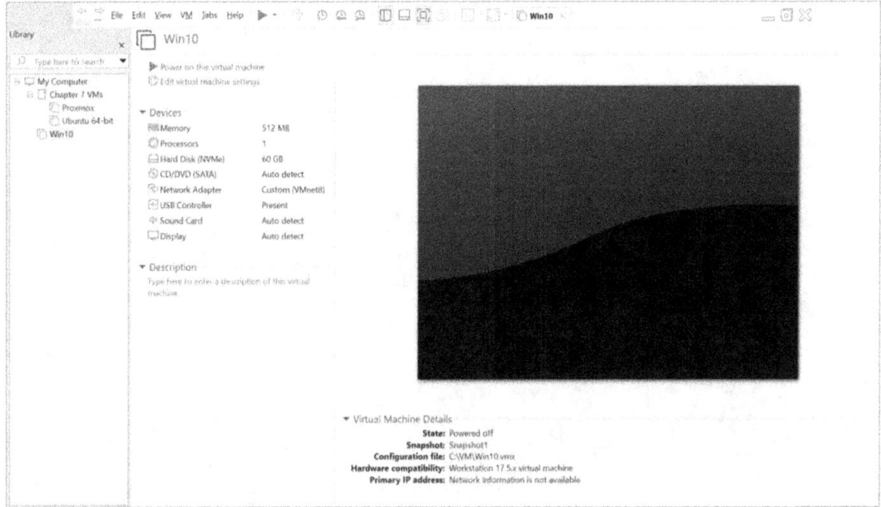

Figure 2-10. *Workstation Pro Launched in Full Screen with Focus VM*

You will also see that the virtual machine is not powered on, just merely in focus. That's because we haven't added the command option to tell Workstation Pro to power it on.

In the next example, we are going to add a final command option to the two previous examples and power the virtual machine on in full screen mode.

To do this command, follow the steps described:

1. Open a command prompt.
2. Navigate to the **C:\Program Files (x86)\VMware\VMware Workstation** folder.
3. At the command prompt, type **`vmware -f - x C:\VM\Win10.vmx`** and then press Enter.
4. Workstation Pro will now launch and power on the virtual as shown in Figure 2-11.

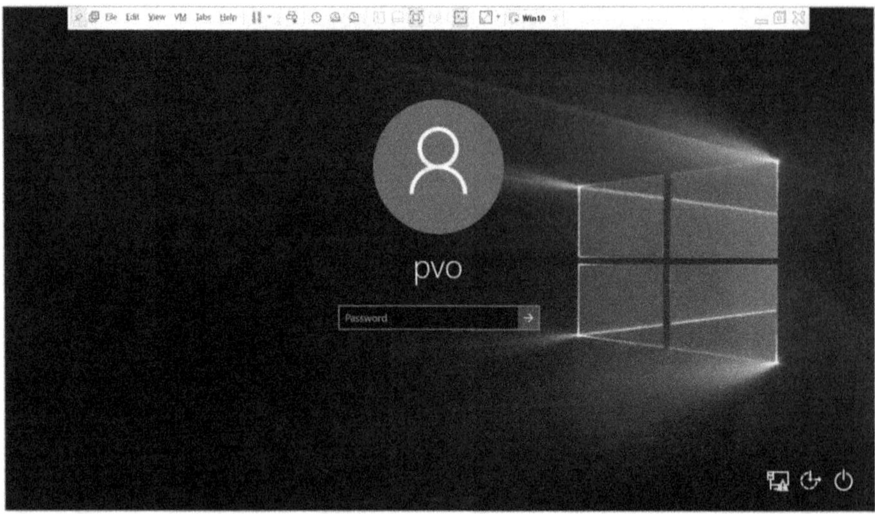

Figure 2-11. *Workstation Pro Launched in Full Screen with VM Powered On*

One final example is that you could also add the **-q** command option which would then close the virtual machine when you power it off. If this was the only virtual machine that was running, then it would also exit and close the Workstation Pro app as well.

If other virtual machines are running at the same time, then it would just close that particular tab for the virtual machine you specified in the command.

To do this command, follow the steps described:

1. Open a command prompt.
2. Navigate to the **C:\Program Files (x86)\VMware\VMware Workstation** folder.
3. At the command prompt, type **`vmware -f - x -q C:\VM\Win10.vmx`** and then press Enter.

4. Workstation Pro will now launch in full screen with the virtual machine powered on. When you power off the virtual machine, then Workstation Pro will exit. This is hard to show in static screenshots.

To finish up on the subject of adding command options, you could also add the -n command option into the mix too. The outcome would be that Workstation Pro would launch in a new window and power on the specific virtual machine in full screen, and then when you power of the virtual machine, then Workstation Pro would exit and close that new window that was opened.

The command to do all of this, using the example Windows 10 virtual machine, would look something like the following:

```
vmware -n -f - x -q C:\VM|Win10.vmx
```

We have now looked at the various different command options for powering on virtual machines, closing them, and setting variables. The final set of command options is for automatically connecting to remote consoles.

In the next section, we are going to look at how you can automatically make those connections when Workstation Pro is launched from the command line.

Console Connections

As a reminder, in Workstation Pro, this means connecting to vCenter Servers or ESXi host servers so that they appear in the inventory within Workstation Pro to enable them to be managed from the same user interface and to copy virtual machines between the platforms.

In this section, we are going to look at how to remotely connect to remote vSphere infrastructure in the form of vCenter Servers and ESXi host servers.

The use case for this is when you use Workstation Pro for development and testing. You may need to download a virtual machine from the data center to a local device running Workstation Pro in order to complete development work or you need to upload a virtual machine built on Workstation Pro. It may just be that you need to manage vSphere infrastructure.

There are three command options for connecting to remote VMware infrastructure which equate to the following required information in order to both connect and authenticate:

- Hostname
- Username
- Password

Taking these three command options, the syntax for this command is as follows:

```
vmware.exe -H <HOSTNAME> -U <USERNAME> -P <PASSWORD>
```

When running the command, replace the <**HOSTNAME**> field with the hostname or IP address of the vCenter Server or ESXi host you want to connect to and then supply the name of the user you want to login as in the <**USERNAME**> field followed by the password for that user in the <**PASSOWRD**> field.

It is basically the same as the **Connect to Server** option discussed in Chapter 11 of Volume 1 of the *Learning VMware Workstation Pro* book and the dialog box shown in Figure 2-12.

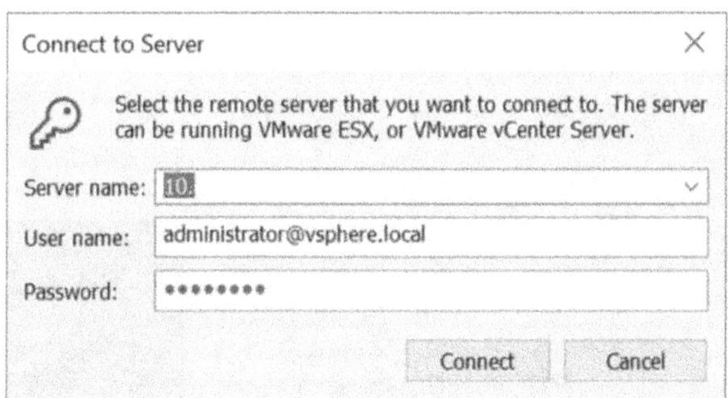

Figure 2-12. *Workstation Pro Connect to Server Dialog Box*

If we follow that example and do this from the command line as we launch Workstation Pro, then follow the steps described:

1. Open a command prompt.
2. Navigate to the **C:\Program Files (x86)\VMware\VMware Workstation** folder.
3. At the command prompt, type **`vmware.exe -H 192.168.1.1 -U PVO -P P@ssw0rd1`** and then press Enter.
4. Workstation Pro will now launch, and as long as you have specified the correct hostname and corresponding credentials, then you will see the vCenter Server or ESXi host you connected to appear in the Workstation Pro library view ready for navigation as shown in the example screenshot in Figure 2-13.

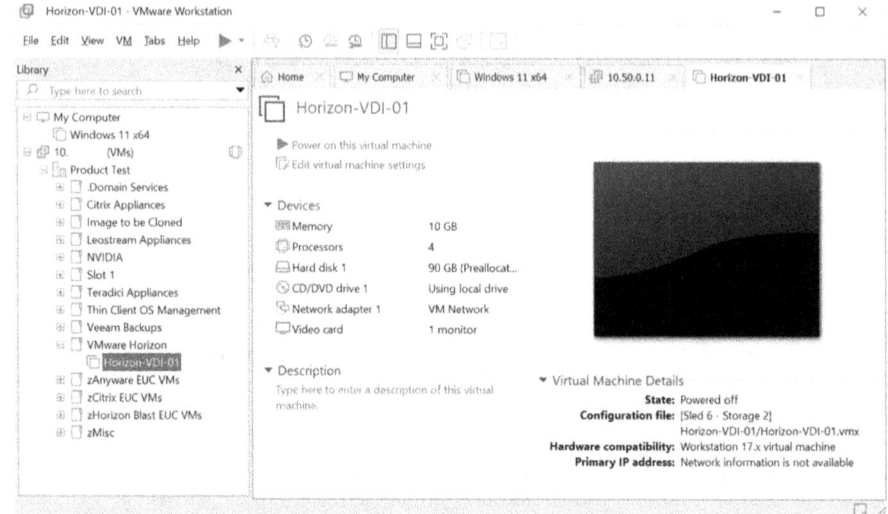

Figure 2-13. *Workstation Pro Connected to Remote Resources*

We have now covered all the available command options for running and launching VMware Workstation Pro from the command line.

Just in case you want a quick recap of the available command options, then there is a way of displaying these which we will cover in the next section.

Display the Command Options

If you want to display a list of all the command options that we have covered in this chapter, then there is one final command we are going to look at to display these.

To display the command options, follow the steps described:

1. Open a command prompt.

2. Navigate to the **C:\Program Files (x86)\VMware\VMware** Workstation folder.

3. At the command prompt, type **`vmware.exe /?`** Or alternatively type **`vmware.exe --help`** and then press Enter.

4. You will see the following dialog box appear as shown in Figure 2-14.

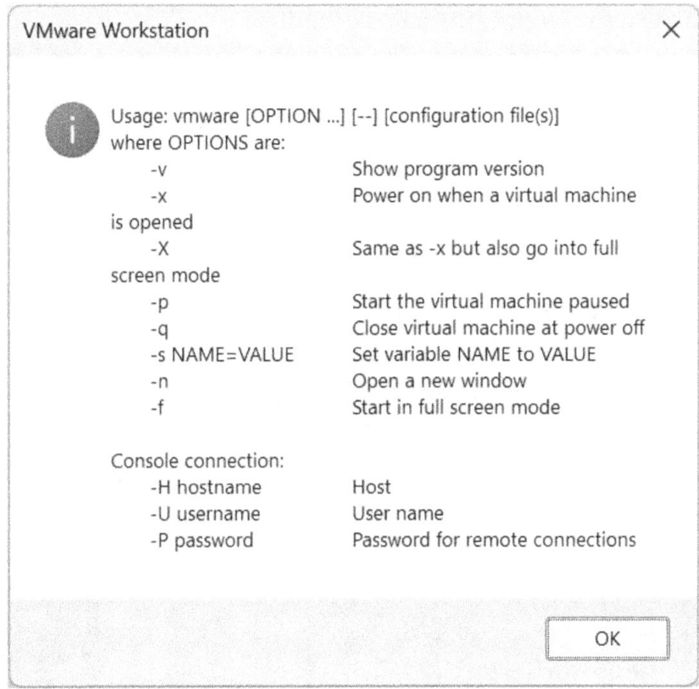
```
VMware Workstation

Usage: vmware [OPTION ...] [--] [configuration file(s)]
where OPTIONS are:
     -v                  Show program version
     -x                  Power on when a virtual machine
is opened
     -X                  Same as -x but also go into full
screen mode
     -p                  Start the virtual machine paused
     -q                  Close virtual machine at power off
     -s NAME=VALUE       Set variable NAME to VALUE
     -n                  Open a new window
     -f                  Start in full screen mode

Console connection:
     -H hostname         Host
     -U username         User name
     -P password         Password for remote connections

                                               OK
```

Figure 2-14. *Command Options Help Dialog Box*

Now we have looked at all the command options available; in the penultimate section, we are, just as an example, going to create a desktop shortcut that demonstrates the use case.

Shortcut Example

In this section, we are going to quickly demonstrate how to create a desktop shortcut that launches VMware Workstation Pro and powers on the example Windows 10 virtual machine.

We are going to create a desktop shortcut on the desktop of the host machine. To do this, follow the steps described:

1. On the host machine that is running VMware Workstation Pro, right-click somewhere on the desktop to display the contextual menu.

2. From that menu, click to expand the **New** option, and then from the pop-out menu that appears, click **Shortcut** as shown in Figure 2-15.

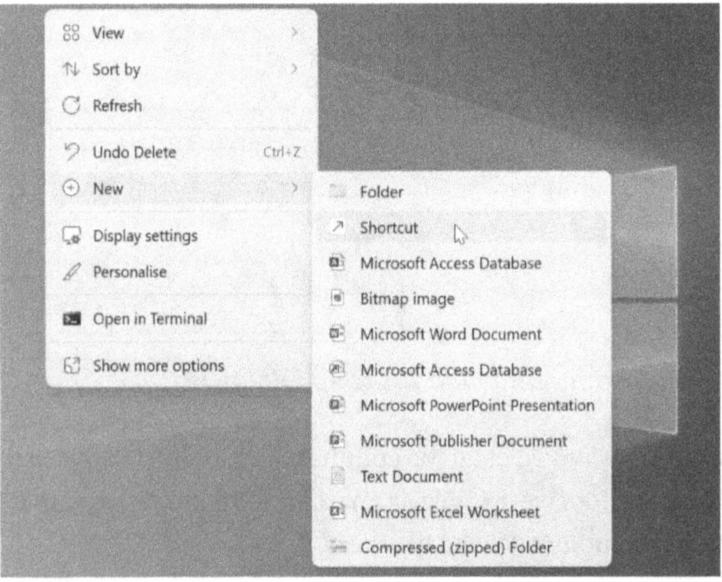

***Figure 2-15.** Desktop Contextual Menu*

3. You will now see the ***Create Shortcut*** screen as shown in Figure 2-16.

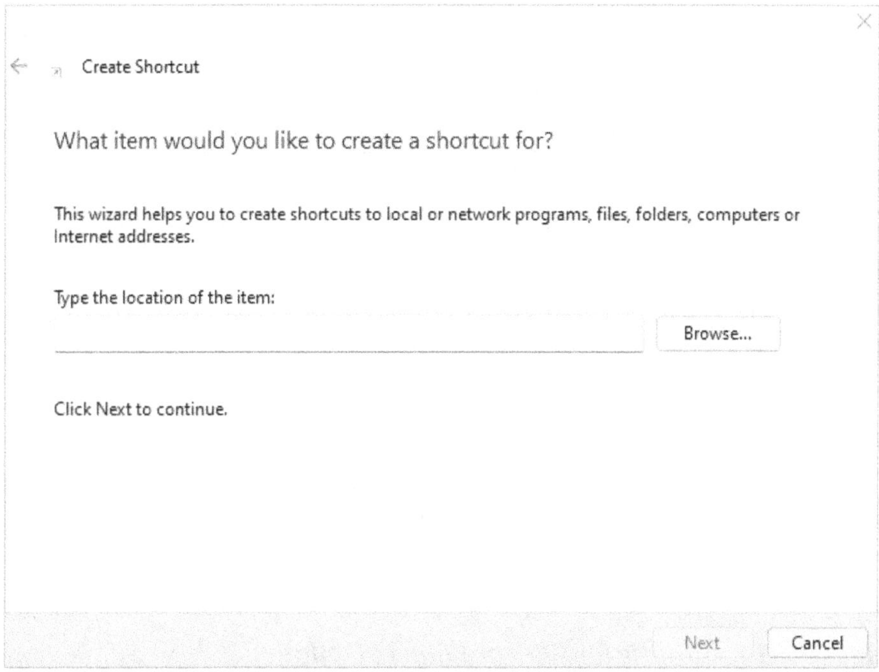

Figure 2-16. *Create Shortcut Configuration Screen*

4. In the **Type the location of the item** box, type in the full path to the vmware.exe file. The full path is as follows:

   "C:\Program Files (x86)\VMware\VMware Workstation\vmware.exe"

   Note that this will need to be in quotes as shown.

5. You could alternatively click the **Browse...** button, which will open the **Browse for File or Folders** dialog box where you can then navigate to the location of the vmware.exe file by clicking through

the folders, so click **This PC**, then **Local Disk (C:)**, **Program Files (x86)**, **VMware**, **VMware Workstation**, and then finally the **vmware.exe** file itself.

This file is easy to identify as it will have the VMware Workstation Pro icon as shown in Figure 2-17.

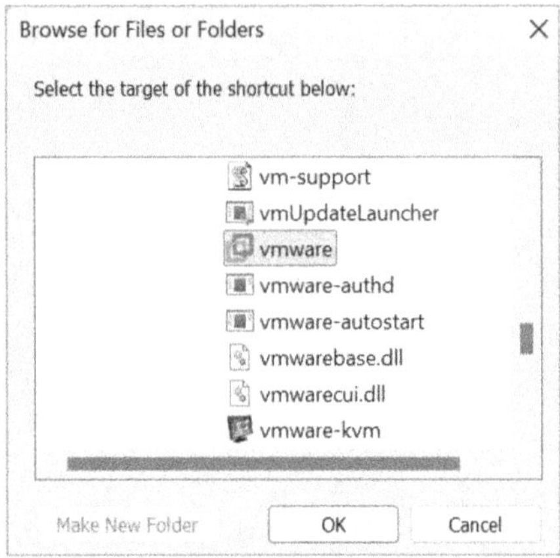

***Figure 2-17.** Browse for Files or Folders Dialog Box*

6. Click ***OK*** and then path will be added to the ***Create Shortcut*** screen as shown in Figure 2-18.

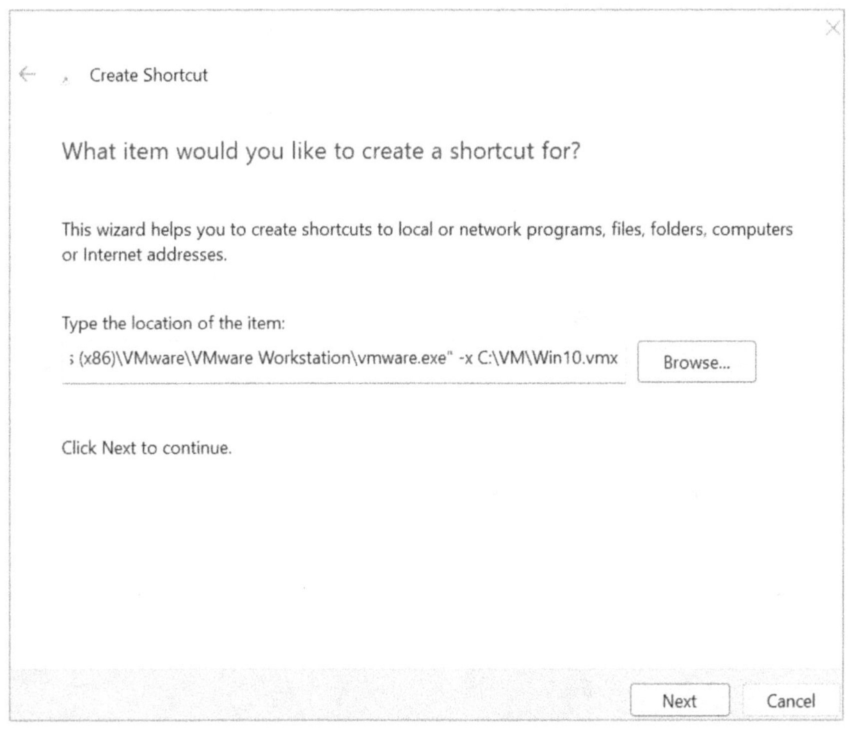

***Figure 2-18.** Path Added for the New Shortcut*

7. With the path and the executable for Workstation Pro configured, you can now add any of your command options or specific virtual machine details to the end of the command, after the quote marks.

8. In this example, we are going to power on the example Windows 10 virtual machine so we would add the -x command option followed by the path to where the virtual machine is stored. This would be like the following:

   ```
   "C:\Program Files (x86)\VMware\VMware
   Workstation\vmware.exe" -x C:\VM\Win10.vmx
   ```

You can of course add any other command options such as -f for full screen or -q to close the virtual machine. Just add these as we have described throughout this chapter.

9. Click **Next** to continue.

10. You will see the ***What would you like to name the shortcut*** screen as shown in Figure 2-19.

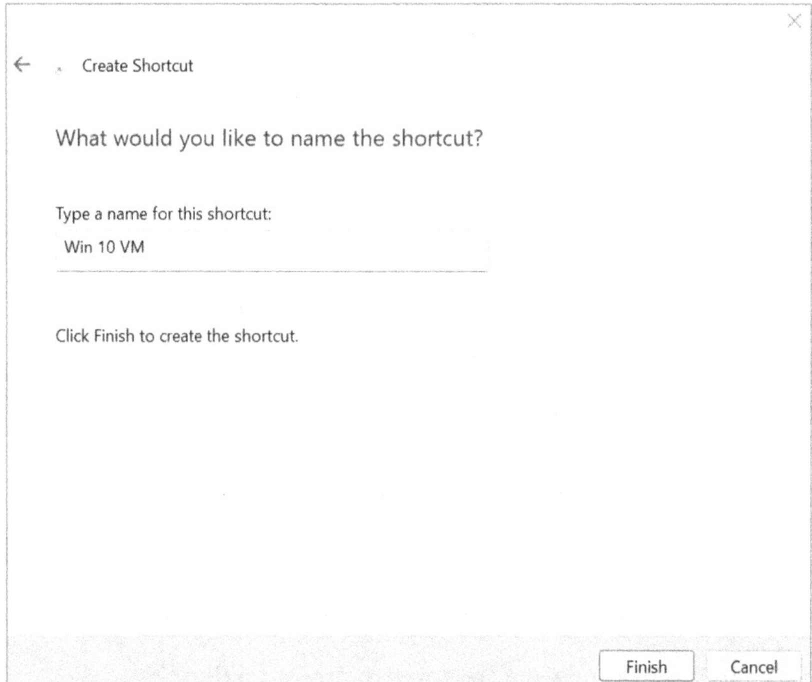

Figure 2-19. *Name the Shortcut Screen*

11. In the **Type a name for this shortcut** box, enter a name for the shortcut that will appear on the desktop of the host machine. You will likely want to name it something meaningful and that is clear on the screen, so don't make the name too long so that you can see it all.

12. In this example, we have simply called this **Win 10 VM**.

13. Once you have entered the name, click the **Finish** button to create the shortcut.

14. The shortcut has now been created, and the icon will appear on the desktop of the host machine with the name you provided as shown in Figure 2-20.

Figure 2-20. *Shortcut Created on the Desktop*

The final step is to test that the shortcut works. To do this, simply double-click the icon.

The result should be that Workstation Pro will launch and that the Windows 10 virtual machine will power on and be available to use. If you have added any other command options such as the full screen option, then you should see that result too.

In our example, we have just added the command to power on the Windows 10 virtual machine, and so the result would look like that shown in Figure 2-21.

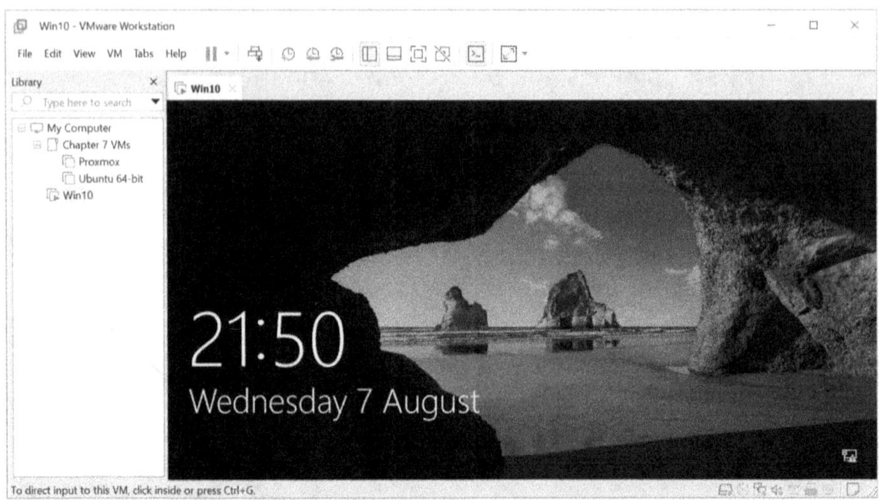

Figure 2-21. *Shortcut Launching Workstation Pro and Powering on VM*

We have now completed our overview of the **vmware.exe** command.

Summary

In this chapter, we have looked at the command, in this case the vmware.exe command for launching Workstation Pro, then followed by looking at all the additional command options that are available as part of this command, their syntax, and examples of what they do.

This is used to specify different options when launching Workstation Pro from a shortcut that you have created on the host machine for example.

With this approach, you can launch Workstation Pro with the correct variables, whether it is in full screen, or just to simply close the application when powering off a virtual machine.

We finished the chapter by creating an example shortcut and bringing together some of those different command options.

In the next chapter, we are going to take a closer look at the **vmrun** command.

CHAPTER 3

Using the vmrun Command

The **vmrun** command is a command line utility available in Workstation Pro that allows you to control virtual machines and automate guest operating system actions on virtual machines.

It is associated with the VIX API which is a library that is used for writing scripts and programs to manipulate virtual machines. The functionality can be broken down into different sections that relate to the various categories of what can be controlled as listed below:

- Power commands
- Snapshot commands
- Network commands
- Guest OS commands
- General commands
- Template VM commands

In the next sections, we are going to look at how to run the **vmrun** command and then look at each one of those categories in the above list individually in more detail and the command line options associated with that category.

P. von Oven, *Learning VMware Workstation Pro for Windows: Volume 2*,
https://doi.org/10.1007/979-8-8688-0864-7_3

How to Use the vmrun Command

The **vmrun** command is installed by default when you install the Workstation Pro software. It doesn't require any additional configuration or settings to be able to use it.

To run the command, follow the steps described.

1. On the host machine running Workstation Pro, open a command prompt window.

2. At the command prompt, navigate to the directory in which Workstation Pro is installed. By default, this will be **C:\Program Files (x86)\VMware\VMware Workstation** or add this to your path.

3. From here, you can now run the **vmrun** commands. If you simply type **vmrun** at the command prompt and then press Enter, you will see the list of the available commands and parameters as shown in Figure 3-1.

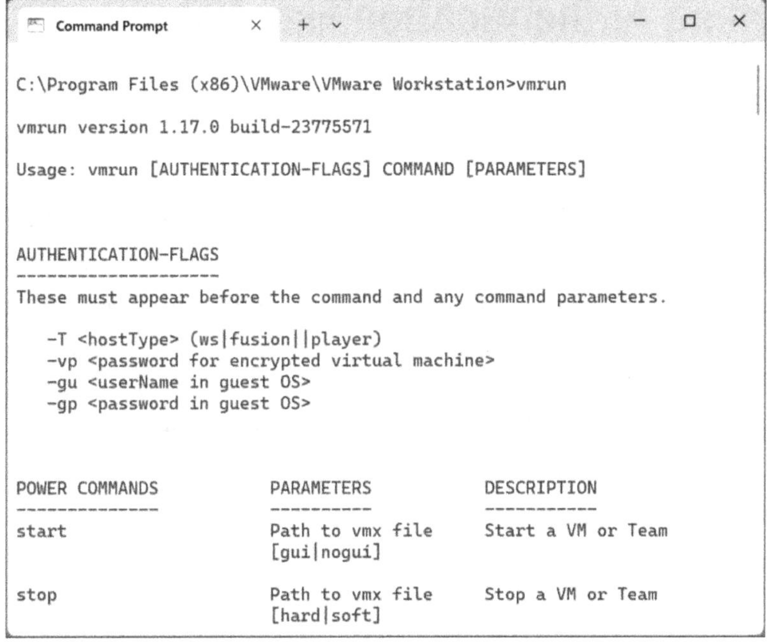

Figure 3-1. *Running the vmrun Command*

To run a vmrun command, you need to follow the following syntax as shown below with the options input in the order shown too. That means that the authentication flags need to come before any commands and any command parameters:

```
vmrun [AUTHENTICATION-FLAGS] COMMAND [PARAMETERS]
```

In the following sections, we are going to work through the commands and the command parameters, along with the authentication flags. As we work through the various commands, we will look at real examples including exact command syntax and screenshots to demonstrate the output.

Running Authentication Flag Commands

As we stated in the previous section, authentication flags need to be added at the start of any **vmrun** command and before any commands and command parameters are added.

This is so that you have access to the system to enable the commands to run. Like any other machine, virtual or otherwise, to run an application or execute some form of action, then you need to be authenticated in the first place when you access guest operating systems. And as we move to Windows 11 where encrypted machines are a requirement, you will need to provide the credentials for accessing encrypted virtual machines.

As part of this authentication process, you also have the option to specify what type of host you are going to run the command against. This is because the **vmrun** command can be used on Workstation Pro, Workstation Player, or Fusion (the Apple macOS version of Workstation). Therefore, you can specify which of these you are running.

The following authentication flag commands are available:

- **-T <host_type>** (select from either ws, fusion, or player depending on the platform). For example, if you were running on Workstation Pro, then the command would be **vmrun -T ws**.
- **-vp <password>** would be used to access an encrypted virtual machine on which you wanted to run commands. The command would be **vmrun -vp <type in password here>**.
- **-gu <Guest OS Username>** would be used to access the virtual machines operating system to run guest OS commands. The command would be **vmrun -vp <type in username here>**. This would also require the password for this user as per the next command.

- **-gp <Guest OS Password>** is used to enter the password for the username you entered in the previous command. The command would be **vmrun -gp <type in password here>**.

As an example of authentication flags using the above commands to authenticate to a virtual machine running on Workstation Pro with Windows 11 running as an encrypted guest operating system with a user on that VM called PVO, the command would look like the following:

```
vmrun -T ws -vp PASSWORD -gu PVO -gp PASSWORD
```

Now that we have looked at authenticating and gaining access to the virtual machines on the chosen platform, the next thing we are going to look at is to look at some of the guest operating system commands that you can now run.

Guest OS Commands

Now that you have authenticated with the virtual machine running the guest operating system by using the commands we looked at previously, you can now start to run commands from the command line of the host machine directly on the operating system of the virtual machine.

The following guest operating system commands are available when the virtual machine is running:

- **runProgramInGuest** allows you to launch and run an application that is hosted on the operating system of the virtual machine. You then have several parameters that can be used with the command as listed below:
    - First you need to enter the full path details to where the vmx virtual machine configuration file is stored. By default, this will be a folder called Virtual

Machines which can be found in the Document folder of the end user that created the virtual machine. The path is entered exactly as it appears.

- **`-activeWindow`** ensures that when the application launches that it doesn't launch the application user interface minimized, and so it is visible to the end user.
- **`-interactive`** forces an interactive guest login. This is useful for Windows 7 or later to make the program visible in the console window.
- **`-noWait`** means that once the application has launched on the virtual machine, then the command prompt returns to the host machine to allow you to run other commands. If you don't use this option, then the command line will not be available until the application is closed.

You will need to enter the full path to the application on the virtual machines operating system that you want to run, for example, C:\Windows\System32\paint.exe.

Finally, you can add arguments or options to the application itself. These are the standard switch options that go with the application, for example, paint.exe /p to print directly to the default printer.

Having now covered the options for running applications from the command line of the host machine on the virtual machine as one final example, we will bring all the commands together to show you the outcome.

In this example, we are going to login to a Windows 10 virtual machine that is stored in a folder called VM on the C: drive and launch Windows Notepad ensuring that the command line is returned to the host machine.

The command would look something like the following:

```
vmrun -T ws -gu pvo -gp PASSWORD runProgramInGuest C:\VM\win10.
vmx -activeWindow -noWait C:\windows\system32\notepad.exe
```

It is difficult to show the outcome properly using static screenshots, but the following screenshot in Figure 3-2 shows the command line on the host machine and the application running on the virtual machine.

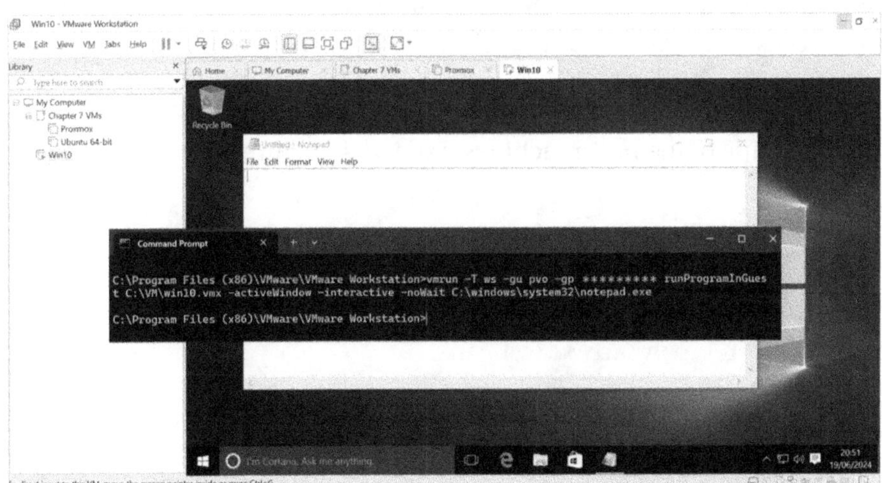

***Figure 3-2.** Launching Notepad Using the vmrun Command*

The next command allows you to check whether a particular file is present on the selected virtual machine. The command is detailed below:

- **fileExistsInGuest** allows you to check on the operating system of a specific virtual machine, which is specified by adding the full path details to where the vmx virtual machine configuration file is stored, the existence of a specific file on the operating system of that specified virtual machine. You then specify the file you are checking for by adding the full path to where that file should be stored.

As an example of this command, we are going to login to a Windows 10 virtual machine that is stored in a folder called VM on the C: drive and check for the presence of a file called pvo.txt that should be stored in the C:\Temp folder on that virtual machine.

The command would look something like the following:

```
vmrun -T ws -gu pvo -gp PASSWORD runProgramInGuest C:\VM\win10.
vmx fileExistsInGuest c:\vm\win10.vmx c:\temp\pvo.txt
```

If the file exists, then you will see the following displayed on the command line of the host machine as shown in Figure 3-3.

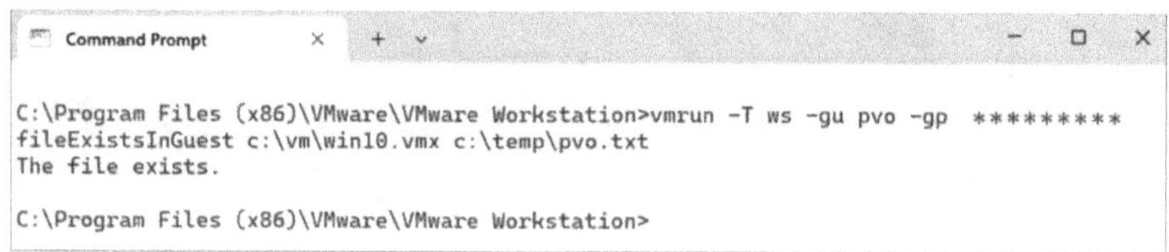

Figure 3-3. *File Exists on the Virtual Machine*

If the file does not exist, then you will see the following displayed on the command line of the host machine as shown in Figure 3-4.

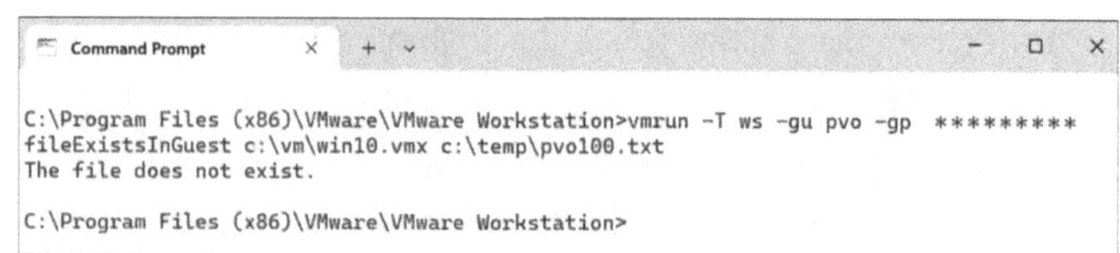

Figure 3-4. *File Does Not Exist on the Virtual Machine*

Like the command for checking for the existence of a file, the next command is used to check whether a folder or directory exists on the virtual machine. The command is detailed below:

- **directoryExistsInGuest** allows you to check on the operating system of a specific virtual machine, which is specified by adding the full path details to where the vmx virtual machine configuration file is stored, the existence of a specific folder or directory on the operating system of that specified virtual machine. You then specify the directory or folder you are checking for by adding the full path to where that directory or folder should be located.

As an example of this command, we are going to login to a Windows 10 virtual machine that is stored in a folder called VM on the C: drive and check for the presence of a folder called C:\Temp.

The command would look something like the following:

```
vmrun -T ws -gu pvo -gp PASSWORD runProgramInGuest C:\VM\win10.
vmx directoryExistsInGuest c:\vm\win10.vmx c:\temp
```

If the directory of folder exists, then you will see the following displayed on the command line of the host machine as shown in Figure 3-5.

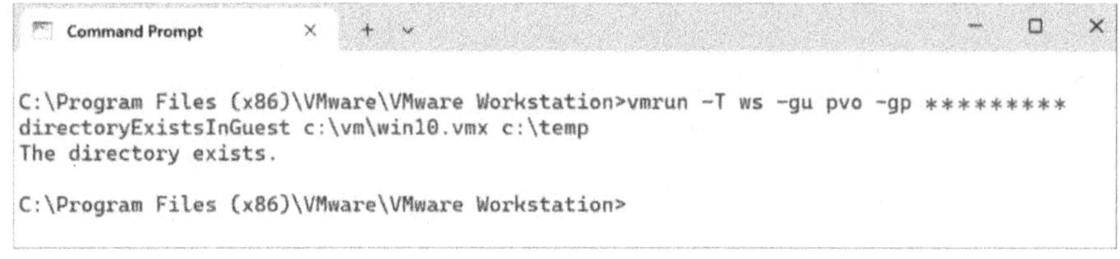

Figure 3-5. *Directory Exists on the Virtual Machine*

If the file does not exist, then you will see the following displayed on the command line of the host machine as shown in Figure 3-6.

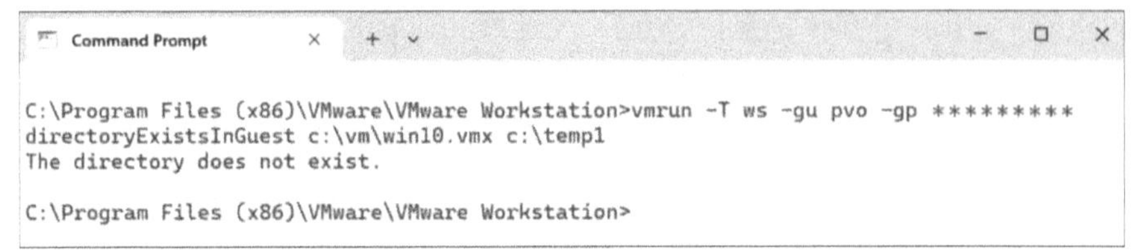
```
C:\Program Files (x86)\VMware\VMware Workstation>vmrun -T ws -gu pvo -gp *********
directoryExistsInGuest c:\vm\win10.vmx c:\templ
The directory does not exist.

C:\Program Files (x86)\VMware\VMware Workstation>
```

Figure 3-6. *Directory Does Not Exist on the Virtual Machine*

The next command is used to modify the host to guest shared folder. This shared folder is used to share files between the virtual machine and the host machine. Any file saved or copied to the shared folder on the virtual machine will automatically be available in a folder on the host and vice versa meaning that any file saved or copied to the shared folder on the host machine will be available to the virtual machine when it is powered on.

If the virtual machine is powered off, as the contents of the shared folder are shared with the host, then the files will still be available even though the virtual machine is powered off. The command is detailed below:

- **setSharedFolderState** allows you to set the specified folder, on the specified virtual machine to be either read-only or writable.

  That means there are two parameters that can be used with this command:

  - **readonly** - Sets the folder to be read-only
  - **writable** - Allows files to be written to the shared folder

As an example of this command, we are going to login to a Windows 10 virtual machine that is stored in a folder called VM on the C: drive where we have a share name called Share and the path to that folder on the host is c:\share.

The command would look something like the following:

```
vmrun -T ws -gu pvo -gp PASSWORD setSharedFolderState
C:\VM\win10.vmx Shared C:\ Shared readonly
```

If you log on to the virtual machine and try to create a file in the shared folder, you will see the following error message stating that access to the folder is denied as shown in Figure 3-7.

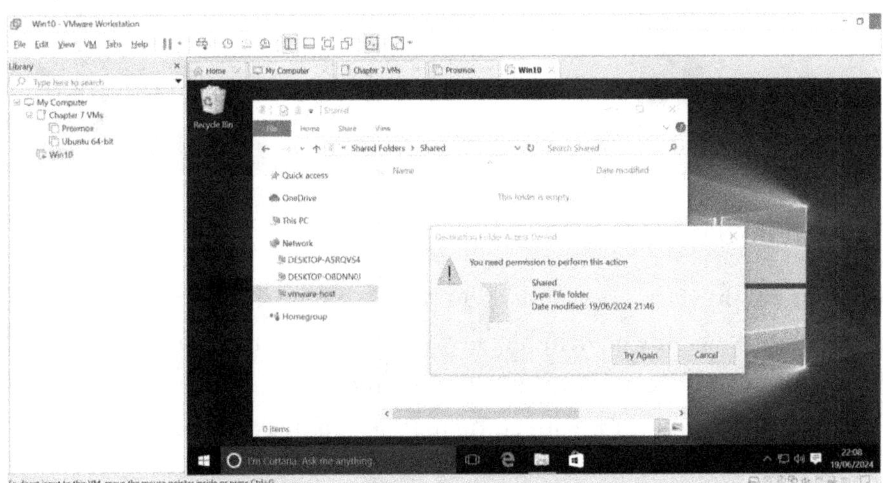

Figure 3-7. Shared Folder State Set to Read-Only

As a second example, we are going to set the shared folder to be writable using the command as follows:

```
vmrun -T ws -gu pvo -gp PASSWORD setSharedFolderState
C:\VM\win10.vmx Shared C:\ Shared writable
```

If you log on to the virtual machine again and now try to create a file in the shared folder as you did in the previous example, then you will see that you can now create a file as shown in the following screenshot in Figure 3-8.

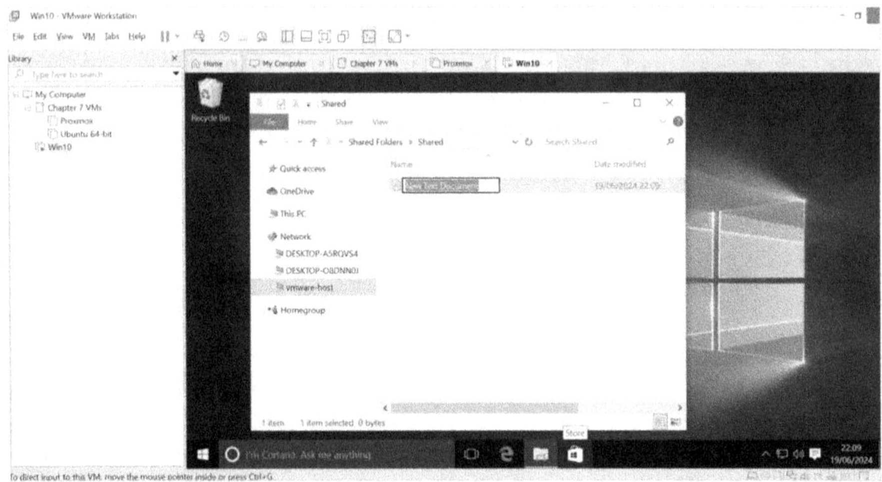

Figure 3-8. *Shared Folder State Set to Writable*

With the previous command, you could change the shared folder state to be either read-only or writable; however, that command requires the shared folder to have already been configured.

The next command we are going to look at allows you to create the shared folder.

You need to create the folder on the host machine first. The vmrun command for creating a shared folder does not create the folder on the host machine automatically as part of running the command.

The command is detailed below:

- **`addSharedFolder`** allows you to create a shared folder between the virtual machine and the host machine.

As an example of this command, we are going to login to a Windows 10 virtual machine that is stored in a folder called VM on the C: drive. We are then going to create a shared folder using the folder called **pvoshare** which has already been created on the host machine.

The command would look something like the following:

```
vmrun -T ws -gu pvo -gp PASSWORD addSharedFolder C:\VM\win10.
vmx pvoshare C:\pvoshare
```

If you now log on to the virtual machine, by selecting the virtual machine you created the shared folder for, open the virtual machine settings for that virtual machine, click the **Options** tab, and then click **Shared Folders**, you will see that the new shared folder called **pvoshare** has been created as shown in Figure 3-9.

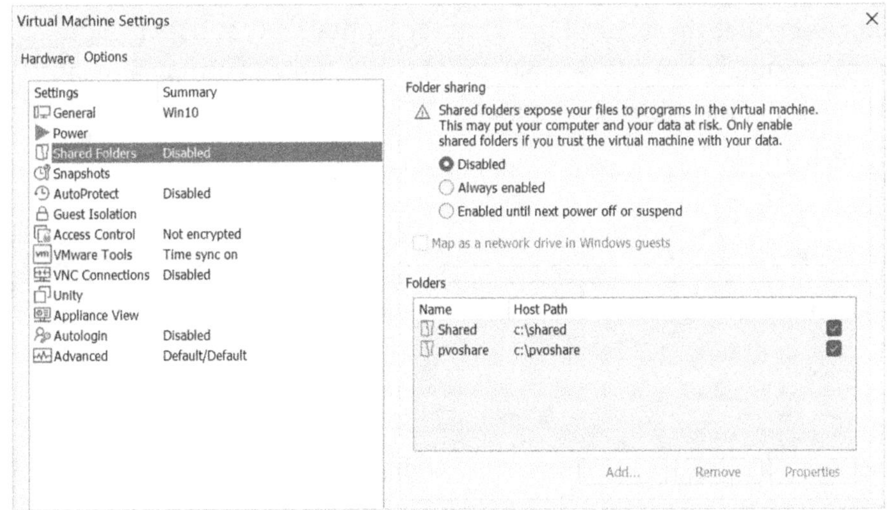

Figure 3-9. *New Shared Folder Created*

You will have also noticed that that this new shared folder is currently set to **Disabled**, which leads us nicely on to the next command which is used to enable shared folders.

The command is detailed below:

- **enableSharedFolders** allows you to enable the shared folder feature for shared folders between the virtual machine and the host machine.

As an example of this command, we are going to login to a Windows 10 virtual machine that is stored in a folder called VM on the C: drive. We are then going to enable the shared folders feature on that virtual machine.

The command would look something like the following:

```
vmrun -T ws -gu pvo -gp PASSWORD enableSharedFolders
C:\VM\win10.vmx
```

If you now log on to the virtual machine, by selecting the virtual machine you enabled the shared folders for, open the virtual machine settings for that virtual machine, click the **Options** tab, and then click **Shared Folders**, you will see that the **Always enabled** button has been selected, and therefore, shared folders have been enabled as shown in Figure 3-10.

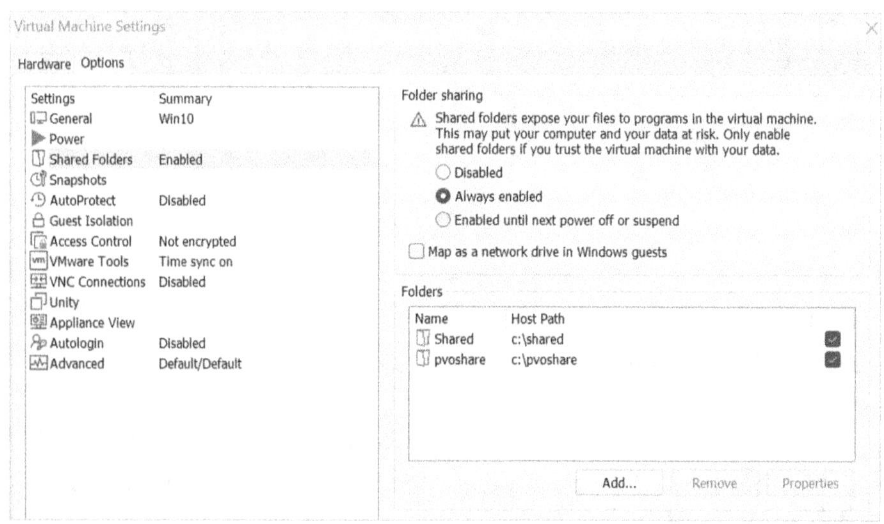

Figure 3-10. *Shared Folders Enabled*

With this command, there is the option to add the **runtime** argument which when applied will limit the shared folder feature until the virtual machine is powered off. Otherwise, the setting will persist when the virtual machine is next powered on.

So, we have now looked at how to add a shared folder and then how to enable that shared folder, as adding it does not enable it. The next two commands deliver the reverse actions and disable the shared folders feature and then remove a shared folder.

We will start by looking at the command for disabling shared folders. The command is detailed below:

- **disableSharedFolders** allows you to disable the shared folder feature for shared folders between the virtual machine and the host machine.

As an example of this command, we are going to login to a Windows 10 virtual machine that is stored in a folder called VM on the C: drive. We are then going to disable the shared folders feature on that virtual machine.

The command would look something like the following:

```
vmrun -T ws -gu pvo -gp PASSWORD disableSharedFolders
C:\VM\win10.vmx
```

If you now log on to the virtual machine, by selecting the virtual machine you enabled the shared folders for, open the virtual machine settings for that virtual machine, click the **Options** tab, and then click **Shared Folders**, you will see that the **Disabled** button has been selected, and therefore, shared folders have been enabled as shown in Figure 3-10.

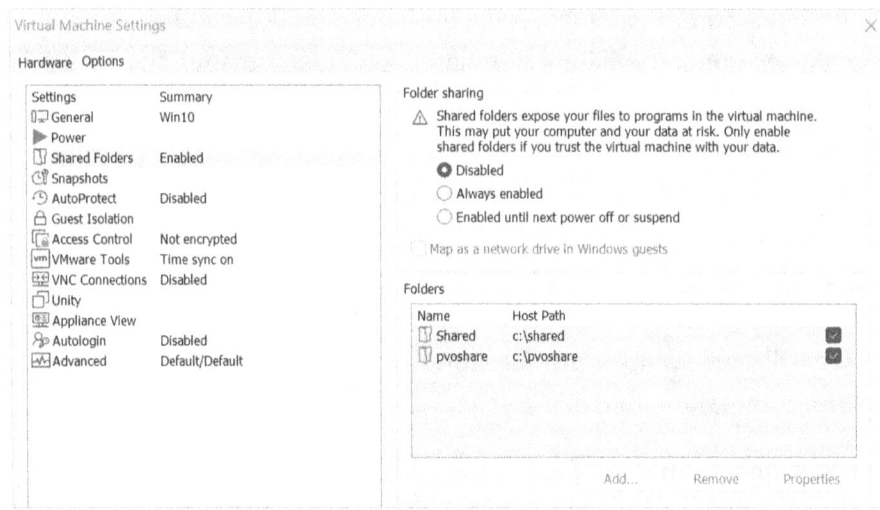

Figure 3-11. *Shared Folders Disabled*

Now that you have disabled the shared folder feature, you can now optionally remove it if you don't need it again.

The command is detailed below:

- **removeSharedFolder** allows you to remove the shared folder that was created for sharing files between the virtual machine and the host machine.

As an example of this command, we are going to login to a Windows 10 virtual machine that is stored in a folder called VM on the C: drive. We are then going to remove the shared folder from that virtual machine.

The command would look something like the following:

```
vmrun -T ws -gu pvo -gp PASSWORD
removeSharedFolder C:\VM\win10.vmx pvoshare
```

If you now log on to the virtual machine, by selecting the virtual machine you enabled the shared folders for, open the virtual machine settings for that virtual machine, click the **Options** tab, and then click **Shared Folders**, you will see that the **pvoshare** shared folder has been removed as shown in Figure 3-12.

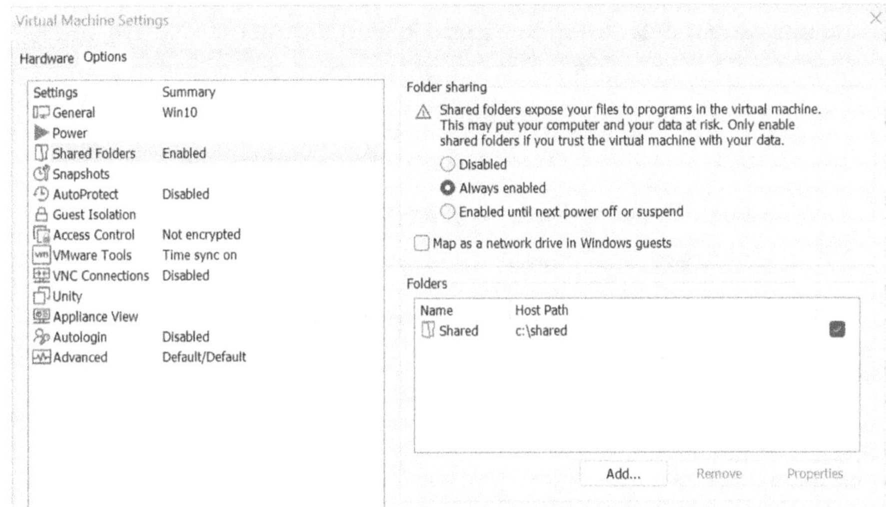

Figure 3-12. *Shared Folder Removed*

Note that the actual folder that was created on the host machine for the shared folder feature is not removed when you remove the shared folder. All the remove command does is effectively remove the folder from being available to the virtual machine.

To delete the folder, you will need to do this manually using Windows Explorer on the host machine.

Next, we are going to look at a command that can be used to list all the processes that are running on the virtual machine.

The command is detailed below:

- **listProcessesInGuest** allows you to list all the processes that are running in the operating system of the virtual machine specified in the command line.

As an example of this command, we are going to login to a Windows 10 virtual machine that is stored in a folder called VM on the C: drive and list the processes that are running on that virtual machine. We are then going to remove the shared folder from that virtual machine.

The command would look something like the following:

```
vmrun -T ws -gu pvo -gp PASSWORD
listProcessesInGuest C:\VM\win10.vmx
```

You will then see the list of processes running on the virtual machine displayed in the command prompt windows as shown in Figure 3-13.

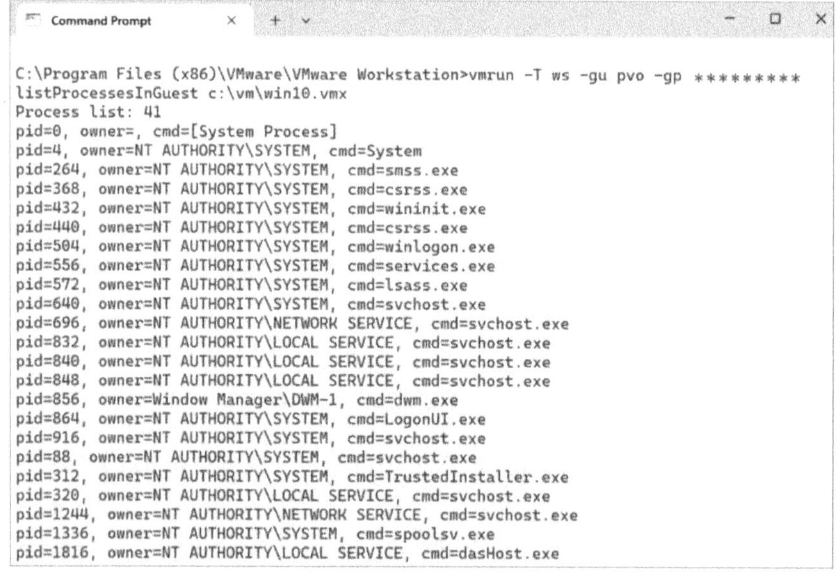

***Figure 3-13.** List of Processes Running on the Virtual Machine*

With the next command, we are going to look at how you can kill a process running on the virtual machine.

The command is detailed below:

- **killProcessInGuest** allows you to kill a process (specified as part of the command) that is running in the operating system of the virtual machine that is also specified in the command line.

As an example of this command, we are going to login to a Windows 10 virtual machine that is stored in a folder called VM on the C: drive upon which we have Notepad running. We are then going to kill the Notepad process which has a process ID (PID) value of 364. Notepad will be closed.

The command would look something like the following:

```
vmrun -T ws -gu pvo -gp PASSWORD
killProcessInGuest C:\VM\win10.vmx 364
```

This is another one of those commands that is difficult to demonstrate properly using static screenshots; however, if you were now open a console to the virtual machine, you will see that Notepad is no longer running. You could of course also use the previous listProcessesInGuest command to check the list of running processes to ensure that Notepad is no longer running.

Next, we have a command that allows you to execute scripts on a VM. The command is detailed below:

- **runScriptInGuest** allows you to run a script using the script interpreter that you specify as part of the command, which then runs the script (which you enter as a script rather than point to a script file, on the operating system of the virtual machine that is also specified in the command line).

You also have the following additional commands:

- **-activeWindow** ensures that when the script interpreter launches, it doesn't launch the application user interface minimized, and so it is visible to the end user.
- **-interactive** forces an interactive guest login. This is useful for Windows 7 or later to make the program visible in the console window.
- **-noWait** means that once the script interpreter has launched on the virtual machine, then the command prompt returns to the host machine to allow you to run other commands. If you don't use this option, then the command line will not be available until the script interpreter is closed.

As an example of this command, we are going to login to a Windows 10 virtual machine that is stored in a folder called VM on the C: drive. We are then going to launch the script interpreter which in this case is Perl. The "**-e**" switch allows you specify a single line of code on the command line. As previously mentioned, you need to add the script text to the command.

The command would look something like the following:

```
vmrun -T ws -gu pvo -gp PASSWORD
runScriptInGuest C:\VM\win10.vmx c:\cygwin\
bin\perl.exe -e "<TYPE SCRIPT HERE>"
```

If you want to delete a file from the virtual machine, then you can use the following command detailed below:

- **deleteFileInGuest** allows you to delete a file, specified in the command line, from the virtual machine that you also specify on the command line.

As an example of this command, we are going to login to a Windows 10 virtual machine that is stored in a folder called VM on the C: drive. We are then going to delete the file pvo.txt from the c:\temp folder.

The command would look something like the following:

```
vmrun -T ws -gu pvo -gp PASSWORD
deleteFileInGuest C:\VM\win10.vmx
c:\temp\pvo.txt
```

If you now log on to the virtual machine you selected in the command line and open Windows Explorer and if you then navigate to the c:\temp folder, you will see that the pvo.txt file will no longer exist.

Deleting a file using this process means that the file is completely deleted meaning it won't appear in the Recycle Bin for restoring.

The next command allows you to create a directory on the virtual machine and is detailed below:

- **createDirectoryInGuest** allows you to create a new directory or folder that you specify the name of in the command line, on the virtual machine that you also specify on the command line.

As an example of this command, we are going to login to a Windows 10 virtual machine that is stored in a folder called VM on the C: drive. We are then going to create a folder on the C:\ drive called pvo-new-folder.

The command would look something like the following and is also shown in Figure 3-14 below.

```
vmrun -T ws -gu pvo -gp PASSWORD
createDirectoryInGuest C:\VM\win10.vmx
c:\pvo-new-folder
```

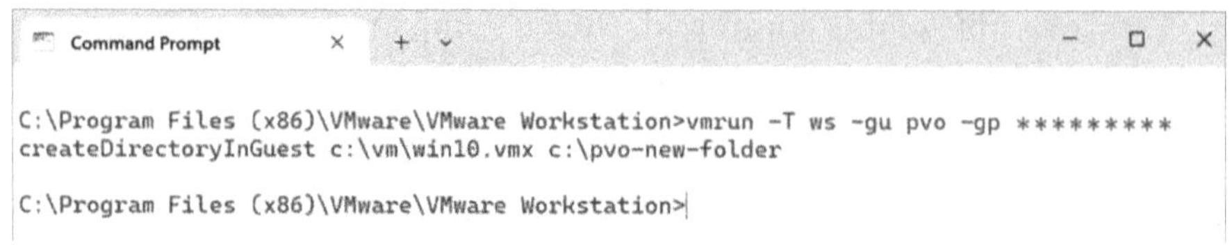

Figure 3-14. *Create a New Folder on the Virtual Machine*

If you now log on to the virtual machine you selected in the command line and open Windows Explorer and if you then navigate to the c:\ drive, you will see that the pvo-new-folder has been created as shown in Figure 3-15.

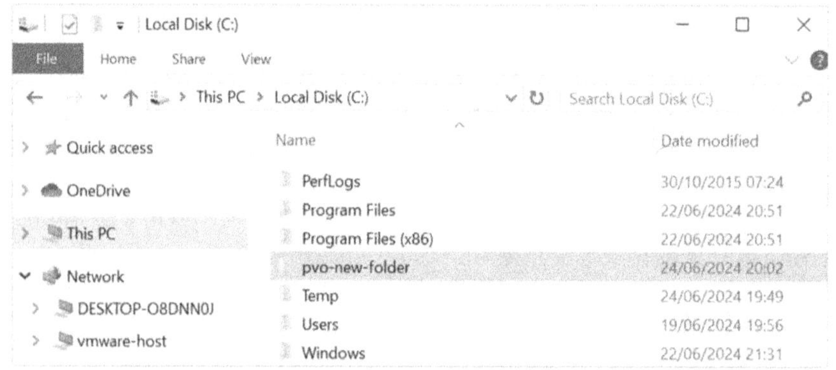

Figure 3-15. *New folder successfully created*

Having just created a new directory in the virtual machine, with the next command, we are going to delete the directory. The command to do this is detailed below:

- **deleteDirectoryInGuest** allows you to delete a directory or folder that you specify the name of in the command line, on the virtual machine that you also specify on the command line.

As an example of this command, we are going to login to a Windows 10 virtual machine that is stored in a folder called VM on the C: drive. We are then going to delete a folder on the C:\ drive called pvo-new-folder.

The command would look something like the following:

```
vmrun -T ws -gu pvo -gp PASSWORD
deleteDirectoryInGuest C:\VM\win10.vmx
c:\pvo-new-folder
```

If you now log on to the virtual machine you selected in the command line and open Windows Explorer and if you then navigate to the c:\ drive, you will see that the pvo-new-folder has been deleted.

The next command allows you to create a temporary file on the virtual machine. The command to do this is detailed below:

- **createTempfileInGuest** allows you to create a temporary file on the virtual machine.

As an example of this command, we are going to login to a Windows 10 virtual machine that is stored in a folder called VM on the C: drive. We are then going to create a temporary file.

It's worth noting that you can't specify the name of the temp file in the command line and instead the file will be name using the format vmwareXXX where XXX will be substituted with a number.

It will also be created in the following folder location on the virtual machine – C:\Users\pvo\AppData\Local\Temp.

The command would look something like the following:

```
vmrun -T ws -gu pvo -gp PASSWORD
createTempfileInGuest C:\VM\win10.vmx
```

If you now log on to the virtual machine you selected in the command line and open Windows Explorer and navigate to the C:\Users\pvo\AppData\Local\Temp folder, you will see that a file called vmware161 has been created. This is shown in Figure 3-16.

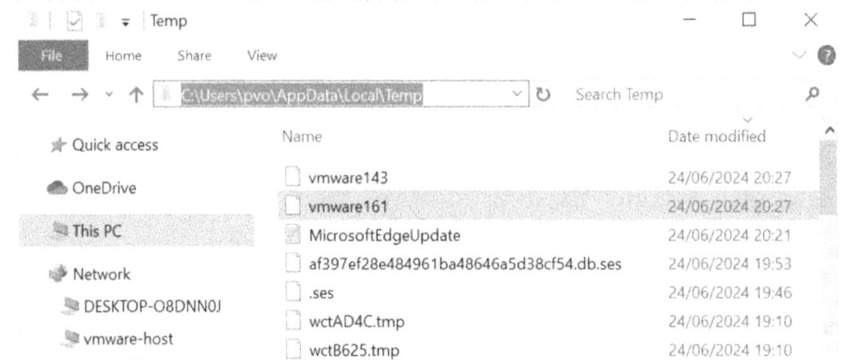

Figure 3-16. *Creating a Temp File on the Virtual Machine*

With the next command, you can show the contents of a particular directory on the virtual machine.

The command to do this is detailed below:

- **`listDirectoryInGuest`** allows you to list the contents of the directory or folder that you specify in the command line on the virtual machine that you also specify on the command line.

As an example of this command, we are going to login to a Windows 10 virtual machine that is stored in a folder called VM on the C: drive. We are then going to list the contents of the c:\temp folder on the virtual machine.

The command would look something like the following:

- **`vmrun -T ws -gu pvo -gp PASSWORD listDirectoryInGuest C:\VM\win10.vmx`**

The output is displayed in the command line on the host machine as shown in Figure 3-17.

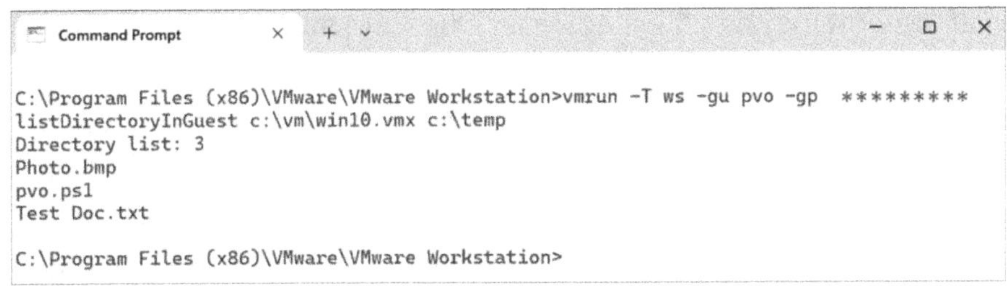

```
C:\Program Files (x86)\VMware\VMware Workstation>vmrun -T ws -gu pvo -gp  *********
listDirectoryInGuest c:\vm\win10.vmx c:\temp
Directory list: 3
Photo.bmp
pvo.ps1
Test Doc.txt

C:\Program Files (x86)\VMware\VMware Workstation>
```

Figure 3-17. *Directory Listing of the Virtual Machine*

With the next two commands, we are going to look at copying files from the host machine to the virtual machine and then vice versa, from the virtual machine to the host machine. We will start with the former.

The command to do this is detailed below:

- **`CopyFileFromHostToGuest`** allows you to copy a file from the host machine, for which the path is specified on the command line to a folder on the virtual machine, both of which is also specified as part of the command line.

As an example of this command, we are going to login to a Windows 10 virtual machine that is stored in a folder called VM on the C: drive. We are then going to copy the files from the c:\pvoshare folder on the host machine to the c:\temp folder on the virtual machine.

You cannot specify individual file names, and so this command will copy the entire file contents of the specified folder.

The command would look something like the following:

- **`vmrun -T ws -gu pvo -gp PASSWORD CopyFileFromHostToGuest C:\VM\win10.vmx c:\pvoshare c:\temp`**

If you now log on to the virtual machine you selected in the command line and open Windows Explorer and navigate to the target folder on the virtual machine, in this case the c:\temp folder, you will see that the files from the host machine and the files within the specified source folder have now been copied to the virtual machine.

You can also copy files the other way around, from the virtual machine to the host machine.

The command to do this is detailed below:

- **CopyFileFromGuestToHost** allows you to copy a file from the virtual machine, for which the path and virtual machine are both specified on the command line to a folder on the host machine, which has also been specified as part of the command line.

As an example of this command, we are going to login to a Windows 10 virtual machine that is stored in a folder called VM on the C: drive. We are then going to copy the files from the c:\temp folder on the virtual machine to the c:\pvoshare folder on the host machine.

Remember, you cannot specify individual file names, and so this command will copy the entire file contents of the specified folder.

The command would look something like the following:

```
vmrun -T ws -gu pvo -gp PASSWORD
CopyFileFromGuestToHost C:\VM\win10.vmx
c:\temp c:\pvoshare
```

If you now log on to the host machine and open Windows Explorer and navigate to the target folder, in this case the c:\pvoshare folder, you will see that the files from the c:\temp folder on the virtual machine have now been copied to the host machine.

The next file-based command we are going to look at allows you to rename a file on the virtual machine.

The command to do this is detailed below:

- **renameFileInGuest** allows you to rename a file on the virtual machine.

As an example of this command, we are going to login to a Windows 10 virtual machine that is stored in a folder called VM on the C: drive. We are then going to rename the file photo.bmp in the c:\temp folder on the virtual machine to the photo-pvo.bmp.

The command would look something like the following:

- **vmrun -T ws -gu pvo -gp PASSWORD renameFileInGuest C:\VM\win10.vmx c:\temp\photo.bmp c:\temp\photo-pvo.bmp**

If you now log on to the virtual machine and open Windows Explorer and navigate to the c:\temp folder, you will see that the file has been renamed.

The next two commands allow you to either connect or disconnect a device to and from the virtual machine. The first one we will look at in more detail is for connecting devices.

The command to do this is detailed below:

- **connectNamedDevice** allows you to connect the device that you name in the command to the virtual machine that you specify in the command.

As an example of this command, we are going to login to a Windows 10 virtual machine that is stored in a folder called VM on the C: drive. We are then going to connect a second hard drive to the virtual machine.

The command would look something like the following:

```
vmrun -T ws -gu pvo -gp PASSWORD
connectNamedDevice C:\VM\win10.vmx sata0:2
```

If you now log on to the virtual machine and open Windows Explorer, you will see that a second virtual hard drive will have been connected. It is worth noting that with something like a virtual hard drive, you will need to create the hardware first. This command does not do that for you.

If you then want to disconnect that same device, you will use the following command:

- **disconnectNamedDevice** allows you to disconnect the device that you name in the command to the virtual machine that you specify in the command.

The command would look something like the following:

```
vmrun -T ws -gu pvo -gp PASSWORD
disconnectNamedDevice C:\VM\win10.
vmx sata0:2
```

If you were now to log on to the same virtual machine and open Windows Explorer, you will see that the second virtual hard drive will no longer be visible and has been disconnected. This doesn't delete the virtual hard drive; it is just disconnected so the virtual disk file will still be available.

You can only run the connect and disconnect device command when the virtual machine is powered on.

The next command allows you to take a screen capture or screenshot of the virtual machine.

The command to do this is detailed below:

- **captureScreen** allows you to take a screen capture of the virtual machine and the contents that are currently displayed. The file containing the screen capture is saved on the host machine.

As an example of this command, we are going to take a screenshot of the Windows 10 example machine.

The command would look something like the following:

```
vmrun -T ws -gu pvo -gp PASSWORD
captureScreen C:\VM\win10.vmx c:\pvoshare\
capture.png
```

If you were now to log on to the host machine and open Windows Explorer and navigate to the folder you saved the capture to, you would see something like the screenshot that is shown in Figure 3-18.

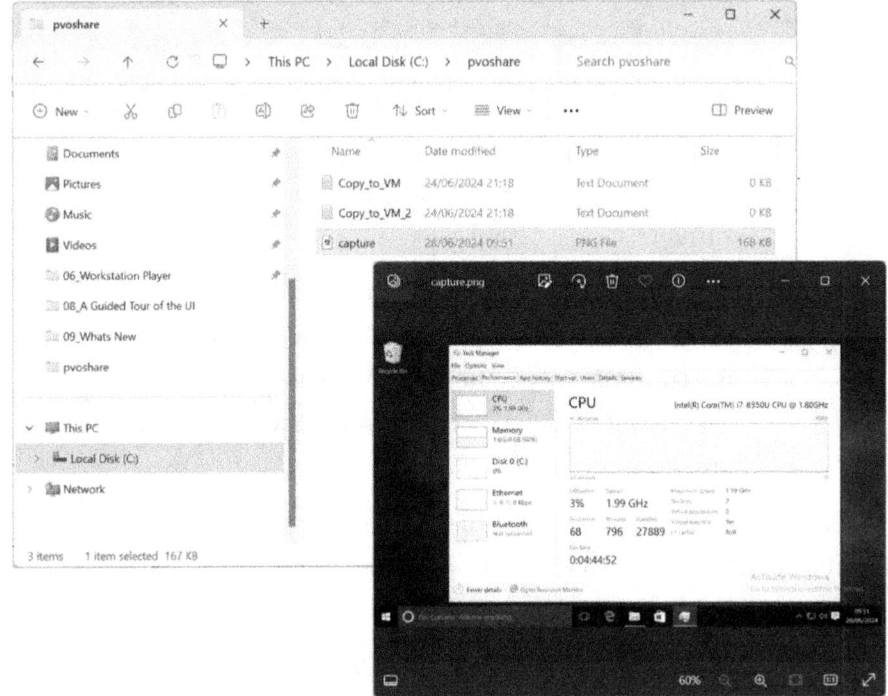

Figure 3-18. *Screen Capture of the Virtual Machine*

When using the screen capture command, ensure that you specify both a folder and file name on the host machine for saving the captured screenshot.

The next command allows you to write a variable to the virtual machine state or guest. The command to do this is detailed below:

- **writeVariable** allows you to write a variable to the virtual machine. You then have several parameters that can be used with the command as listed below:
  - **runtimeConfig** allows you to specify the variable written is for a runtime configuration as stored in the .vmx file.
  - **guestEnv** allows you to set an environment variable.
  - **guestVar** allows you to set a nonpersistent guest variable on the virtual machine. The guest variable is a runtime-only value that gives you a quick and easy way in which you can pass runtime values to and from the virtual machine.

As an example of this command, we are going to set a guest variable for the vmstartdate on the Windows 10 example machine.

The command would look something like the following:

```
vmrun -T ws -gu pvo -gp PASSWORD
writeVariable C:\VM\win10.vmx guestVar
vmstartdate 28June2024
```

If you were now to log on to the virtual machine, open a command prompt, and run the **rptool.exe "info-get guestinfo.vmstartdate"** command, you will see the following as shown in Figure 3-19.

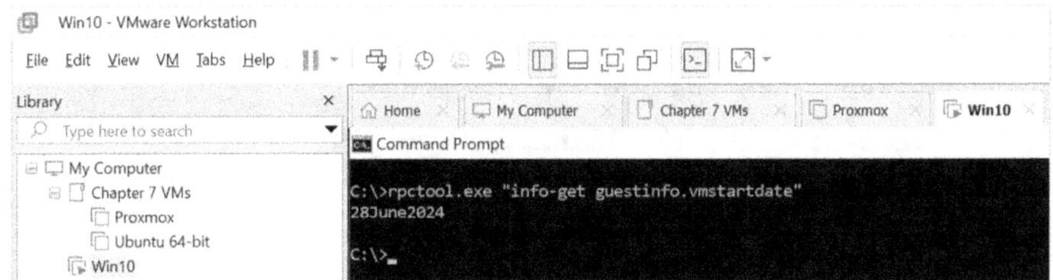

***Figure 3-19.** Reading the Newly Written Variable*

As you can see, the variable has been successfully written to the virtual machine. One point to note, by default, the **rpctool** command is not included in the path so you either need to run it from the directory in which it resides or add the location to the path.

You could also use the read variable command too.

The command to do this is detailed below:

- **readVariable** allows you to read a variable from the virtual machine. You then have several parameters that can be used with the command as listed below:
    - **runtimeConfig** allows you to specify the variable read is for a runtime configuration as stored in the .vmx file.
    - **guestEnv** allows you to read an environment variable.
    - **guestVar** allows you to read a nonpersistent guest variable on the virtual machine. The guest variable is a runtime-only value that gives you a quick and easy way in which you can pass runtime values to and from the virtual machine.

As an example of this command, we are going to read the guest variable for the vmstartdate on the Windows 10 example machine.

The command would look something like the following:

```
vmrun -T ws -gu pvo -gp PASSWORD
readVariable C:\VM\win10.vmx guestVar
vmstartdate
```

The result of the command will be displayed in the command prompt from where you ran the command as shown in Figure 3-20.

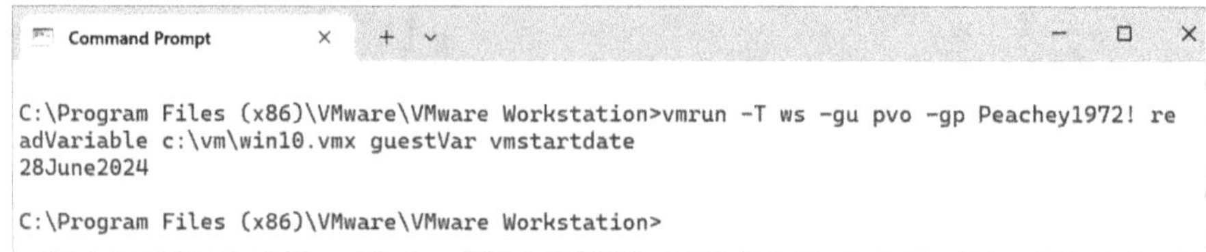

Figure 3-20. *Reading the Variable Using the vmrun Command*

The final Guest OS command we are going to look at is for displaying the IP address of the virtual machine.

The command to do this is detailed below:

- **getGuestIPAddress** allows you to show the IP address of the virtual machine.

As an example of this command, we are going to get the IP address of the Windows 10 example machine.

The command would look something like the following:

```
vmrun -T ws -gu pvo -gp PASSWORD
getGuestIPAddress C:\VM\win10.vmx
```

The result of the command will be displayed in the command prompt from where you ran the command as shown in Figure 3-21.

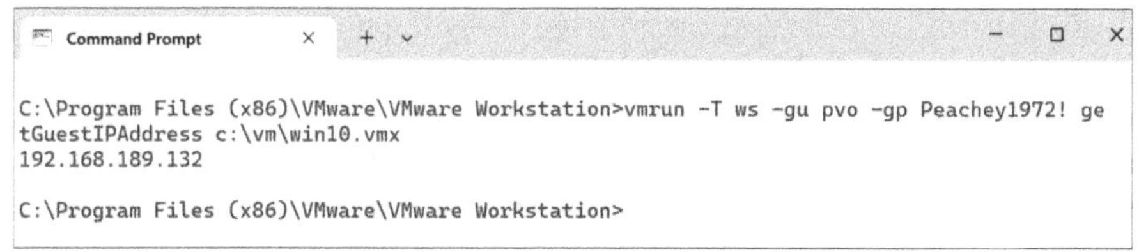

Figure 3-21. *Displaying the IP Address of the Virtual Machine*

In the next section, we are going to take a look at the power-based commands for controlling the power state of virtual machines.

Power Commands

The next set of vmrun commands that we are going to look at is for controlling the power state of the virtual machines. We are going to start with powering on a virtual machine.

To start a virtual machine or power it on, you would use the command detailed below:

- **start** allows you to power on or resume a suspended virtual machine. You have the following parameters that can be used with this command:
    - **gui** allows the virtual machine to be started interactively, which is required if you want to display the user interface. This is the default setting.
    - **nogui** suppresses the user interface, which includes the startup dialog box. This allows you to run noninteractive scripting as part of startup if required.

As an example of this command, we are going power on the example Windows 10 virtual machine with the user interface.

The command would look something like the following:

```
vmrun -T ws -gu pvo -gp PASSWORD start
C:\VM\win10.vmx gui
```

The result of the command will be that the virtual machine will be powered on and ready for you to login and use.

If you want to power off the virtual machine, then you would use the command detailed below:

- **stop** allows you to power off or shut down a virtual machine. You have the following parameters that can be used with this command:
    - **hard** performs a hard power off as if you pressed the power button or pulled the power plug out to turn the virtual machine off.
    - **soft** performs a graceful shutdown of the virtual machine which runs all the shutdown scripts.

As an example of this command, we are going power off the example Windows 10 virtual machine with the graceful shutdown option.

The command would look something like the following:

```
vmrun -T ws -gu pvo -gp PASSWORD stop
C:\VM\win10.vmx soft
```

You will now see the virtual machine power down gracefully.

The next command is for resetting the virtual machine. If you want to reset the virtual machine, then you would use the command detailed below:

- **reset** allows you to reset or reboot a virtual machine. You have the following parameters that can be used with this command:
  - **hard** performs a hard reset as if you pressed the reset button.
  - **soft** performs a graceful reboot of the virtual machine which runs all the shutdown and reboot scripts.

As an example of this command, we are going reset the example Windows 10 virtual machine with the graceful reset option.

The command would look something like the following:

```
vmrun -T ws -gu pvo -gp PASSWORD reset
C:\VM\win10.vmx soft
```

You will now see the virtual machine reboot gracefully.

Next, we have a command that is used suspending the virtual machine. If you want to suspend the virtual machine, then you would use the command detailed below:

- **suspend** allows you to suspend a virtual machine without shutting it down so that it can quickly be resumed from the same point in time as when you suspended it.

  Effectively, it puts the virtual machine to sleep without shutting it down. You have the following parameters that can be used with this command:
  - **hard** suspends a virtual machine without running any scripts.
  - **soft** suspends the virtual machine after running system scripts such as releasing the IP address.

As an example of this command, we are going suspend the example Windows 10 virtual machine with the graceful reset option.

The command would look something like the following:

```
vmrun -T ws -gu pvo -gp PASSWORD suspend
C:\VM\win10.vmx soft
```

You will now see the virtual machine suspended.

Finally, we have two commands that fall under the heading of power commands that are for pausing and unpausing a virtual machine.

The first one we will look at is how to pause a virtual machine. This feature you will notice can't be found on any of the menu options in Workstation Pro.

If you want to pause the virtual machine, then you would use the command detailed below:

- **pause** allows you to stop a virtual machine exactly where it is without suspending or shutting it down. It is literally like pressing the pause button when watching live streaming. There are no other parameter options for this command.

As an example of this command, we are going pause the example Windows 10 virtual machine.

The command would look something like the following:

```
vmrun -T ws -gu pvo -gp PASSWORD pause
C:\VM\win10.vmx
```

You will now see the virtual machine suspended as shown in Figure 3-22.

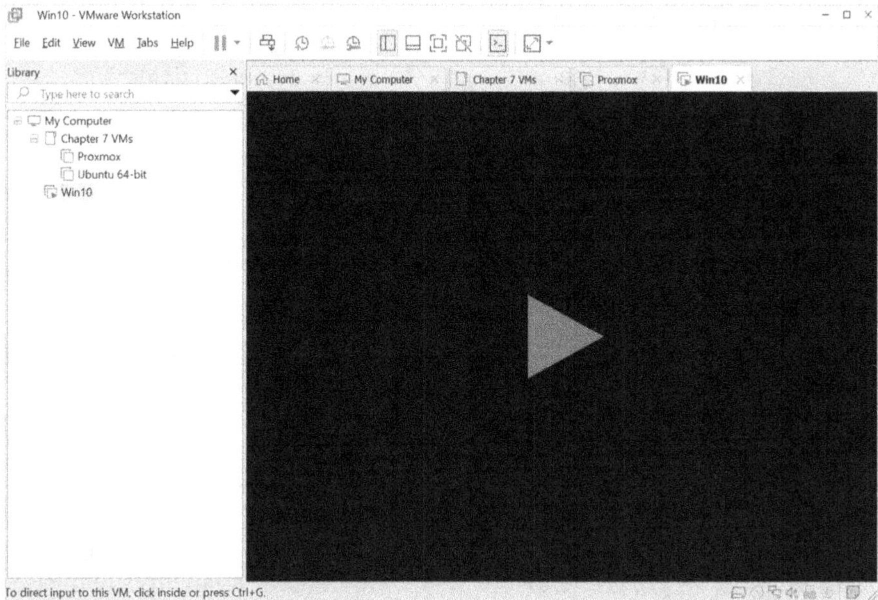

***Figure 3-22.** Virtual Machine Paused*

If you now want to unpause the virtual machine, then you would use the command detailed below:

- **unpause** allows you to resume the virtual machine from its paused state. Unpause may sound like the wrong word for this feature, and resume would be a better name, but resume is used for resuming a machine from a suspended state which is not the same as pausing; hence, the two commands need to be differentiated, although technically pause and unpause don't appear as menu options.

As an example of this command, we are going to unpause the example Windows 10 virtual machine.

The command would look something like the following:

- **vmrun -T ws -gu pvo -gp PASSWORD unpause C:\VM\win10.vmx**

You will now see the virtual machine has resumed from exactly the same place as where you paused it and available to carry on using.

We have now covered all the power commands available when using the vmrun command line. In the next section, we are going to look at commands that enable you to use the vmrun command to manage virtual machine snapshots.

Snapshot Commands

In this section, we are going to look at how to manage snapshots using the vmrun command and the different snapshot-based commands available.

The first of these commands is used to list snapshots.

If you want to list the snapshots for a specific virtual machine, then you would use the command detailed below:

- **listSnapshots** enables you to list all the current snapshots for the virtual machine you specify in the command line. You also have an additional parameter:
    - **showTree** enables you to display snapshots using a tree view where child snapshots are shown indented under their parent snapshot.

As an example of this command, we are going to list the current snapshots for the Windows 10 example virtual machine.

The command would look something like the following:

```
vmrun -T ws -gu pvo -gp PASSWORD
listSnapshots C:\VM\win10.vmx
```

You will now see the snapshots listed in the command prompt window as shown in Figure 3-23.

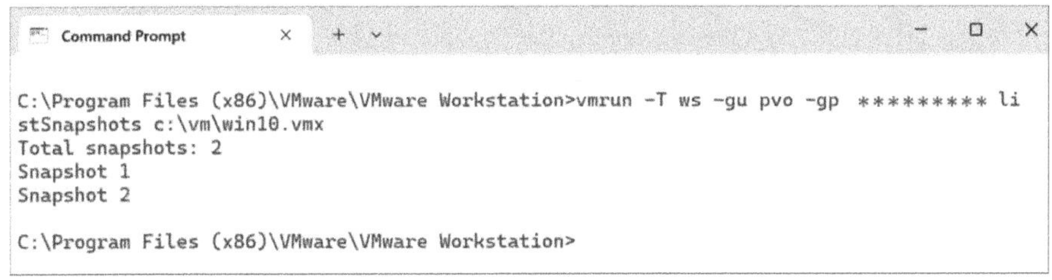

Figure 3-23. *List of Virtual Machine Snapshots*

The next command we are going to look at creates a snapshot.

If you want to create a new snapshot for a specific virtual machine, then you would use the command detailed below:

- **snapshot** allows you to create a snapshot of the virtual machine's current state.

As an example of this command, we are going to create a new snapshot for the Windows 10 example virtual machine.

The command would look something like the following:

```
vmrun -T ws -gu pvo -gp PASSWORD snapshot
C:\VM\win10.vmx pvosnapshot
```

If you now log on to the virtual machine for which you created the snapshot for and open the Snapshot Manager, you will now see that the snapshot has been created as shown in Figure 3-24.

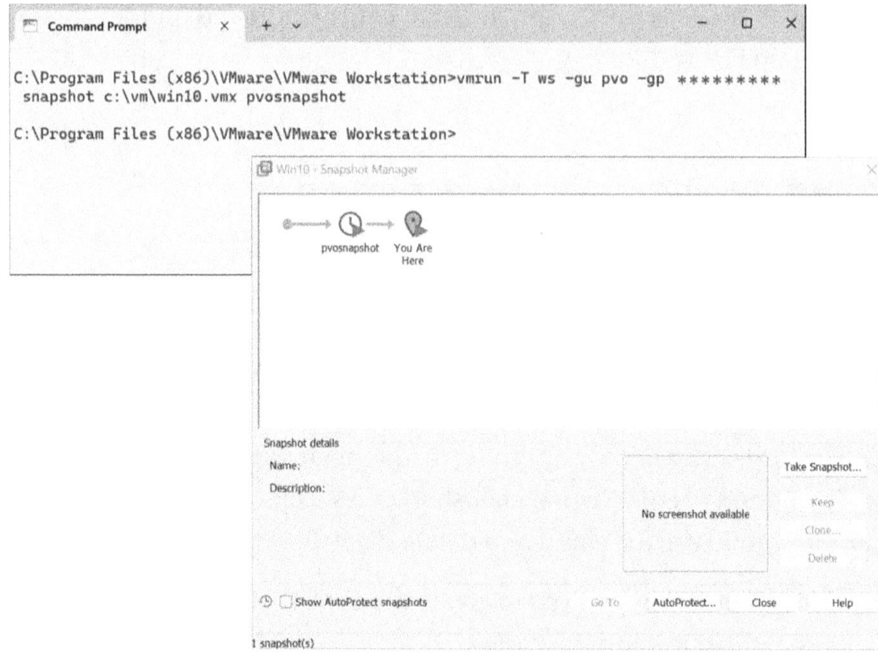

Figure 3-24. *Snapshot Created*

Having created a new snapshot, you can also delete it. If you want to delete an existing snapshot for a specific virtual machine, then you would use the command detailed below:

- **deleteSnapshot** allows you to delete the specified snapshot from the specified virtual machine. Note that the virtual machine needs to be either powered off or suspended to delete the snapshot.

  If the snapshot has any child snapshots, they become children of the deleted snapshot's parent. Any new snapshots after this will continue as before from the last snapshot created.

You also have the additional command parameter:

- **andDeleteChildren** allows you to also delete the specified snapshot and any children it may have, recursively.

As an example of this command, we are going to delete a snapshot called pvosnapshot from the Windows 10 example virtual machine.

The command would look something like the following:

```
vmrun -T ws -gu pvo -gp PASSWORD
deleteSnapshot C:\VM\win10.vmx pvosnapshot
```

If you log on to the virtual machine that originally held that snapshot and open the Snapshot Manager, you will see that the specified snapshot has been deleted.

The final snapshot command is to revert to an already existing snapshot.

If you want to revert to an existing snapshot for a specific virtual machine, then you would use the command detailed below:

- **revertToSnapshot** allows you to revert to the specified named snapshot on the specified named virtual machine. Both virtual machine and snapshot are named in the command line.

  However, if the virtual machine was powered on when the snapshot was created, the vmrun command reverts the virtual machine to its suspended state.

  In the case where you may have several snapshots with the same name, then you would need to specify the snapshot by including the full pathname to the snapshot. In the world of snapshots, the pathname is a series of snapshot names that are separated by a forward slash "/". Each name specifies a new snapshot in the snapshot tree.

If we take an example with a pathname of Snapshot1/ Snapshot2, that would mean that a snapshot named **Snapshot2** would have been taken from the state of a snapshot named **Snapshot1**.

As an example of this command, we are going to revert to a snapshot called pvosnapshot from the Windows 10 example virtual machine.

The command would look something like the following:

```
vmrun -T ws -gu pvo -gp PASSWORD
revertToSnapshot C:\VM\win10.vmx pvosnapshot
```

If you log on to the virtual machine and open the Snapshot Manager, you will see that it has reverted to the specified named snapshot.

We have now covered all the available snapshot commands available using the vmrun command.

In the next section, we are going to look at network commands available on the host machine.

Host Network Commands

The next set of commands is designed around the host network and in particular port forwarding.

Before you start configuring port forwarding, you first have a command that lists the available networks on the host machine. To show the available networks, then you would use the command detailed below:

- **`listHostNetworks`** allows you to list the networks that are available to the host machine.

As an example of this command, we are going to list the host networks that are available to the host machine we are using in the examples that is currently running VMware Workstation and the example virtual machines.

The command would look something like the following:

```
vmrun listHostNetworks
```

The output, i.e., the list of host networks, will be displayed in the command prompt window as shown in Figure 3-25.

```
C:\Program Files (x86)\VMware\VMware Workstation>vmrun listHostNetworks
Total host networks: 2
INDEX  NAME         TYPE         DHCP         SUBNET            MASK
1      vmnet1       hostOnly     true         192.168.83.0      255.255.255.0
8      vmnet8       nat          true         192.168.189.0     255.255.255.0

C:\Program Files (x86)\VMware\VMware Workstation>
```

Figure 3-25. *List Host Machine Networks*

As we said previously, most of the commands under the heading of host network commands are around port forwarding. With the previous command, we listed all the networks available to the host machine, so with the next command, you can show any currently configured port forwarding rules.

To show the current port forwarding rules, then you would use the command detailed below:

- **listPortForwardings** allows you to list the currently configured port forwarding rules networks that have been configured on the host machine. You need to specify the network name as part of the command to show the port forwardings for that network.

As an example of this command, we are going to list the port forwarding rule that are currently configured on the host machine we are using in the examples that is currently running VMware Workstation and the example virtual machines, specifically port forwardings for the vmnet8 network.

The command would look something like the following:

```
vmrun listPortForwardings vmnet8
```

The output, i.e., the list of port forwardings for the vmnet8 network, will be displayed in the command prompt window as shown in Figure 3-26.

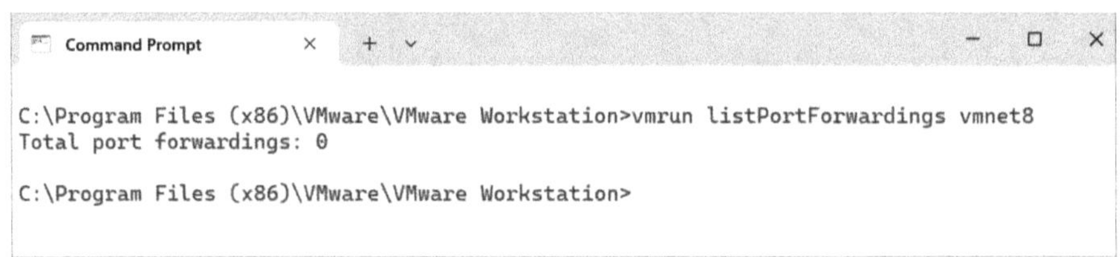

***Figure 3-26.** List of Port Forwardings for the Specified Network*

As you can see in this example, currently there are no port forwarding rules for the vmnet8 network. With the next command we are going to look at, you can create port forwarding rules with the command detailed below:

- **setPortForwarding** allows you to set port forwarding for the selected network on the host machine.

As an example of this command, using the vmnet8 as the network we are going to create the port forwarding rule on, we are then going to forward tcp port 8082 on the host network to the IP address of the virtual machine on port 88. Finally, we will create a description of this port forwarding rule.

The command would look something like the following:

```
vmrun setPortForwarding vmnet8 tcp 8082
10.10.10.1 88 pvo-portforwarding
```

To run this command, you need to run it from an elevated command prompt or use the sudo command for Windows. In this example, we were running in an elevated command prompt. If you do not run as elevated, then running the command will result in an error.

After you have run the command, you will just return to the command prompt, unless the command fails. This is shown in Figure 3-27.

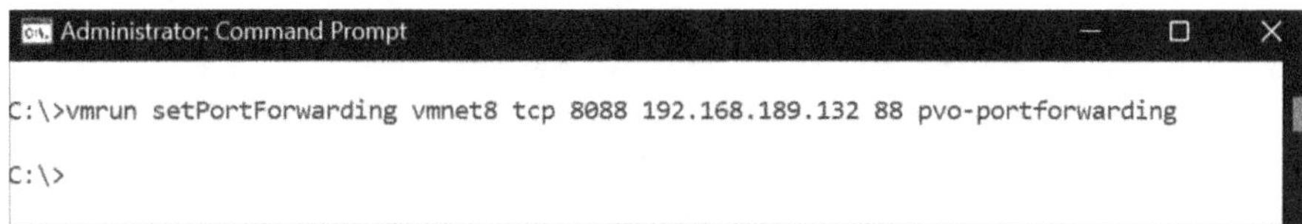

Figure 3-27. *Running the Port Forwarding Command*

To check that the port forwarding has been created, you can run the **listPortForwardings** command making sure you specify which network you want to check the port forwarding rules for, in this case the vmnet8 network. The command would look like the following:

```
vmrun listPortForwardings vmnet8
```

The output of the command is shown in the Figure 3-28.

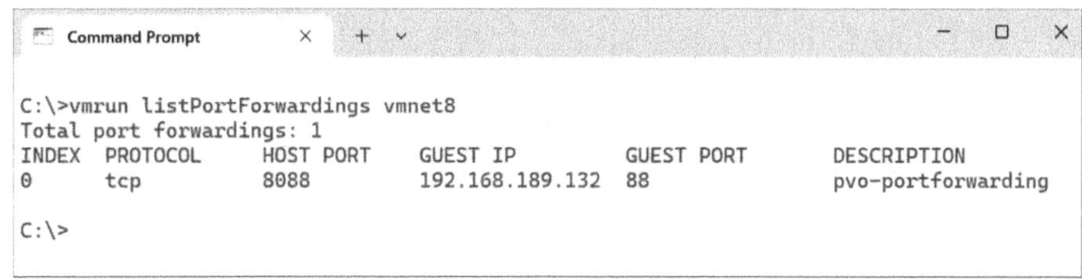

Figure 3-28. *Listing the Port Forwarding Rules*

The final host networking command is for deleting any port forwarding rules, and the command for this is detailed below:

- **deletePortForwarding** allows you to delete a port forwarding rule for the selected network on the host machine.

As an example of this command, we are going to delete the port forwarding rule we created on the vmnet8 network in the previous step. The command would look something like the following:

```
vmrun deletePortForwarding vmnet8 tcp 8082
```

Remember, this command also needs to run with elevated privileges and so should be run from an Administrator command prompt.

As with running the command for creating the port forwarding rule, you will just return to the command prompt unless an error has occurred. To check that the port forwarding rule has been deleted, run the **listPortForwardings** command making sure you specify which network you want to check the port forwarding rules for.

To check that the port forwarding has been deleted, you can run the **listPortForwardings** command making sure you specify which network you want to check the port forwarding rules for, in this case the vmnet8 network. The command would look like the following:

```
vmrun listPortForwardings vmnet8
```

The output of the command is shown in the Figure 3-29.

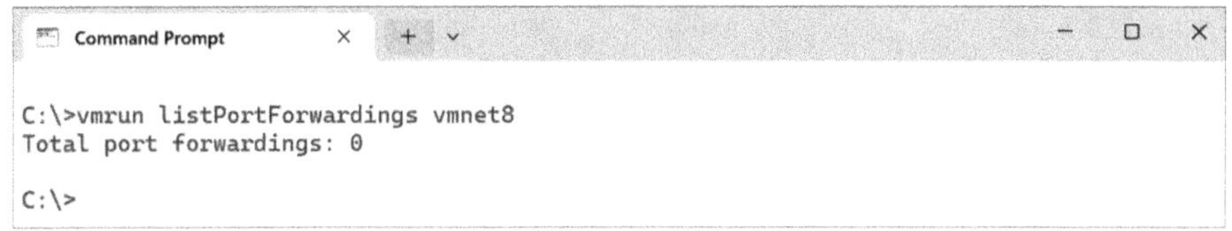
```
C:\>vmrun listPortForwardings vmnet8
Total port forwardings: 0

C:\>
```

***Figure 3-29.** Listing the Port Forwarding Rules*

As you can see, there are no port forwardings listed, and so the port forwarding rule we created previously has now been deleted.

We have now covered the host networking commands. In the next section, we are going to look at some of the more generic commands that you can use.

General Commands

In this section, we are going to look at some commands that fall under the heading of general. These range from commands for VMware Tools to deleting and cloning a virtual machine.

The first command we are going to look at is for listing all the currently running virtual machines. This command is detailed below:

- **list** lists all the currently running virtual machines.

As an example of this command, we are going to list all the running virtual machines on the host machine that is hosting the example labs. The command would look like the following:

```
vmrun list
```

The output, i.e., the list of running virtual machines, is shown in the command prompt window as shown in Figure 3-30.

Figure 3-30. *Listing the Running Virtual Machines*

As you can see, there is currently a total of one running virtual machine, and you will see the virtual machines configuration file and path to that configuration file displayed.

The next command is for upgrading the virtual machine hardware compatibility version, typically required should you upgrade to a newer version of VMware Workstation and want to take advantage of new and extended hardware features.

To upgrade the hardware compatibility version using the vmrun command, the virtual machine you want to upgrade needs to be powered off.

The command is detailed below:

- **upgradevm** allows you to upgrade to the lasted version of virtual machine hardware.

As an example of this command, we are going to upgrade the hardware compatibility version of the example Windows 10 virtual machine. For this example, we have first set the hardware compatibility version to a lower version.

The command to do this would look like the following:

```
vmrun upgradevm c:\vm\win10.vmx
```

If the virtual machine is already running the latest hardware compatibility version, then this command will have no effect. But if it is running an older version, then it will be upgraded.

Figure 3-31 below shows, on the left-hand screenshot, the virtual machine running hardware compatibility Workstation 15.x. The **upgradevm** command is then run, and if you then check the hardware compatibility version, then you will see that it has now been upgraded to the latest version, in this case Workstation 17.5.x.

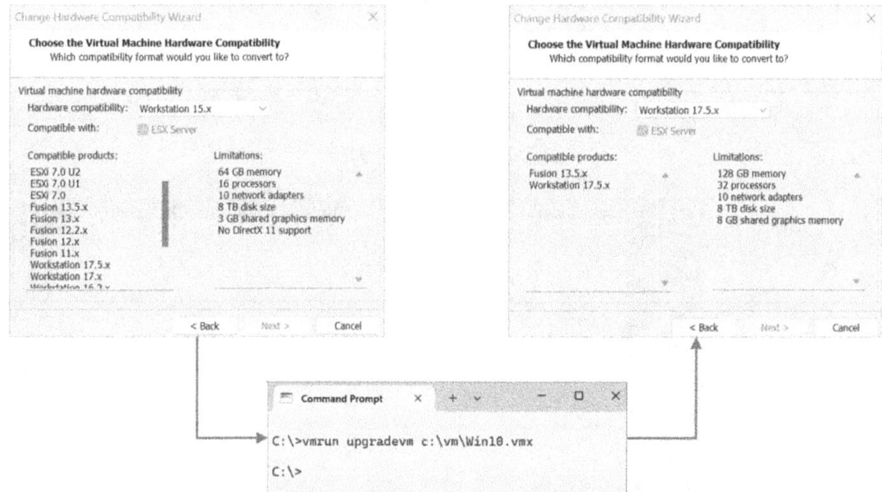

Figure 3-31. *Upgrading the Hardware Compatibility Version*

Next, we are going to look at installing VMware Tools. The command is detailed below:

- **installTools** enables you to install VMware Tools on the specified virtual machine.

As an example of this, we are going to install VMware Tools on the Windows 10 virtual machine. The command to do this would look like the following:

```
vmrun installTools c:\vm\win10.vmx
```

How you install VMware Tools depends on how you have the virtual machine configured. If you have autorun enabled, then running the **installTools** command will mount the VMware Tools ISO and automatically launch the setup utility for you to complete the installation.

If autorun is disabled, then the **installTools** command will only mount the ISO and make the disk available to the virtual machines operating system. You will have to launch the installer manually.

The virtual machine needs to be powered on to install VMware Tools.

In our example, autorun is disabled, and so we will just see the mounted ISO image when you open Windows Explorer as shown is Figure 3-32.

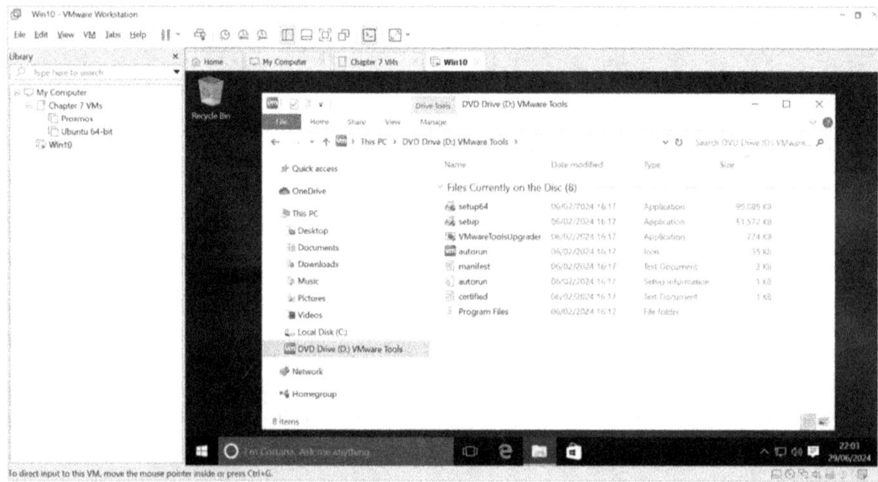

Figure 3-32. *Install VMware Tools*

The next command checks whether VMware Tools is running. The command is detailed below:

- **checkToolsState** allows you to check whether VMware Tools is running on the specified virtual machine.

As an example of this, we are going to check to see if VMware Tools is running on the Windows 10 virtual machine used in the example labs.

The command to do this would look like the following:

```
vmrun checkToolsState c:\vm\win10.vmx
```

The output of the command is displayed in the command prompt window and will state whether VMware Tools is running on the virtual machine that was specified in the command line.

In the case of our example, then you can see that VMware Tools is running on the Windows 10 example lab virtual machine as shown in Figure 3-33.

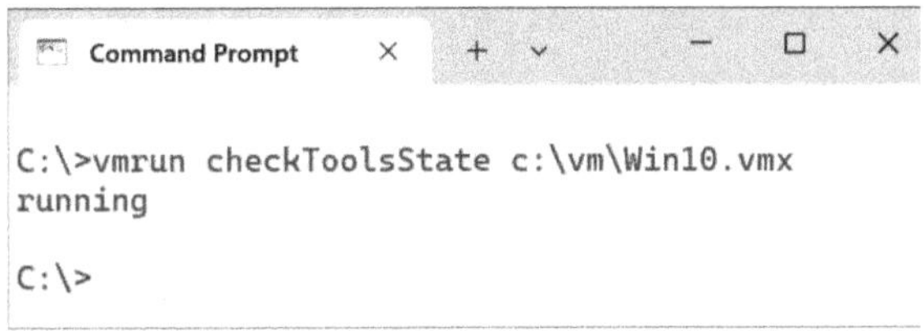

Figure 3-33. *Checking the Status of VMware Tools*

The next command we are going to look at deletes a virtual machine. The command is detailed below:

- **deleteVM** allows you to delete the specified virtual machine.

As an example of this, we have another example virtual machine called win10pvo which we are now going to delete.

The virtual machine will need to be powered off before you can use the vmrun command to delete it.

The command to do this would look like the following:

```
vmrun deleteVM c:\vm1\win10pvo.vmx
```

Once the command has been successfully executed, you will return to the command prompt again with no messages displayed.

To check to see if the virtual machine has been deleted, you need to launch Workstation Pro and check the inventory and the library pane on the left-hand side of the screen.

You will see that there is a red X next to the entry for the virtual machine that was just deleted. If you click the virtual machine, you will also see a pop-up message stating that the virtual machine could not be opened and that the vmx file could not be found. That proves that the virtual machine was deleted; however, as you can see, it does not get removed from the inventory a shown in Figure 3-34.

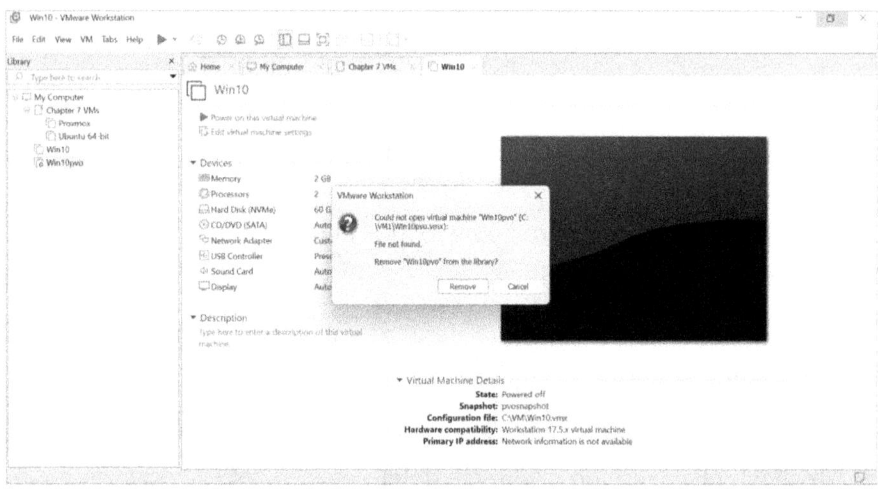

Figure 3-34. *Deleting a Virtual Machine*

Click the **Remove** button to delete the virtual machine from the inventory.

In the previous example of deleting a virtual machine, the machine we created to use in that example was created by making a clone of the existing Windows 10 example virtual machine. This was done using the final that we are going to look at that falls under the heading of general commands.

The command is detailed below:

- **clone** allows you to create a copy of the specified virtual machine. You also have the following additional parameters:
    - **full** creates a full clone of the specified virtual machine.
    - **Linked** creates a linked clone of the specified virtual machine.

You can also specify a snapshot name in the command line to create a clone from that snapshot instead of the current state of the virtual machine.

As an example of this, we are going to clone the Windows 10 virtual machine that we have been using as an example throughout this book.

The command to do this would look like the following:

```
vmrun -T ws clone \vm\win10.vmx
\clonevm\win10pvoclone.vmx full
-cloneName=win10pvoclone
```

The command prompt will look like it has hung for a while but that is to be expected as you won't see the prompt again until the cloning process has completed. This could take several minutes depending on the size of the virtual machine and the speed of your host machine.

Once the command has been successfully completed, you won't see any messages pop-up in the command prompt, and even if you launch Workstation Pro, you will not see the cloned virtual machine appear in the inventory.

To check that the clone has been successfully created, open Windows Explorer on the host machine and navigate to the folder in which the clone was created. In this example, that was the **c:\CloneVM** folder as shown in Figure 3-35.

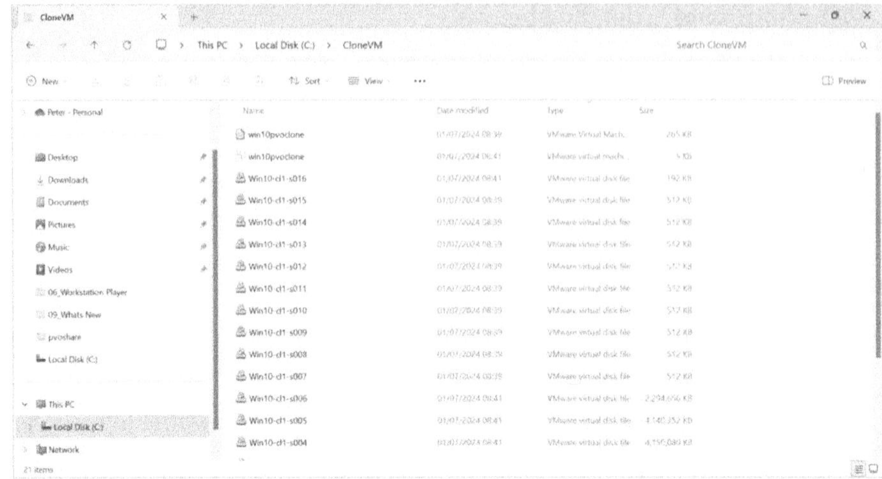

Figure 3-35. *Cloning a Virtual Machine*

We have now covered the general commands and have completed our overview of the vmrun command.

The commands that we have covered in this chapter are those commands that are available when you type vmrun at the command prompt. This lists the available commands on this version of Workstation Pro.

There may be other commands available for other platforms, such as the Linux version of Workstation Pro, Fusion, or even vSphere; however, if you know these commands and they are not discussed here, then they don't apply to this version of Workstation Pro.

Summary

In this chapter, we have introduced you to the vmrun command that you can run from the command prompt and allows you to control and configure the virtual machines running on the host machine from where you run them.

We then discussed each command individually, what it does, and what the syntax for running the commands looks like.

As part of this, we demonstrated several example commands illustrating the screenshots to show the expected outcome of running that command.

In the next chapter, we are going to look at the REST API.

CHAPTER 4

VMware Workstation Pro REST API

In the previous chapter, we discussed how you could use the vmrun command to control and manage virtual machines, running on VMware Workstation, from the command line.

In this chapter, we are going to build on that and look at another way to manage and control virtual machines using a command line-based approach, and that is via the Workstation Pro REST API.

What Is the REST API?

A REST API, or RESTful API, is based on the HTTP protocol and uses HTTP requests to send commands to a target machine.

These APIs are often typically sent by using a simple URL. For example, a command may look like this: `https://example.com/api/users`. This allows applications to be able to interact with this API by making HTTP requests to this URL/endpoint.

As stated in the opening paragraph of this chapter, the Vmware Workstation Pro REST API enables you to interact with the core VMware Workstation Pro solution and the virtual machines that are running on it, by using a set of API calls or commands. The REST API standard commands are discussed in the next section.

P. von Oven, *Learning VMware Workstation Pro for Windows: Volume 2*,
https://doi.org/10.1007/979-8-8688-0864-7_4

REST API Standard Commands

As a standard REST API, it means that you can send the standard REST API commands which are listed below:

- **GET** - reads or retrieves information
- **PUT** - updates the current information or configuration
- **POST** - creates new a configuration
- **DELETE** - deletes existing information and data

Taking one of these standard commands, coupled with specific additional configuration parameters where required, the command is then sent using either HTTP or HTTPS to perform whatever the REST API action is that you have selected along with the additional parameters.

Next, we are going to look at the categories in which these API commands can be used. These are the things that you can use the API to manage or control.

Workstation Pro API Categories

Like the categories we discussed in the previous chapter, the REST API can also be used to control and manage either virtual machines or host machines. The following are the categories within Workstation Pro:

- Host network management
- VM management
- VM network adapter management
- VM power management
- VM shared folders management

When running REST API commands, there are a few points to be aware of. The first and most obvious one is that the Workstation Pro API is only for use with Workstation Pro and not for use with other VMware products or solutions.

It is reliant on using the vmrest process which will run as the end user who launches it so you need to make sure that end user has the appropriate privileges. We will look at how to set and run this in the next section.

Setting Up the REST API

The REST API is available to use on the host machine once Workstation Pro has been installed. You will find it located in the **C:\Program File (x86)\VMware\VMware Workstation** folder.

To make it easier to run, you might want to add this folder location to your current path.

Before you start running the API service, there are a few things you need to complete first. The first of these is to create the credentials that will be used by the API service to authenticate commands. These credentials will be used when you send the commands.

To do this, follow the instructions below:

1. On the host machine that is running Workstation Pro, open a command prompt.
2. Now run the following command: **`vmrest.exe -C`**.
3. At the **Username** prompt, enter a username and press the Enter key. In this example, we have created a user called pvonoven. This is shown in Figure 4-1.

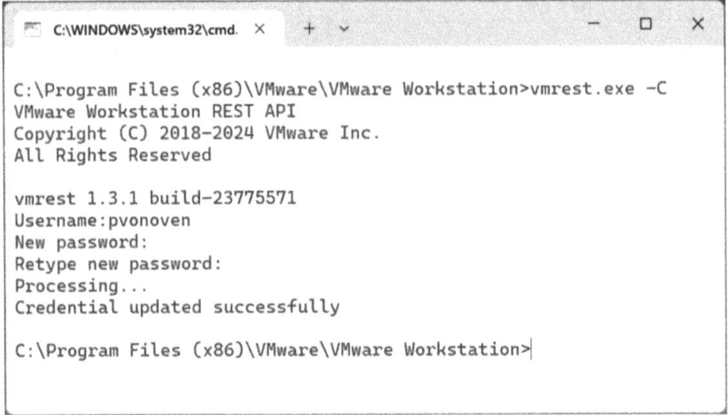
```
C:\Program Files (x86)\VMware\VMware Workstation>vmrest.exe -C
VMware Workstation REST API
Copyright (C) 2018-2024 VMware Inc.
All Rights Reserved

vmrest 1.3.1 build-23775571
Username:pvonoven
New password:
Retype new password:
Processing...
Credential updated successfully

C:\Program Files (x86)\VMware\VMware Workstation>
```

Figure 4-1. *Updating the vmrest Credentials*

4. Then in the **New password** prompt, enter a password for this user account followed by pressing the Enter key.
5. Next, type the password again at the **Retype new password** prompt.
6. You will see the message stating **Processing....**
7. Once completed, you will see a message stating **Credential updated successfully** and you will return to the command prompt. Again, this is shown in Figure 4-1.

If you want to check that the credentials have been successfully saved, then you will find a file called **vmrest.cfg** saved in the user profile folder for the user that was currently logged in when you created the credentials for the REST API.

An example of this is shown highlighted in Figure 4-2.

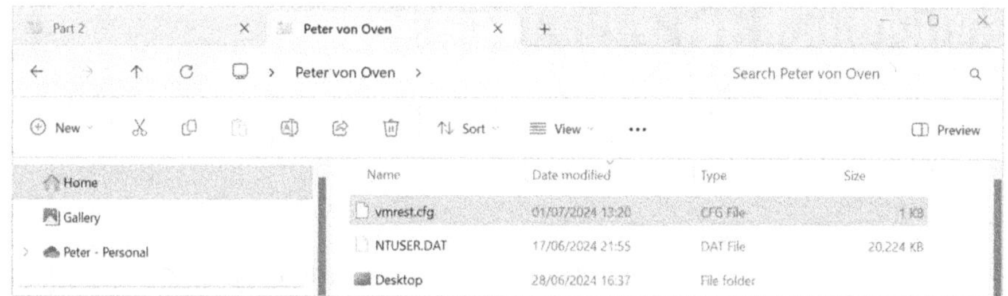

***Figure 4-2.** Credentials Successfully Created*

If you open the file using Notepad for example, then you will see something like the text shown in the following screenshot in Figure 4-3. Note the password is not visible in plain text.

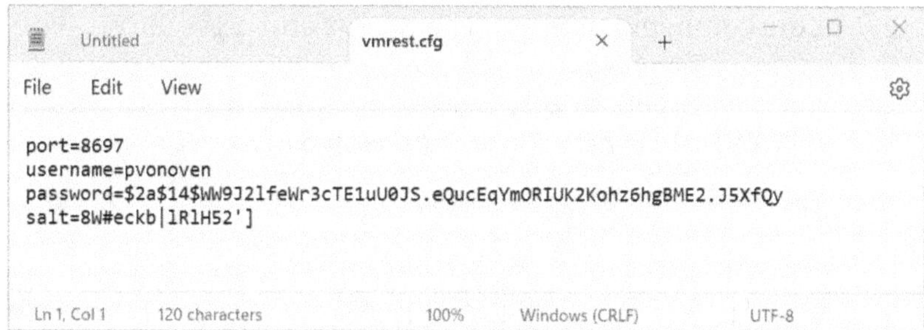

***Figure 4-3.** vmrest.cfg Credentials File Created*

You will now be able to run the **vmrest** command without having to specify credentials each time. In the next sections, we are going to look at how to connect to the API service.

Connecting to the API Service

Now that we have created the credentials for the vmrest API, we can now configure access to it using either HTTP or HTTPS. First, we will look at how to configure HTTP access.

Configuring HTTP API Access

In this section, we are going to look at how to configure access to the API service using HTTP.

Note, it is not recommended to continue to use Workstation Pro while API calls are being actioned and processed.

To configure HTTP API Access, follow the steps described:

1. On the host machine, open a command prompt window.
2. At the command prompt, type **vmrest** and press the Enter key.
3. The REST API is now running as shown in Figure 4-4.

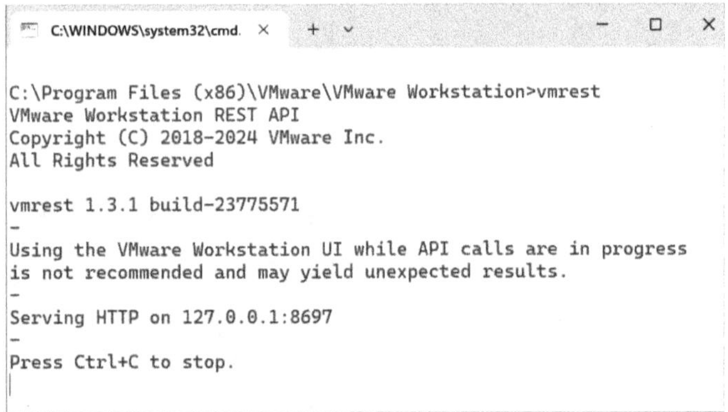

Figure 4-4. *vmrest Running and Serving HTTP*

From the information in the command prompt shown in Figure 4-4, make a note of the IP address for the serving HTTP. We will need this to connect to when sending API commands.

Workstation Pro API Explorer

VMware includes a built-in tool called the REST API Explorer that provides a web-based interface into the available API commands that you can run.

It allows you to configure and run the API commands by building the command syntax and enabling you to add the relevant parameters to those commands that require them.

We will use this in some of the examples, but in order to do that, you need to authorize the web page so that REST API service accepts the commands that are sent to it.

To configure authorization for the API Explorer, follow the steps:

1. Open a browser on the host machine.
2. In the address bar of the browser, type in the IP address recorded in the above step, also noting the port number.

   In this example, you would type **http://127.0.0.1:8697** and then press the Enter key
3. You will see the **VMware Workstation REST API** page as shown in Figure 4-5.

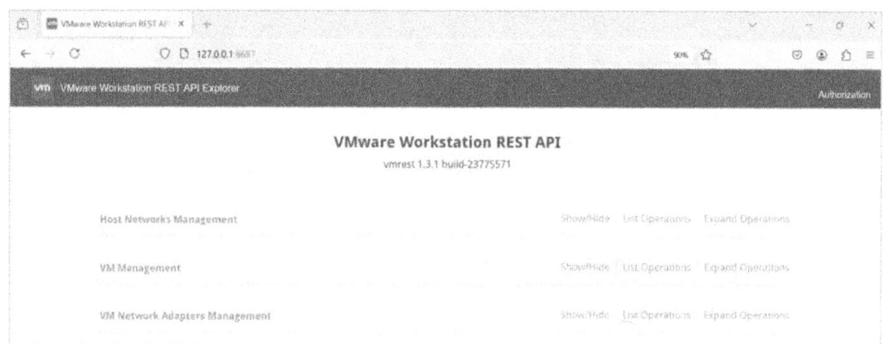

Figure 4-5. *VMware Workstation REST API Explorer Page*

With the page displayed, you can now configure the authorization. To do this, follow the steps described:

4. Click **Authorization** located at the top right-hand corner of the web page as shown in Figure 4-6.

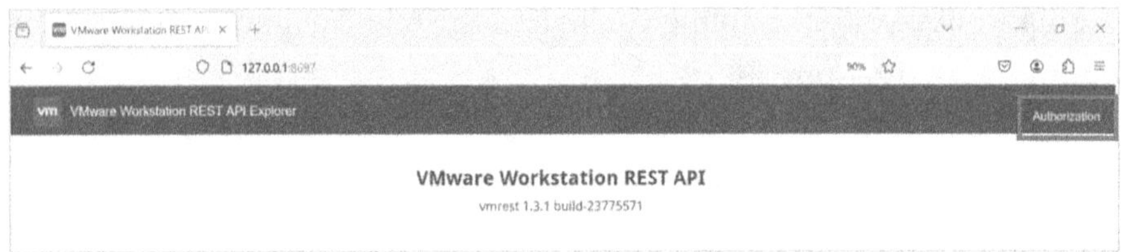

Figure 4-6. *Authorizing the REST API*

5. You will now see the **Configure authorizations** dialog box as shown on Figure 4-7.

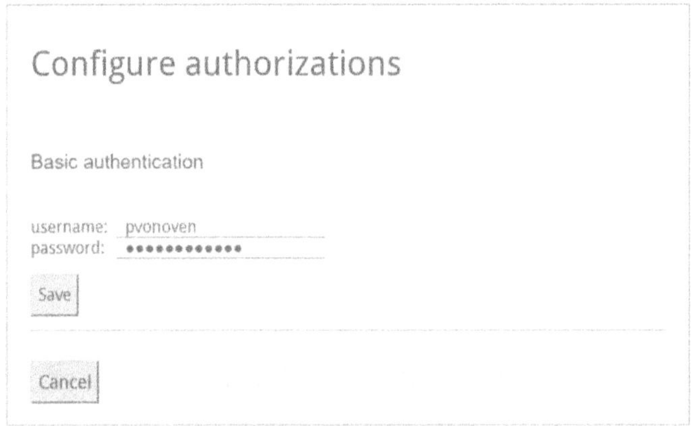

Figure 4-7. *Configuring Authorizations*

6. In the **username** field, enter the password you created in the "Setting Up the REST API" section of this chapter.

7. In the **password** field, enter password that you set for the above username.

8. Now click the **Save** button.

9. You will return to the **VMware Workstation REST API** page.

You have now successfully authorized the user to use API calls via HTTP using the API Explorer.

In the next section, we are going to look at the process for authorizing API calls using HTTPS.

Configuring HTTPS API Access

Following on from the previous section, in this section, we are going to look at how to configure access to the Workstation Pro API using HTTPS. This process is like the process we covered in the HTTP section but now with the additional step of creating certificates to enable security elements.

To configure HTTPS API Access, follow the steps described:

1. On the host machine, open a command prompt window.

2. The first task is to create a certificate that can be used. You may well have a certificate that you use already, but in this example, we are going to generate a self-signed OpenSSL-based certificate along with the associated private key. To download OpenSSL for Windows, follow the link `https://slproweb.com/download/Win64OpenSSL-3_3_1.exe`; then launch the .exe file to install OpenSSL on the host machine.

3. With OpenSSL now installed, open a command prompt with administrator privileges.

4. At the command prompt, change to the OpenSSL directory – **c:\Program Files\OpenSSL-Win64\bin**.

5. Now create the certificate using the following command: **`openssl req -x509 -newkey rsa:4096 -keyout wsapi-key.pem -out wsapi-cert.pem -days 365 -nodes`**.

6. You will be prompted to add information for country code, state, city, organization name, OU name, common name, and email address. This is shown in Figure 4-8.

***Figure 4-8.** Creating a Certificate with OpenSSL*

Once the command has successfully completed, you will see that the certificate and the key file have been created. You will find these in the **C:\Program Files\OpenSSL-Win64\Bin** folder as shown in Figure 4-9.

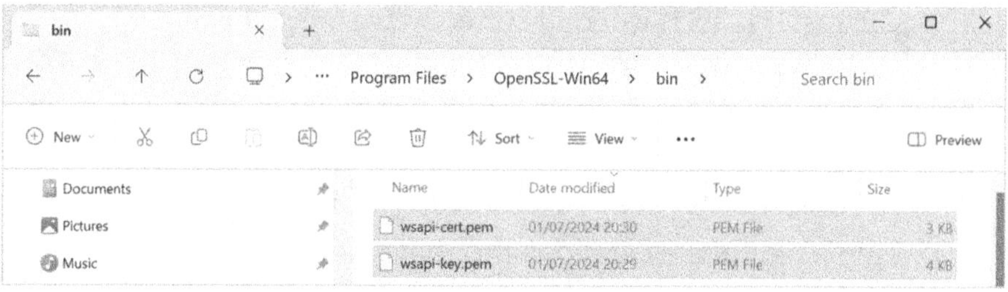

Figure 4-9. *Certificate and Key Files Created*

The next step is to start the vmrest API service but now using the certificate and key files that we just created.

7. On the host machine, open a command prompt window.

8. At the command prompt, type **vmrest -c c:\program files\OpenSSL-Win64\bin\wsapi-cert.pem -k c:\program files\OpenSSL-Win64\bin\wsapi-key.pem** and press the Enter key.

9. The REST API is now running as shown in Figure 4-10.

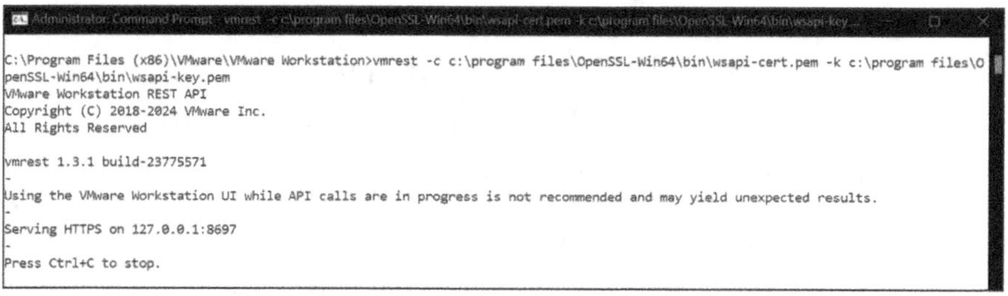

```
C:\Program Files (x86)\VMware\VMware Workstation>vmrest -c c:\program files\OpenSSL-Win64\bin\wsapi-cert.pem -k c:\program files\OpenSSL-Win64\bin\wsapi-key.pem
VMware Workstation REST API
Copyright (C) 2018-2024 VMware Inc.
All Rights Reserved

vmrest 1.3.1 build-23775571
-
Using the VMware Workstation UI while API calls are in progress is not recommended and may yield unexpected results.
-
Serving HTTPS on 127.0.0.1:8697
-
Press Ctrl+C to stop.
```

Figure 4-10. *vmrest Launched Serving HTTPS*

From the information in the command prompt shown in Figure 4-10, make a note of the IP address for the serving HTTPS. We will need this to connect to.

To test HTTPS is working correctly, we are going to connect to the REST API Explorer using HTTPS.

10. Open a browser on the host machine.

11. In the address bar of the browser, type in the IP address recorded in the above step, also noting the port number, in this example **https://127.0.0.1:8697**, and press the Enter key.

12. You will see the **VMware Workstation REST API** page as shown in Figure 4-11.

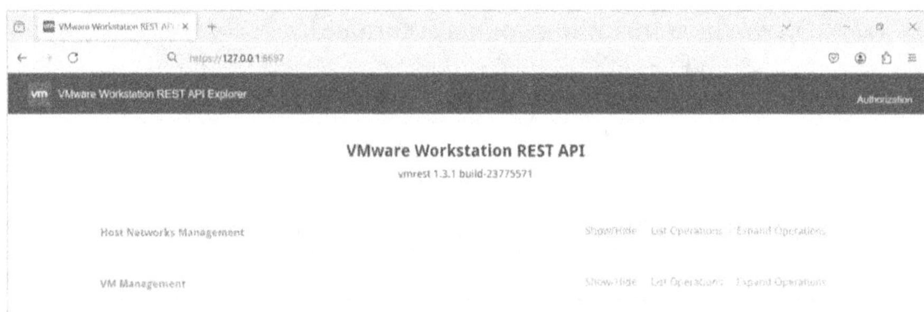

***Figure 4-11.** VMware Workstation REST API screen*

Next you need to "authorize" the API Explorer using the credentials that were configured previously in the "Setting Up the REST API" section of this chapter. To do this, follow the steps described:

13. Click **Authorization** located at the top right-hand corner of the web page as shown in Figure 4-12.

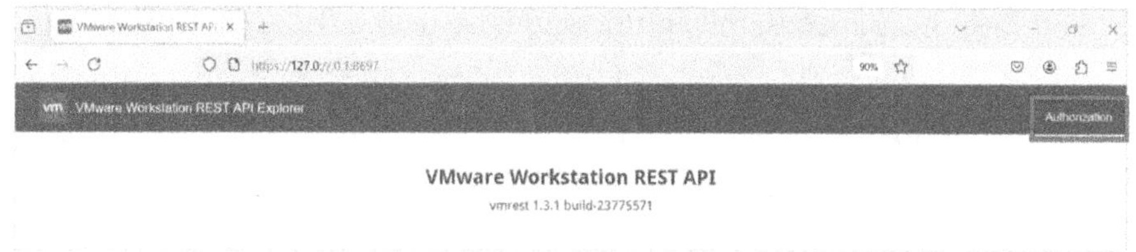

Figure 4-12. *Authorizing the REST API*

14. You will now see the **Configure authorization** dialog box as shown on Figure 4-13.

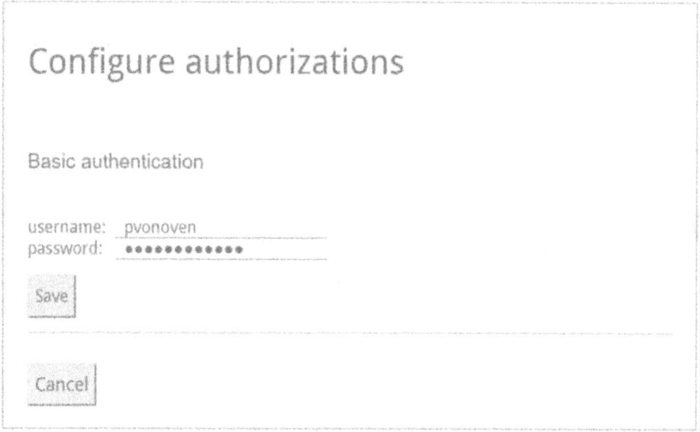

Figure 4-13. *Configuring Authorizations*

15. In the **username** field, enter the password you created in the “Setting Up the REST API” section of this chapter.
16. In the **password** field, enter password that you set for the above username.
17. Now click the **Save** button.
18. You will return to the **VMware Workstation REST API** page.

You have now successfully authorized the user to use API calls via HTTPS.

In this section, we have looked at enabling the API service to be ready to send API calls to using HTTPS, and in the previous section, we did the same but for HTTP.

We then took a look at the REST API Explorer so as to quickly test that authorization was working. As previously mentioned, we are going to use the API Explorer in some of the upcoming examples of using the API commands.

In the next sections of this chapter, with the API service now running, we are going to look at the individual API calls and how they work and the expected responses.

Configuring API Calls

In this section, we are going work through the API calls, look at the syntax of each call, and show some examples, using real-life screenshots of the responses you should expect to receive.

As highlighted at the beginning of this chapter, these API calls cover the following categories:

- Host network management
- VM management
- VM network adapter management
- VM power management
- VM shared folders management

We are going to start with API calls for the host network management.

Host Network Management API Calls

In this section, we are going to focus on API calls that are used for configuring and managing the networking of the host machine running VMware Workstation Pro.

We are going to work through each API call and provide examples of the command syntax, how it works, and with some examples show the screenshots of the responses and output you would expect to see.

To send the API calls, we are going to use the Postman solution which we have installed on the host machine, and therefore, the screenshots of the output will show the Postman UI.

We are also going to show other examples using the REST API Explorer.

Ensure the REST API server is running by launching the **vmrest** command before running any of the API calls.

To show the available API calls, we are going to break these down into the categories of command, starting with the GET API call.

GET Commands

The GET command is used to get the status of and, if available, the results from a currently executing command. The following is a breakdown of the available GET API calls:

Return Virtual Networks Configuration

The command for returning or showing the currently configured networks on the host machine is as follows:

```
GET /vmnet
```

In the following example, we have sent the command **http://127.0.0.1:8697/api/vmnet** to the API service using Postman with the results showing the details returned of the currently configured host networks.

As a reminder, each of the API commands needs to be prefixed with the address of the API server that is listening for the commands.

In the examples shown in this chapter, the host machine running VMware Workstation Pro and therefore the API service is running locally using the local http address of 127.0.0.1.

The service is listening on port 8697.

In this example, you will see that we have virtual networks configured for vmnet1 and vmnet8.

The details of each of the configured networks are then displayed.

For example, for vmnet1, you will also see that the type of network is set to host only, DHCP is enabled, the IP subnet is set to 192.168.83.0, and finally, the IP subnet mask is set to 255.255.255.0.

This is shown in Figure 4-14.

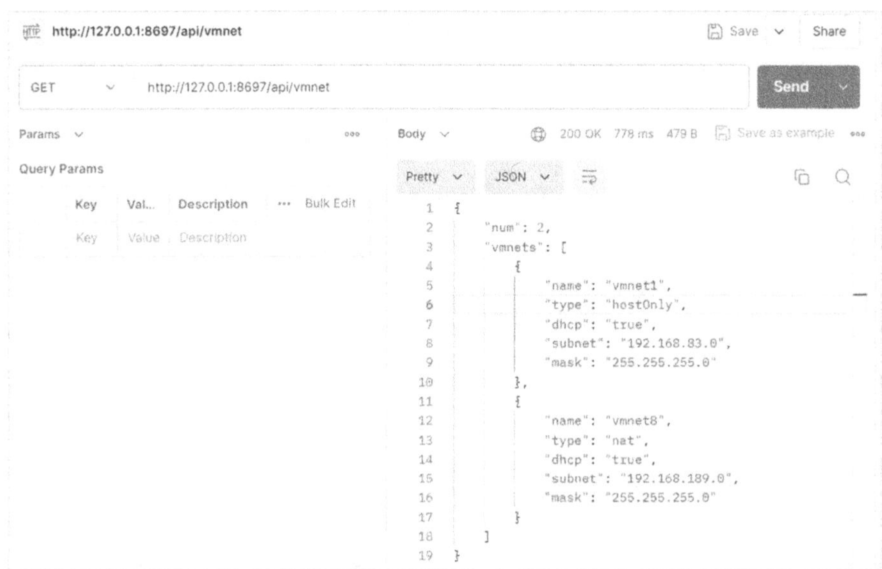

***Figure 4-14.** Return Virtual Networks Configuration Using GET*

The next API call is used to return the DHCP service MAC to IP settings.

DHCP Service MAC to IP Settings

The command for returning or showing the currently configured DHCP service for the MAC to IP settings on the host machine is as follows:

```
GET api/vmnet/<network ID>/mactoip
```

In the above command, you need to replace the **`<network ID>`** with the name of the host network you want to return the information for, for example, vmnet1 or vmnet8.

In the following example, we have sent the following command `http://127.0.0.1:8697/api/vmnet/vmnet8/mactoip` to the API service using Postman with the results showing the details returned of the currently configured MAC to IP settings for the vmnet8 network which was specified in the API call.

In the results in this example, you will see that there is no MAC to IP settings currently configured, detailed as **"num" : 0** as shown in Figure 4-15.

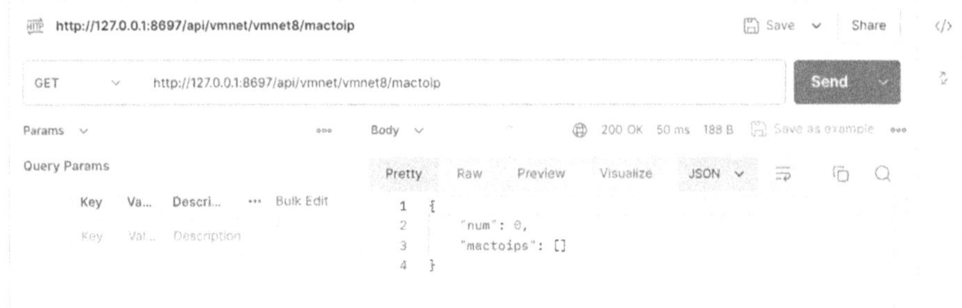

Figure 4-15. *MAC to IP Settings*

If there were any MAC to IP settings, then these would be shown inside the square brackets of the **"mactoips": [ ]** entry in the output.

Next, we are going to look at port forwardings.

Port Forwardings

The command for returning or showing the currently configured port forwardings on the host machine is as follows:

```
GET api/vmnet/<network ID>/portforward
```

In the above command, you need to replace the <network ID> with the name of the host network you want to return the information for, for example, vmnet1 or vmnet8.

In the following example, we have sent the following command `http://127.0.0.1:8697/api/vmnet/vmnet8/portforward` to the API service using Postman with the results showing the details returned of the currently configured port forwarding rules for the vmnet8 network which was specified in the API call.

In the results in this example, you will see that **"num" : 1** indicates that there is one currently configured portforwarding rule in place.

You will also see that the details of the port forwarding rule are also shown. In this case, you will see the protocol, the port being forwarded from the host, and then the IP and port number of the virtual machine that the port is being forwarded to, along with any optional description that you entered when you configured the port forwarding rule.

This is shown in Figure 4-16.

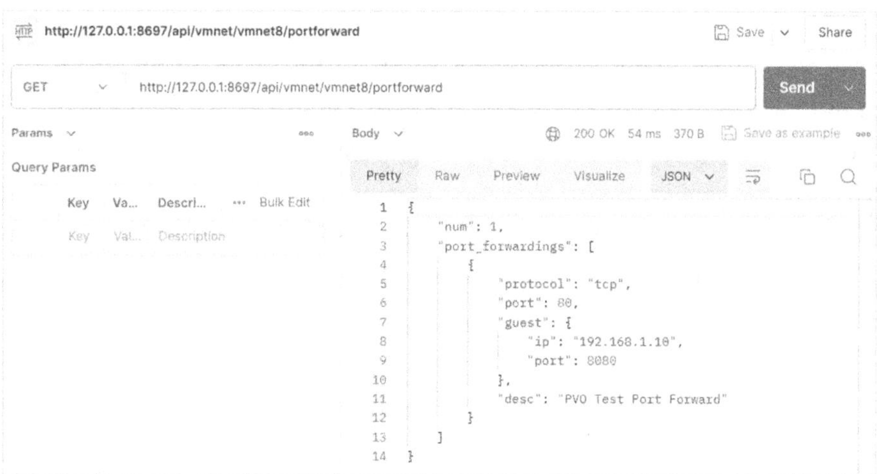

Figure 4-16. *Port Forwarding Rules*

In the next section, we are going to look at the PUT API calls for host network management.

PUT Commands

The PUT command is used to replace an existing variable with a new one. The following is a breakdown of the available GET API calls, starting with updating MAC to IP bindings.

Update MAC to IP Bindings

The command for updating or replacing the currently configured MAC to IP bindings on the host machine is as follows:

```
PUT api/vmnet/<network ID>/mactoip/<mac address>
```

In the above command, you need to replace the **<network ID>** with the name of the host network you want to update the configuration for and the **<mac address>** you want to be mapped with the specified IP address.

In the following example, we are going to build the command using the API Explorer and then take that command as a Curl command and input that into Postman just to demonstrate another way of running and building the API commands and calls. You could of course just run it directly using API Explorer.

If you open the **VMware Workstation REST API Explorer** by launching a browser and navigating to **127.0.0.1:8697**, you will open the API Explorer page.

Now click **Hosts Network Management** and then click **PUT /vmnet/{vmnet}/mactoip/{mac}** as shown in Figure 4-17.

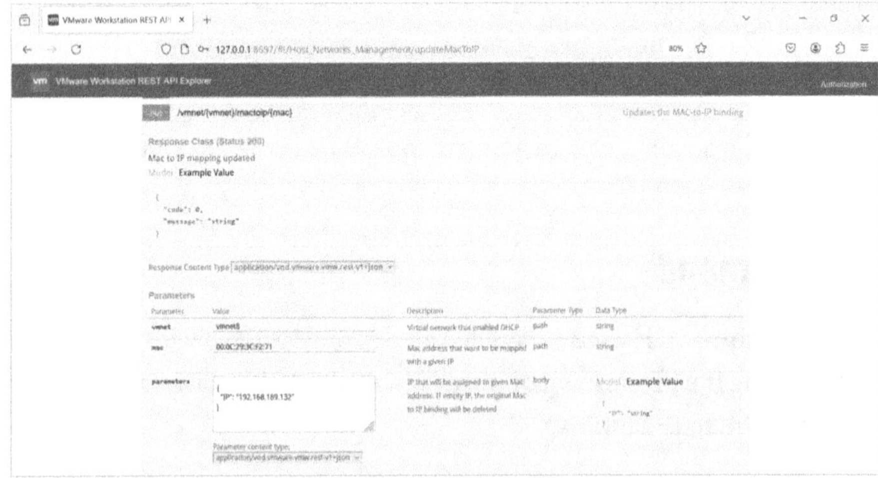

Figure 4-17. Update MAC to IP Bindings

Enter the details for **vmnet**, **mac**, and any parameters as shown in Figure 4-17 and then scroll down to the **TRY IT OUT!** button as shown in Figure 4-18.

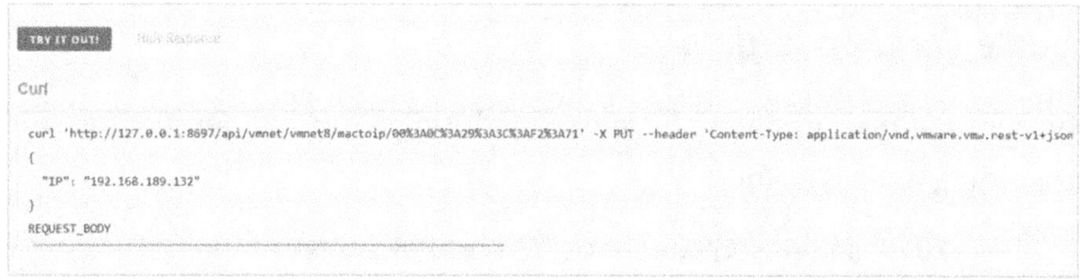

Figure 4-18. *Try Out the API Call*

If you click the **TRY IT OUT!** button, then you will see the commands generated which is also shown in Figure 4-18, in this example the curl command. The command will also have been run by the API Explorer as part of the try it now experience, but for this example, we just want to show another way that command can be taken and used.

Next, we have copied the curl command from the API Explorer and pasted it into Postman as shown in Figure 4-19.

Import cURL into a collection

```
1 curl 'http://127.0.0.1:8697/api/vmnet/vmnet8/mactoip/
    00%3A0C%3A29%3A3C%3AF2%3A71' -X PUT --header 'Content-Type:
    application/vnd.vmware.vmw.rest-v1+json' --header 'Accept: application/
    vnd.vmware.vmw.rest-v1+json' --header 'Authorization: Basic
    cHZvbm92ZW46UGVhY2hleTE5NzIh' -d @- <<REQUEST_BODY
2 {
```

Request name

http://127.0.0.1:8697/api/vmnet/vmnet8/mactoip/00%3A0C%3A29%3A3C%3AF2%3A71<<REQUEST_B

Collection name

New Collection

Import Without Saving | Import Into Collection

Figure 4-19. *Curl Command in Postman*

You can now run the command and make the API call.

Next, we are going to look at how to update the port forwarding using an API call.

Update Port Forwarding

The command for updating or replacing the currently configured port forwarding rules is as follows:

```
PUT api/vmnet/<network ID>/portforward/
<protocol>/<port>
```

When running the command, you need to replace the **<network ID>** with the name of the host network you want to update the configuration for. Then enter the protocol you want to use in the **<protocol>** section, and then finally, enter the network port in the **<port>** section.

In this example, we are going to build the command using the API Explorer to update the port forwarding configuration. To do this, in the **vmnet** section, type in the name of the network you want to update; in the **protocol** section, type in the protocol that will be used; and then finally in **port** section, type in the port number you want to use. In this example, we are going to forward network traffic on port 80 on the vmnet8 network, using TCP.

You then have the parameters section for adding the additional configuration details. In this case, these details provide the target for the updated portforwarding rule. For this example, we are going to forward to port 80 on the virtual machine with the IP address of 192.168.189.132. As an optional parameter, we have given this port forwarding rule the description of "test." This is shown in Figure 4-20.

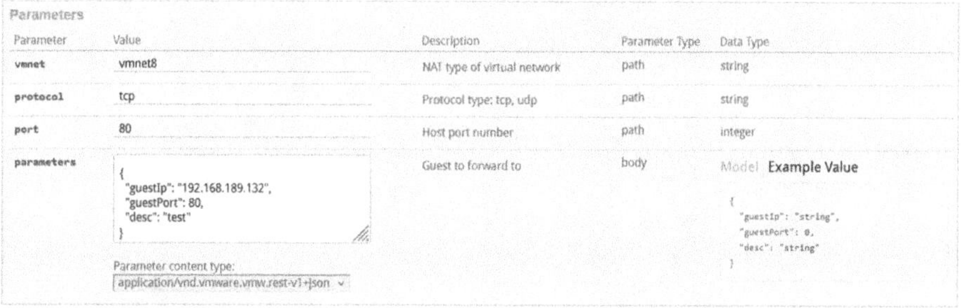

Parameter	Value	Description	Parameter Type	Data Type
vmnet	vmnet8	NAT type of virtual network	path	string
protocol	tcp	Protocol type: tcp, udp	path	string
port	80	Host port number	path	integer
parameters	{ "guestIp": "192.168.189.132", "guestPort": 80, "desc": "test" } Parameter content type: application/vnd.vmware.vmw.rest-v1+json	Guest to forward to	body	Model Example Value { "guestIp": "string", "guestPort": 0, "desc": "string" }

Figure 4-20. Port Forwarding Configuration Parameters

Clicking the **TRY IT NOW** button will execute the command and update the portforwarding rule.

Next, we are going to look at the POST command for the host network management API calls.

POST Commands

A POST command is used to create a new resource on the server. In this section, we are going to look at the single POST command for host network management which is used to create a new virtual network.

Create a New Host Virtual Network

With this next command, you can create a new virtual network on the host machine. This process is the same process as using the Virtual Network Editor on the Workstation Pro UI.

The command is as follows:

```
POST api/vmnets
```

In this example, we are again going to use the API Explorer to build the command. You then need to add the parameters to the command to configure the network name, the type of network, whether or not to use DHCP, the IP subnet, and then the IP subnet mask. This is shown in Figure 4-21.

Parameters

Parameter	Value	Description
parameters	{ "name": "vmnet4", "type": "nat", "dhcp": "true", "subnet": "192.168.73.0", "mask": "255.255.255.0" }	Host network to be created

Parameter content type: application/vnd.vmware.vmw.rest-v1+json

Figure 4-21. *Creating a New Virtual Network*

When you run the command, then a new network will be created. To check this, open the Workstation Pro UI and launch the Virtual Network Editor. You will see that vmnet4 has been created as shown in Figure 4-22.

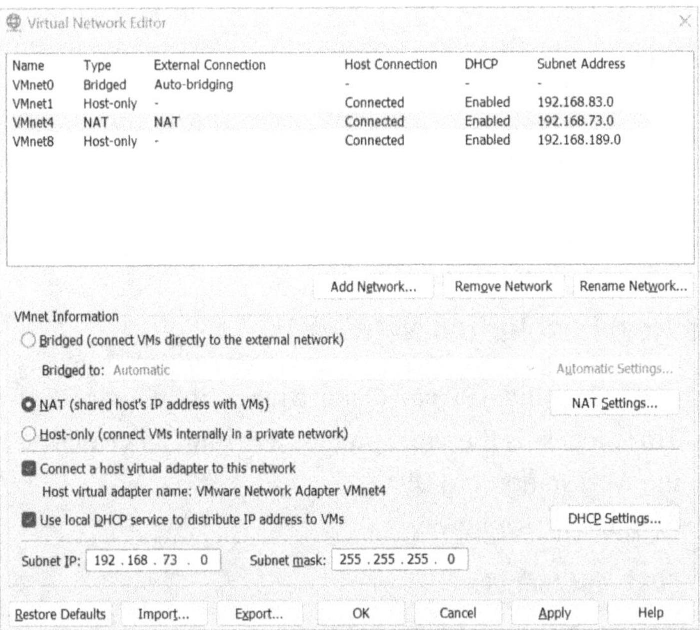

Figure 4-22. *New Virtual Network Created*

The final command under the host network management heading is the delete command.

DELETE Commands

The DELETE command is used to remove a specific resource using a REST API. The DELETE request is sent to the URL of the resource to be deleted, and the API will then remove the resource if it exists.

For host network management, there is just a single command which is used to delete port forwarding rules.

Delete Port Forwarding

This command enables you to delete a current existing port forwarding rule. The command for deleting port forwarding rules is as follows:

```
DELETE api/vmnet/<network ID>/portforward/
<protocol>/<port>
```

When you run the above command, you need to replace the **<network ID>** with the name of the host network you want to delete port forwarding for, enter the protocol in the **<protocol>** section, and then enter the network port in the **<port>** section.

There are no additional parameters with this command as they are all contained within the command line itself.

In this example, we are going to delete the port forwarding configuration we created previously. The command to do this would look like the following:

```
DELETE api/vmnet/vmnet8>/portforward/tcp/80
```

We have now completed the overview of all the available host network management API calls.

In the next section, we are going to look at the API calls that are used for virtual machine management.

Virtual Machine Management

The next set of API calls we are going to look at falls under the heading of virtual machine management. We will start with the GET commands first.

GET Commands

In the following section, we are going to look at the VM management GET commands to retrieve specific information about the virtual machines running on our Workstation Pro example environment.

List VM IDs and Paths

The first of these commands will list the IDs for all the virtual machines running on the host machine, regardless of power state, along with the path to where the virtual machine is stored.

The command for returning for showing the IDs and paths is as follows:

```
GET api/vms
```

In the following example, we have sent the command `http://127.0.0.1:8697/api/vms` to the API service using Postman with the results showing the details returned of the ID of each virtual machine currently hosted on Workstation Pro, along with the path to where the virtual machine files are stored.

This is shown in Figure 4-23.

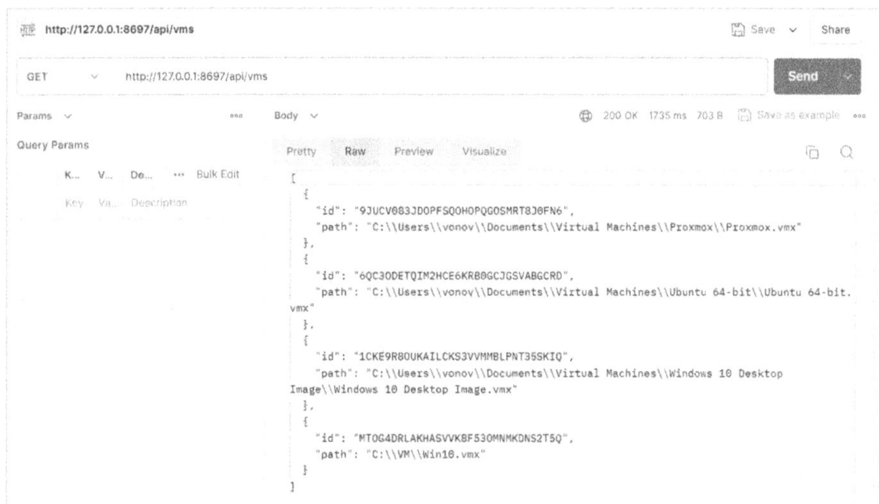

Figure 4-23. *Virtual Machine IDs and Paths*

If we take our example Windows 10 machine that we are going to be using in the majority of the examples, then you can see it has an ID of **MTOG4DRLAKHASVVK8F53OMNMKDNS2T5Q** and that it is stored in a folder on the host called **c:\vm** and the virtual machine files are called Win10.*. As you can see, the **.**vmx virtual machine configuration file is the file that is listed.

We will use this information throughout the examples in this chapter.

The next command is used to retrieve and display the virtual machine settings information.

VM Setting Information

The next command will list the settings for a specific virtual machine using the ID for that virtual machine. Virtual machine IDs can be retrieved using the previous command.

The command for returning or showing the virtual machine settings is as follows:

```
GET api/vms/<VM ID>
```

When running the command, replace the **<VM ID>** with the actual ID of the virtual machine you want to retrieve the settings information for.

In the following example, we have sent the following command **`http://127.0.0.1:8697/api/vms/MTOG4DRLAKHASVVK8F53OMNMKDNS2T5Q`** to the API service using Postman with the results showing the details returned of the settings information for the virtual machine ID that we specified in the command. This virtual machine is the Windows 10 example virtual machine.

This is shown in Figure 4-24.

Figure 4-24. *Virtual Machine Settings Information*

As you can see from the output of running this command, this particular virtual machine is configured with two CPUs and 2GB memory.

Next is the command for retrieving information about specific configuration parameters.

VM Configuration Parameters

The next command will list specific configuration parameter information for a virtual machine using the ID for that virtual machine. You then need to specify which parameter you want to retrieve information for.

The command for returning or showing the virtual machine settings is as follows:

```
GET api/vms/<VM ID>/params/<config parameter>
```

When running the command, replace the **<VM ID>** with the actual ID of the virtual machine you want to retrieve the settings information for and the **<config parameter>** with the specific parameter you want to display.

In the following example, we have sent the following command **`http://127.0.0.1:8697/api/vms/MTOG4DRLAKHASVVK8F53OMNMKDNS2T5Q/params/virtual.HW.version`** to the API service using Postman.

The results show the details returned for the parameter that we specified in the command, for the virtual machine with the ID that we also specified in the command.

The virtual machine used in this example is the Windows 10 example virtual machine, and we have retrieved the information that shows us what hardware compatibility version this virtual machine is running.

This is shown in Figure 4-25.

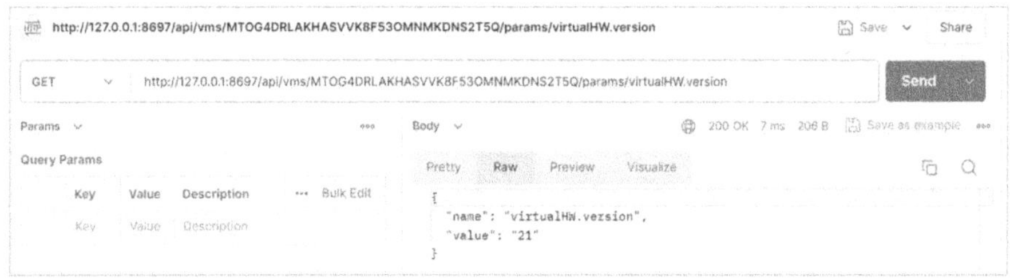

Figure 4-25. *Virtual Machine Configuration Parameter Information*

In this instance, we can see that the Windows 10 example virtual machine is running hardware compatibility version 21.

The next command is for retrieving restriction information.

VM Restriction Information

The next command will list any restriction information for a virtual machine using the ID for that virtual machine.

The command for returning or showing the virtual machine restriction information is as follows:

```
GET api/vms/<VM ID>/restrictions
```

When running the command, replace the **<VM ID>** with the actual ID of the virtual machine you want to retrieve the restriction information for.

In the following example, we have sent the following command **`http://127.0.0.1:8697/api/vms/MTOG4DRLAKHASVVK8F53OMNMKDNS2T5Q/restrictions`** to the API service using Postman with the results showing the details returned of the virtual machine restrictions.

This is shown in Figure 4-26.

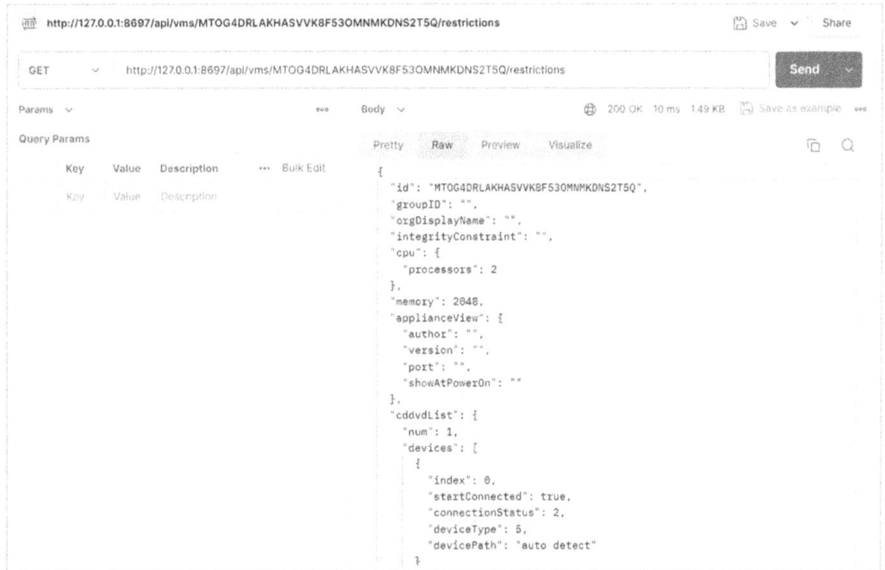

Figure 4-26. *Virtual Machine Restriction Information*

In the next section, we are going to look at the PUT commands for virtual machine management.

PUT Commands

In the following sections, we are going to look at the VM management PUT commands used to replace an existing variable with a new one.

The following is a breakdown of the available PUT API calls, starting with updating virtual machine settings.

Update VM Settings

This first of the PUT API calls is for updating virtual machine settings.

The command for updating the virtual machine settings is as follows:

```
PUT api/vms/<VM ID>/<parameters>
```

When running the command, replace the **<VM ID>** with the actual ID of the virtual machine you want to update the configuration for, and then in the **<parameters>** section, you would enter the request information, i.e., the updated configuration.

An example of this using the cURL command is shown in Figure 4-27.

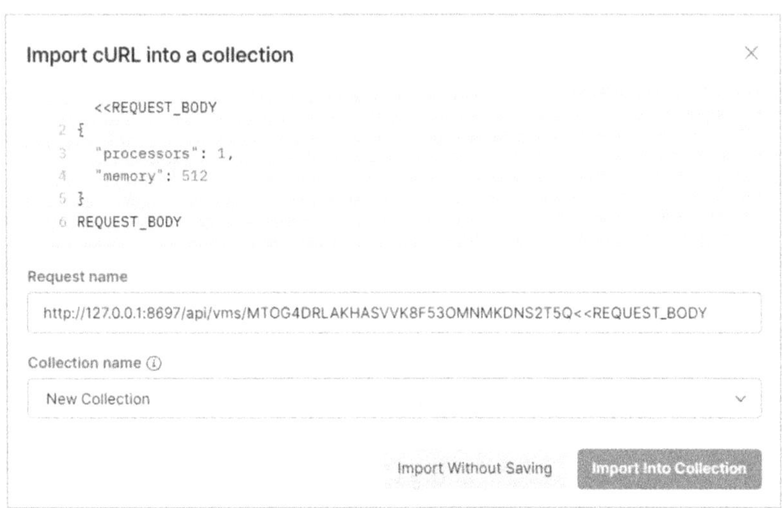

Figure 4-27. *Virtual Machine Settings Update*

In this example, we have changed the virtual machine settings so that the virtual machine now has just a single CPU and 512MB memory.

Next, we are going to look at how you can update configuration parameters of the virtual machine.

Update VM Configuration Parameters

This next API call is for updating the virtual machine configuration parameters.

The command for updating the virtual machine settings is as follows:

```
GET api/vms/<VM ID>/<CONFIG>
```

When running the command, replace the **<VM ID>** with the actual ID of the virtual machine you want to update the configuration parameters for, and then in the **<CONFIG>** section, you would enter the request information, i.e., the updated configuration parameters.

An example of this is shown in Figure 4-28 where we have updated the hardware compatibility version of the virtual machine.

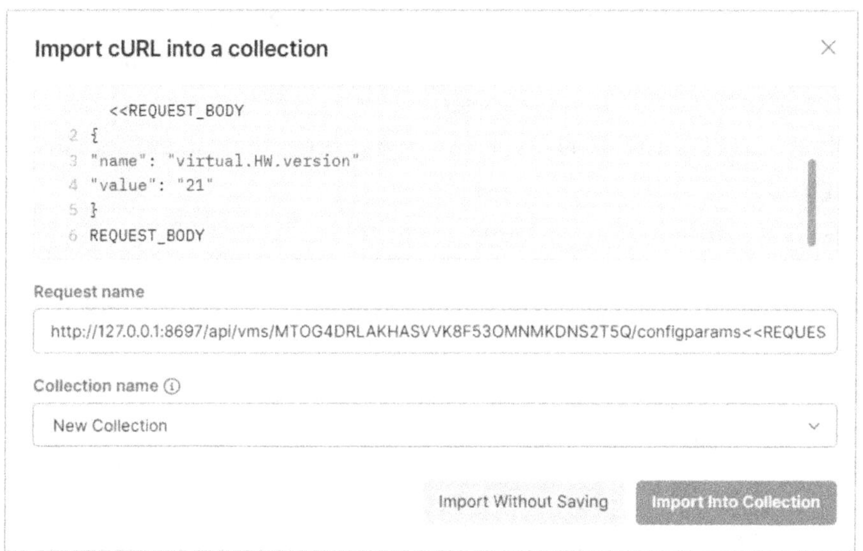

***Figure 4-28.** Virtual Machine Configuration Parameters Update*

Next, we are going to look at the POST commands for virtual machine management.

POST Commands

In this section, we are going to look at POST commands for creating new resources for virtual machine management tasks. We are going to start with an API call that enables you to create a copy of an existing virtual machine.

Create a Copy of a VM

The first command we are going to look at is for creating a copy of an existing virtual machine.

The command for creating a copy of a virtual machine is as follows:

```
POST api/vms
```

When running the command, you need to enter some additional configuration details in the body of the command. These details configure the name of the virtual machine that will be created as a copy of the original (target) and the ID of the virtual machine that you are copying from (source).

This is shown in the Postman screenshot in Figure 4-29.

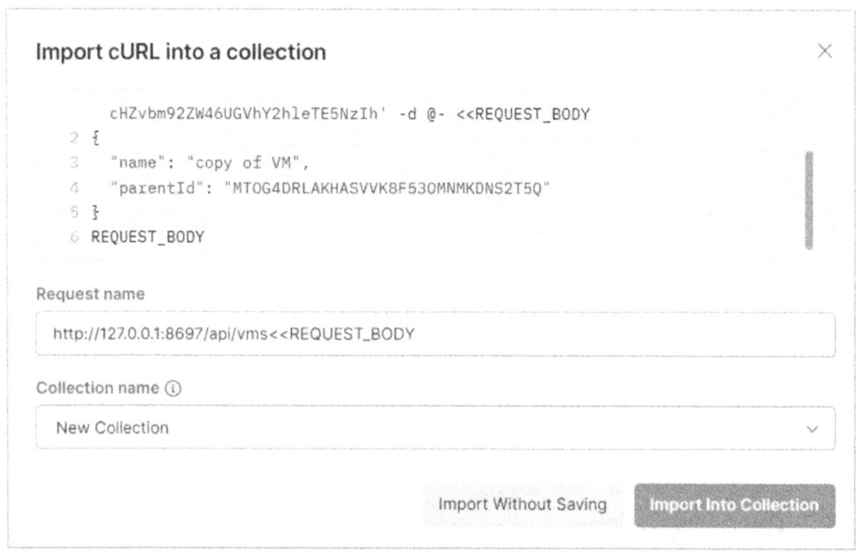

Figure 4-29. *Copy a Virtual Machine*

Following on from the previous command for creating a copy of a virtual machine, although you now have what is effectively a new virtual machine, by default, it will not appear in the library view in Workstation Pro.

You will need to add it manually or by running the next command which will register the newly created virtual machine with the library, making it available for use.

Register VM in the library

This next command is used to register a virtual machine in the Workstation Pro library to make it visible and therefore available for use.

This could be, as we saw with the previous command, a copy of an existing virtual machine, a newly imported or copied virtual machine, or one that still has its virtual disk files stored on the host but has had its entry deleted from the library.

The command for registering a virtual machine in the Workstation Pro library is as follows:

```
POST api/vms/registration
```

When running the command, you need to enter some additional configuration details in the body of the command. These details configure the name of the virtual machine that that will be displayed in the library, plus the path to the virtual machine configuration files.

This is shown in the Postman screenshot in Figure 4-30.

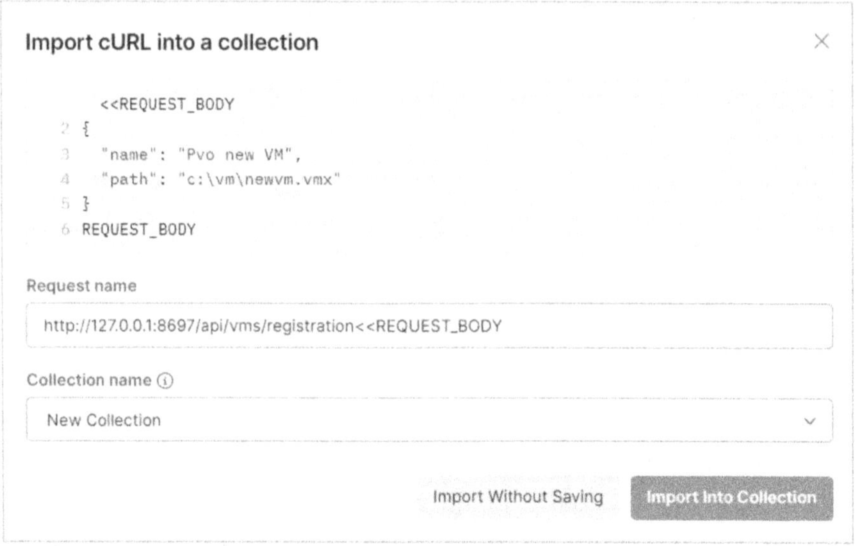

Figure 4-30. *Registering a Virtual Machine in the Library*

Once the command has successfully been run, then the virtual machine specified will now appear in the library.

In the next section we are going to look at the DELETE command.

DELETE Command

In the VM management category of commands, there is just a single delete command which is used to delete a virtual machine.

Delete a VM

This command is used to delete a virtual machine from Workstation Pro. The command for deleting a virtual machine from the Workstation Pro library is as follows:

```
DELETE api/vms/<VM ID>
```

When running the command, replace the **<VM ID>** with the actual ID of the virtual machine you want to delete.

In the following example, we are going to delete a Windows Server 2022 virtual machine which has the VM ID of AO0AGVRHKIIB39UJO9HAFM19JF79IUKJ. The command to do this would look something like the following:

```
DELETE api/vms/AO0AGVRHKIIB39UJO9HA
FM19JF79IUKJ
```

The virtual machine will be deleted.

This command will delete the virtual machines files and folder from the host machine. It does not remove it from the library, and so the virtual machine name will still be visible, but when you click it, you will get an error as the files are no longer there.

You need to now remove the virtual machine from the library.

You also need to ensure that the virtual machine is not locked, so the lock file would need to be deleted, if it exists, first.

We have now discussed all the API calls for virtual machine management.

In the next section, we are going to discuss the API calls that are available for managing the virtual machine network adapter.

VM Network Adapter Management

In this section, we are going to look at the API calls that are used for managing the virtual machine network adapter.

To show the available API calls for managing the virtual machine network adapter, we are going to break these down into the categories of command, starting with the GET API call.

GET Commands

The GET command is used to get the status of different components of the virtual machines network adapter. The following is a breakdown of the available GET API calls.

VM IP Address

The first command enables you to retrieve the IP address for the virtual machine specified.

The command for returning or showing the currently configured IP address for a specific virtual machine is as follows:

```
GET /vms/<VM ID>/ip
```

When running the command, replace the **<VM ID>** with the actual ID of the virtual machine you want to retrieve the IP address for.

In the following example, we are going to retrieve the IP address for the Windows 10 vm which has the VM ID of MTOG4DRLAKHASVVK8F53OMNMKDNS2T5Q. The command to do this would look something like the following:

```
GET api/vms/MTOG4DRLAKHASVVK8F53
OMNMKDNS2T5Q/ip
```

Running this command in Postman will give you the results as shown in Figure 4-31.

***Figure 4-31.** Retrieving a Virtual Machine IP Address*

For this command to work, the virtual machine specified will need to be powered on.

As you can see from the output, the IP address of this Windows 10 virtual machine is 192.168.189.132.

Next, we are going to look at the virtual machine network adapters.

VM Network Adapters

The next command enables you to retrieve the details of the configured network adapters for the virtual machine specified.

The command for returning or showing the network adapter configuration for a specific virtual machine is as follows:

```
GET /vms/<VM ID>/nic
```

When running the command, replace the **<VM ID>** with the actual ID of the virtual machine you want to retrieve the network adapter information for.

In the following example, we are going to retrieve the network adapter information for the Windows 10 vm which has the VM ID of **MTOG4DRLAKHASVVK8F53OMNMKDNS2T5Q**. The command to do this would look something like the following:

```
GET api/vms/MTOG4DRLAKHASVVK8F530
MNMKDNS2T5Q/nic
```

Running this command in Postman will give you the results as shown in Figure 4-32.

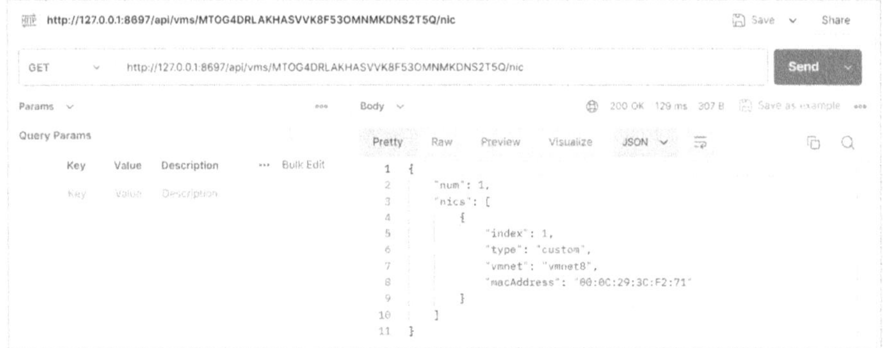

Figure 4-32. *Retrieving a Virtual Machine NIC information*

As you can see from the results, there is a single network adapter configured on this virtual machine, indicated by **"num": 1**.

You can also see that it is a custom network connection, connected to the vmnet8 host machine network. The adapter has the MAC address of 00:0C:29:3C:F2:71.

Unlike the previous command, you can run this command with the virtual machine powered off.

Next, we are going to look at the command for retrieving the IP stack network adapter information.

VM IP Stack NIC Configuration

The next command enables you to retrieve the full details of the complete IP stack for the configured network adapters for the virtual machine specified.

The command for returning or showing the network adapter configuration for a specific virtual machine is as follows:

```
GET /vms/<VM ID>/nicips
```

When running the command, replace the **<VM ID>** with the actual ID of the virtual machine you want to retrieve the IP stack information for.

In the following example, we are going to retrieve the IP stack information for the Windows 10 virtual machine which has the VM ID of MTOG4DRLAKHASVVK8F53OMNMKDNS2T5Q. The command to do this would look something like the following:

```
GET api/vms/MTOG4DRLAKHASVVK8F530
MNMKDNS2T5Q/nicips
```

Running this command in Postman will give you the results as shown in Figure 4-33.

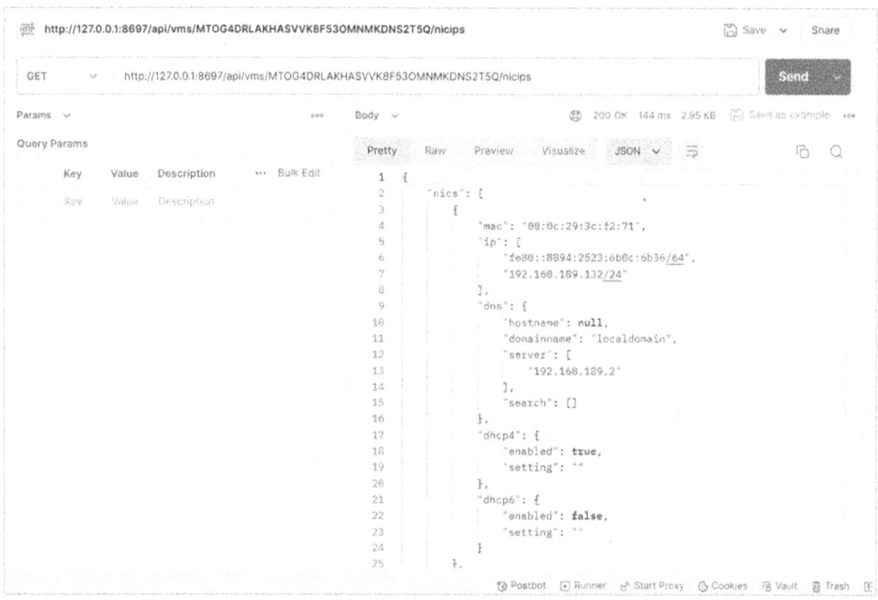

***Figure 4-33.** Retrieving a VM IP Stack*

As you can see from the results, all information regarding the network adapters and the full IP stack is shown in the output.

For this command to work, the virtual machine specified will need to be powered on.

Next, we are going to look at the PUT commands that relate to the virtual machine network adapter management

PUT Commands

With the PUT command for managing virtual machine network adapters, there is just one command which is for updating the virtual machine network adapter configuration.

Update VM Network Adapter

This next command enables you to update and change the settings for the network adapter for the virtual machine specified in the command.

The command for returning or showing the network adapter configuration for a specific virtual machine is as follows:

```
PUT /vms/<VM ID>/<INDEX>
```

When running the command, replace the **<VM ID>** with the actual ID of the virtual machine you want to update the network adapter for. Then replace the **<INDEX>** for the adapter index number for the adapter you want to update.

In the following example, we are going to change the network for the Windows 10 virtual machine with the VM ID of MTOG4DRLAKHASVVK8F53OMNMKDNS2T5Q, from vmnet8 to vmnet4, for the network adapter with the index number 1. The command to do this would look something like the following:

PUT api/vms/MTOG4DRLAKHASVVK8F53 OMNMKDNS2T5Q/nic/1

In addition to this command, you need to add the parameters that contain the details of the parameter that you want to update, in this case changing the network from vmnet8 to vmnet4. You would add the following parameters:

```
"type": "custom",
"vmnet": "vmnet4"
```

Optionally you can also add the parameter for **"macAddress": "string"** if you are updating the MAC address.

When you run the command, you will see the following output shown in Figure 4-34.

```
{
  "index": 1,
  "type": "custom",
  "vmnet": "vmnet4",
  "macAddress": "00:0C:29:3C:F2:71"
}
```

***Figure 4-34.** API Call Output for Updating Network Adapter*

Also, for this example, we are going to take a quick look at the virtual machine itself and show that the network adapter is now connected to vmnet4 as shown in Figure 4-35.

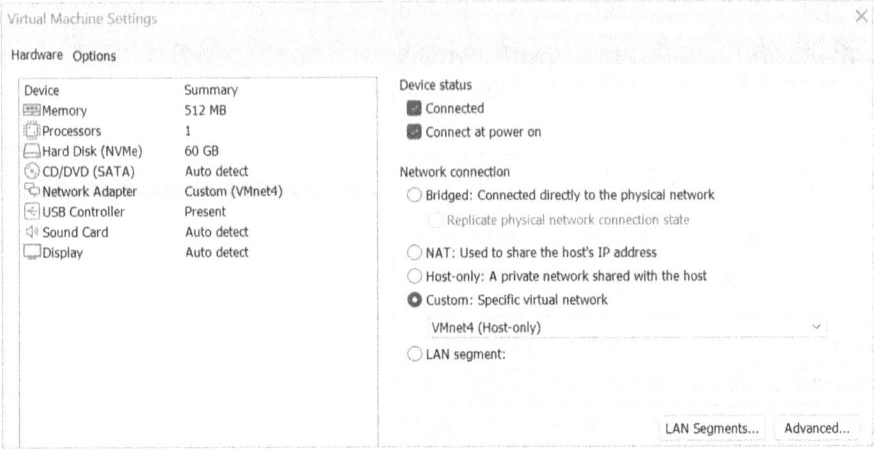

Figure 4-35. *Network Adapter Updated to vmnet4*

Next, we are going to look at the POST commands for managing virtual machine network adapters.

POST Commands

There is just one POST command for managing virtual machine network adapters, and that is to create a new network adapter

Create a Network Adapter

With this command, you can create a new network adapter for the virtual machine specified.

The command for adding a new network adapter for a specific virtual machine is as follows:

```
POST /vms/<VM ID>/nic
```

When running the command, replace the **<VM ID>** with the actual ID of the virtual machine you want to create a new network adapter for.

In the following example, we are going to add a new network adapter to the Windows 10 virtual machine with the VM ID of MTOG4DRLAKHAS VVK8F53OMNMKDNS2T5Q.

The command would look like the following:

```
PUT api/vms/MTOG4DRLAKHASVVK8F530
MNMKDNS2T5Q/nic
```

In addition to this command, you need to add the parameters that contain the details of the new network adapter, in this case the network type and the network you want to connect the network adapter to.

```
"type": "custom",

"vmnet": "vmnet4"
```

Optionally, you can also add the parameter for **"macAddress": "string"** if you want to add the MAC address. If you don't add this, then the MAC address will be generated automatically.

When you run the command, you will see the following output shown in Figure 4-36.

```
{
  "index": 2,
  "type": "custom",
  "vmnet": "vmnet4",
  "macAddress": ""
}
```

Figure 4-36. *Adding a New Network Adapter*

The command output shows that a second network adapter has been added to the virtual mention (index:2). It also shows that it is a custom network connected to the vmnet4 network.

The MAC address is shown as blank as this will have been autogenerated when the additional adapter was created and will be found in the advanced settings of the network adapter configuration.

If we now switch to the Workstation Pro UI and select the virtual machine for which we just created a new network adapter and look in the Virtual Machine Settings, you will see that the second network adapter has been created and connected to vmnet4.

Opening the advanced settings, you will find, at the bottom of the dialog box, details of the MAC address as shown in Figure 4-37.

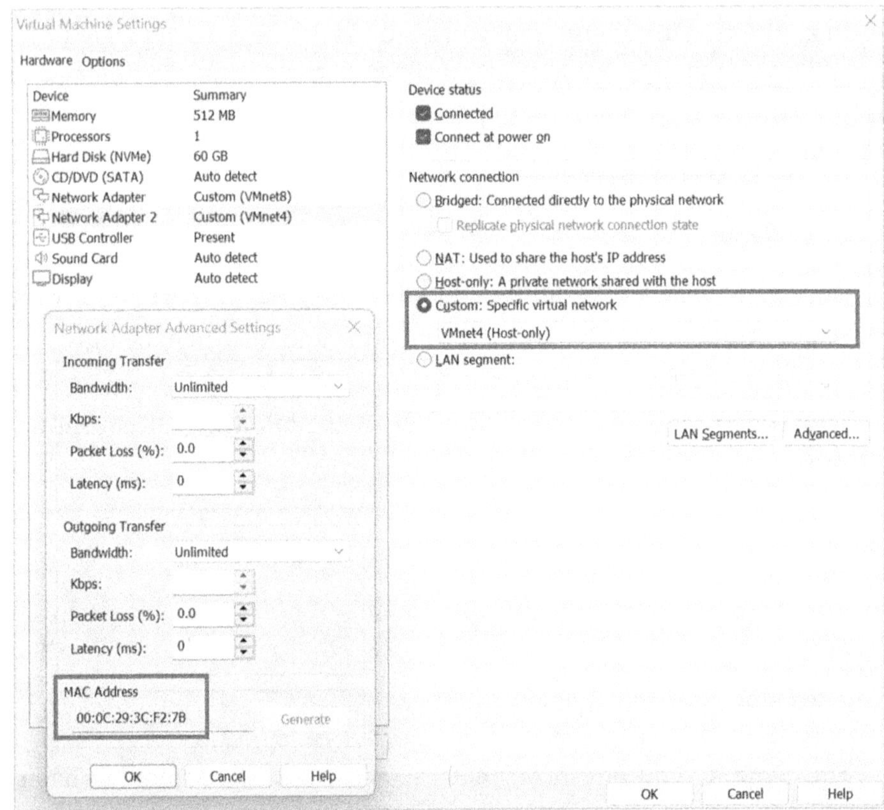

Figure 4-37. *Details of the New Network Adapter*

The final set of commands for managing virtual machine network adapters is for deleting a network adapter.

DELETE Commands

There is just one command for DELETE, and that command enables you to delete a virtual machine network adapter.

Delete a VM Network Adapter

With this command, you can delete a network adapter for the virtual machine specified. The command for deleting a network adapter for a specific virtual machine is as follows:

```
DELETE /vms/<VM ID>/nic/<INDEX>
```

When running the command, replace the **<VM ID>** with the actual ID of the virtual machine you want to delete the network adapter for and replace the **<INDEX>** with the index number of the network adapter.

In the following example, we are going to delete the network adapter that we created on the Windows 10 virtual machine in the previous section. That is the virtual machine with the ID of MTOG4DRLAKHASVVK8F53OMNMKDNS2T5Q.

The command to do this would look like the following:

```
DELETE api/vms/MTOG4DRLAKHASVVK8F530
MNMKDNS2T5Q/nic/2
```

You won't receive a response to running this command other than if you now switch to the Workstation Pro UI and select the virtual machine for which we just deleted the network adapter for and look in the virtual machine settings you will see that the second network adapter has now been deleted.

In the next section, we are going to look at the API calls for managing virtual machine power states.

VM Power Management

In this section, we are going to look at the commands that are used for virtual machine power management. There are only two commands that fall under the GET and PUT API calls. We will start with the GET commands.

GET Commands

There is just a single GET command for virtual machine power management, and that is used to retrieve the power state of a virtual machine.

VM Power State

With this command, you can retrieve the current power state of a specified virtual machine.

The command for displaying the power state of a specific virtual machine is as follows:

```
GET /vms/<VM ID>/power
```

When running the command, replace the **<VM ID>** with the actual ID of the virtual machine you want to show the current power state for.

In this example, we are going to retrieve the power state for the example Windows 10 virtual machine with the VM ID of MTOG4DRLAKHASVVK8F53OMNMKDNS2T5Q.

The command to do this would look like the following:

```
GET api/vms/MTOG4DRLAKHASVVK8F53
OMNMKDNS2T5Q/power
```

If we run this command using Postman, then we will get a response as shown in Figure 4-38.

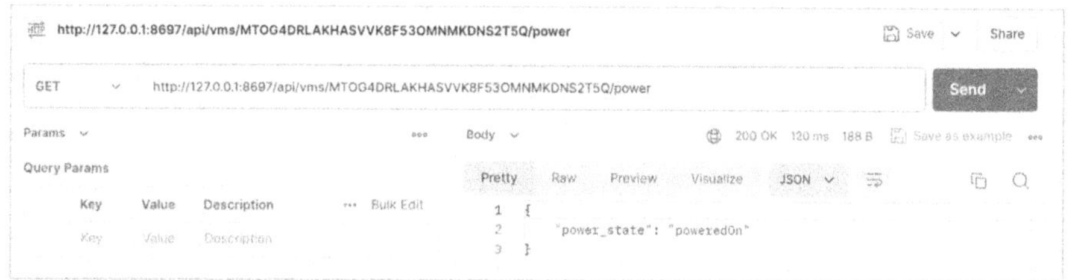

***Figure 4-38.** Details of the Power State of a Virtual Machine*

As you can see in Figure 4-37, the Windows 10 example virtual machine is currently power on.

Next, we are going to look at the PUT commands for vm power management.

PUT Commands

As with the GET command for virtual machine power management, there is just a single PUT command for changing the power state of a virtual machine.

Change VM Power State

With this command, you can change the power state of a virtual machine.

The command for changing the power state of a specific virtual machine is as follows:

```
GET /vms/<VM ID>/power
```

When running the command, replace the **<VM ID>** with the actual ID of the virtual machine you want to change the current power state for.

In this example, we are going to power on the Windows 10 example machine with the VM ID of MTOG4DRLAKHASVVK8F53OMNMKDNS2T5Q.

The command to do this would look like the following:

```
GET api/vms/MTOG4DRLAKHASVVK8F530
MNMKDNS2T5Q/power
```

In addition to this command, you need to add the parameters that contain the details of the power state you want send to the virtual machine. You have the option of the following power states:

- On
- Off
- Shutdown
- Suspend
- Pause
- Unpause

To power on this virtual machine, we are going to use the cURL command as shown in the Figure 4-39.

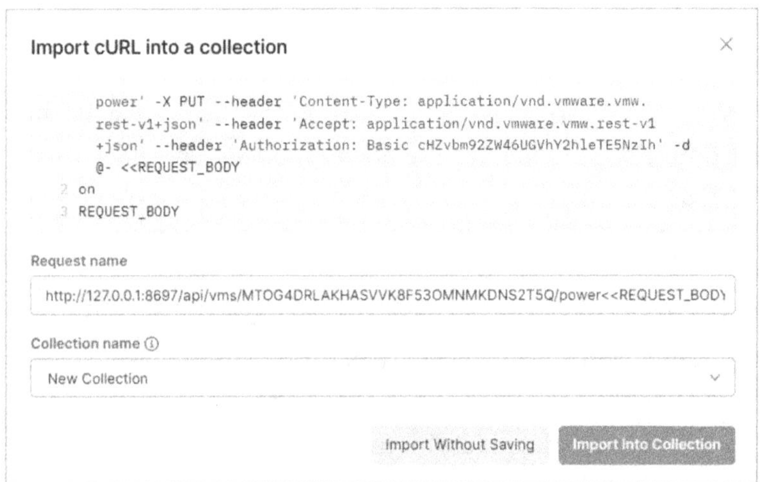

Figure 4-39. *Power on a Virtual Machine Using cURL*

When you run the command, you will see the following response as shown in Figure 4-40.

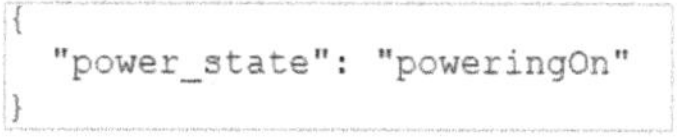

Figure 4-40. *Power on a Virtual Machine Output*

The next set of commands focuses on the management of virtual machine shared folder.

VM Shared Folders Management

In this section, we are going to look at the API calls for managing virtual machine shared folders. These are the folders that are shared by the virtual machine and the host machine for sharing files and data.

We will start with the GET command.

GET Commands

There is just a single GET command for managing virtual machine shared folders. That command just lists the shared folders.

List the Shared Folders

With this command, you can list the currently configured shared folders between a specified virtual machine and the host machine.

The command for displaying the shared folder for a specific virtual machine is as follows:

```
GET /vms/<VM ID>/sharedfolders
```

When running the command, replace the **<VM ID>** with the actual ID of the virtual machine you want to show the sharded folders for.

In this example, we are going to display the shared folders for the example Windows 10 vm with the VM ID of **MTOG4DRLAKHASVVK8F530MN MKDNS2T5Q.**

The command to do this would look like the following:

```
GET api/vms/MTOG4DRLAKHASVVK8F53
OMNMKDNS2T5Q/sharedfolders
```

If we run this command using Postman, then we will get a response as shown in Figure 4-41.

Figure 4-41. *Virtual Machine Shared Folders*

You will see that the folder ID is set to shared and that the host path, or shared folder on the host machine is set to c:\shared.

In the next section, we are going to look at the PUT command for managing virtual machine shared folders.

PUT Commands

There is just a single PUT command for managing virtual machine shared folders.

Update VM Shared Mounted Folder

With this command, you can update the configuration details of the shared folders.

The command for updating the shared folder configuration for a specific virtual machine is as follows:

```
PUT /vms/<VM ID>/sharedfolders/<FOLDER ID>
```

When running the command, replace the **<VM ID>** with the actual ID of the virtual machine you want to show the sharded folders for. Also, in the **<FOLDER ID>**, you need to enter the name of the shared folder.

In this example, we are going to update the shared folder for the example Windows 10 vm with the VM ID of **MTOG4DRLAKHASVVK8F53OMNMKDNS2T5Q** and update the folder with the ID **Shared**. We are going to then set the host path to point to a different folder on the host machine.

The command to do this would look like the following:

```
PUT api/vms/MTOG4DRLAKHASVVK8F53
OMNMKDNS2T5Q/sharedfolders/shared
```

In addition to this command, you need to add the parameters that contain the details of the updated host path you want to set and the flags setting.

So, in this example of updating the host path details, the additional parameters required would look like the following:

```
"host_path": "c:\\vm1",

"flags": 0
```

The output from the command is shown in Figure 4-42.


```
{
  "folder_id": "Shared",
  "host_path": "c:\\vm1",
  "flags": 0
}
```


Figure 4-42. *Checking the VM Shared Folders Config update*

If you now open the Workstation Pro UI, navigate to the virtual machine for which you just updated the shared folder information for, open the virtual machine settings and, on the Options tab, scroll down and click shared folders. You will see that the name of the shared folders host path has been updated. This is shown in Figure 4-43.

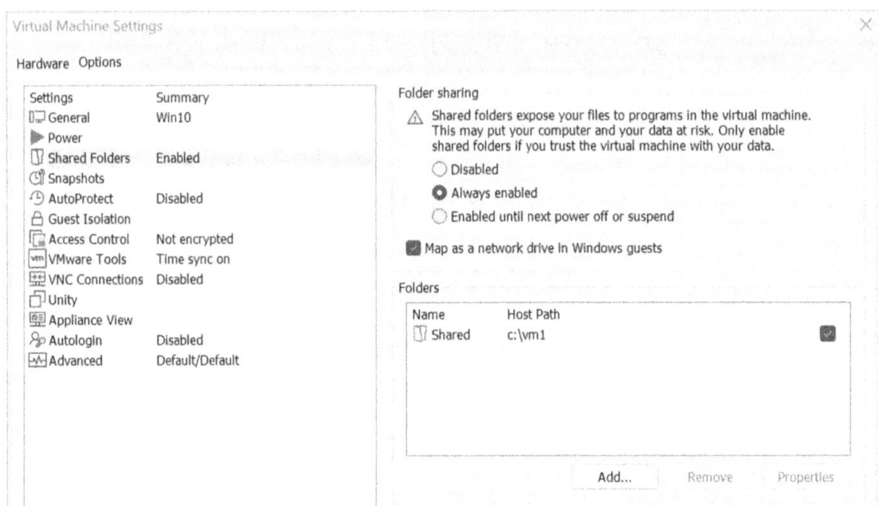

***Figure 4-43.** Updating Virtual Machine Shared Folders*

Next, we are going to look at the POST commands for virtual machine shared folder management.

POST Commands

There is again just a single POST command for managing virtual machine shared folders.

Mount a New Shared Folder

With this command, you can create a new shared folder.

Before you use this command, you need to have already created the folder on the host machine; otherwise, the command will fail.

The command for creating a new shared folder for a specific virtual machine is as follows:

```
POST /vms/<VM ID>/sharedfolders
```

When running the command, replace the **<VM ID>** with the actual ID of the virtual machine you want to show the sharded folders for.

In this example, we are going to create a new shared folder for the example Windows 10 vm with the VM ID of **MTOG4DRLAKHASVVK8F53OMNMKDNS2T5Q. This folder is going to have the folder ID of Shared2 and will map to the C:\vm2 folder on the host machine.**

The command to do this would look like the following:

```
POST api/vms/MTOG4DRLAKHASVVK8F53
OMNMKDNS2T5Q/sharedfolders
```

In addition to this command, you need to add the parameters that contain the details of the new folder ID and the new hot path details.

```
"folder_id": "Shared2",

"host_path": "c:\\vm2",

"flags": 0
```

When you run the command, you will see the following output shown in Figure 4-44.

```
[
  {
    "folder_id": "Shared",
    "host_path": "c:\\vm1",
    "flags": 0
    },
  {
    "folder_id": "Shared2",
    "host_path": "c:\\vm2",
    "flags": 0
  }
]
```

Figure 4-44. *Output from Creating a New Shared Folder*

As you can see from the output, you will see the original shared folder called Shared1 which is mapped to c:\vm1 on the host machine and now also the newly created shared folder called Shared2 which is mapped c:\vm2.

In the next section, we are going to look at the final virtual machine shared folder management and that is for DELETE commands.

DELETE Commands

In this section, we are going to look at the DELETE command for deleting shared folders.

Delete a Shared Folder

With this command, you can delete an existing shared folder.

The command for deleting an existing shared folder for a specific virtual machine is as follows:

```
DELETE /vms/<VM ID>/sharedfolders/<FOLDER ID>
```

When running the command, replace the **<VM ID>** with the actual ID of the virtual machine you want to delete the sharded folders from. Then, replace the **<FOLDER ID>** with the ID of the folder that you want to delete.

In this example, we are going to delete the shared folder we created in the previous section. This was for example Windows 10 virtual machine with the VM ID of **MTOG4DRLAKHASVVK8F53OMNMKDNS2T5Q**. The ID of the folder we are going to delete is the **Shared2** folder.

The folder on the host machine will not be deleted when you run this command.

You will need to do that manually if you want to delete that as well. If you leave it, then you can always share it again at a later stage if required.

The command to do this would look like the following:

```
DELETE api/vms/MTOG4DRLAKHASVVK8F53
OMNMKDNS2T5Q/sharedfolders/Shared2
```

When you run the command, the only output you will get is a message that states no content.

If you now open the Workstation Pro UI, navigate to the virtual machine for which you just updated the shared folder information for (Windows 10), open the virtual machine settings and, on the Options tab, scroll down and click shared folders. You will see that the folder has now been deleted.

We have now discussed all the available API calls and commands that are included with Workstation Pro.

Summary

In this chapter, we have given you an overview of the REST API that comes with Workstation Pro and all the API calls and commands that are available to use in the management of both the host machine and the virtual machines running on it.

We provided an overview of each command, its syntax, and in some examples the output, whether that is the output of the command itself or the outcome of the action it performed on either the host machine or the virtual machines.

In the next chapter, we are going to look at some of the support and troubleshooting tips.

CHAPTER 5

Support and Troubleshooting

In this chapter, we are going to look at how you can support your VMware Workstation Pro installation along with some of the more common issues you may encounter when running virtual machines.

We are going to start by looking at how to gather any information that may be required in order to log a support call with VMware. You can collect information for individual virtual machines, multiple virtual machines, or just the host machine that is running Workstation Pro and is running the virtual machines.

The method of doing that is using a feature called the support script.

Running the Support Script

The support script feature is a tool that is used to all of the Workstation Pro log files from the host machine or virtual machines that are running on the host machine.

These could potentially be required to send to VMware support should you need to log a support call with them where they will ask you to send or upload them.

P. von Oven, *Learning VMware Workstation Pro for Windows: Volume 2*,
https://doi.org/10.1007/979-8-8688-0864-7_5

For example, if a virtual machine crashes or fails, you can run the support script to collect the appropriate log files and system information. You can run the support script directly from the Workstation Pro application.

Before you start this process, there are a few prerequisites that you need to complete. These are as follows:

- Increase the logging level for a VM
- Create a support request

We will start with how to configure the logging levels to ensure the correct and relevant amount of data is collected.

Gathering Debugging Information from a VM

When running in debugging mode, a virtual machine will collect information that can help the VMware technical support teams quickly understand the issue and therefore provide a resolution.

Debugging mode is set to default as the default setting. You also have the following debugging options that you can configure:

- **None** - This is the normal debugging mode. With this mode, no debugging information is collected, and therefore, the virtual machine will run faster than when other debugging modes are selected.

  Once you have identified the issue from the debugging report, then you should switch back to None again.

- **Full** - This mode would be used when you want to collect debugging information when you experience virtual machine crashes.

- **Statistics** – If a virtual machine is experiencing slow performance when running certain workloads, then you can set the logging mode to Statistics.

  This will create a statistics file that can be downloaded and sent to the VMware technical support teams.

So that you can collect as much information as possible, you need to temporarily increase the logging level to collect a greater and more detailed level of information.

To configure debugging mode for a selected virtual machine, follow the steps as described:

You can only configure the debug mode for a virtual machine when the virtual machine is powered off.

---

1. Select the VM you want to collect the debug information by selecting the virtual machine from the library pane. In this case, we have selected a virtual machine called Proxmox.
2. Right-click the virtual machine and then from the contextual menu that appears as shown in Figure 5-1.

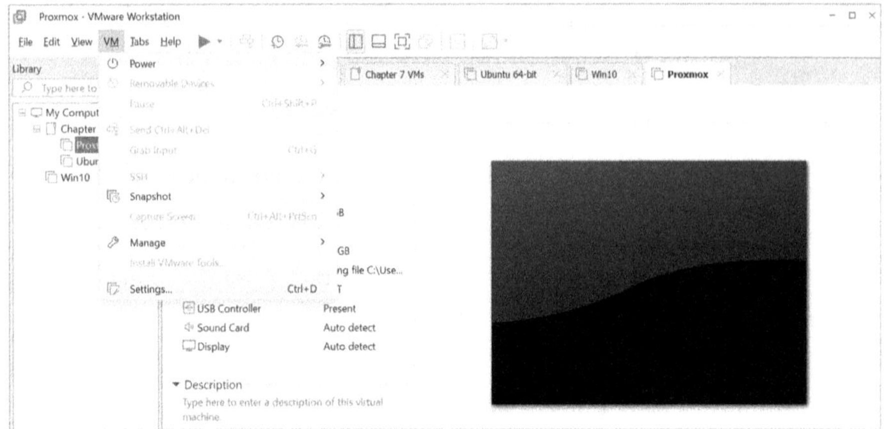

***Figure 5-1.** Select the Settings Menu for a VM*

3. Click the **Settings...** option.

4. You will see the **Virtual Machine Settings** screen as shown in Figure 5-2.

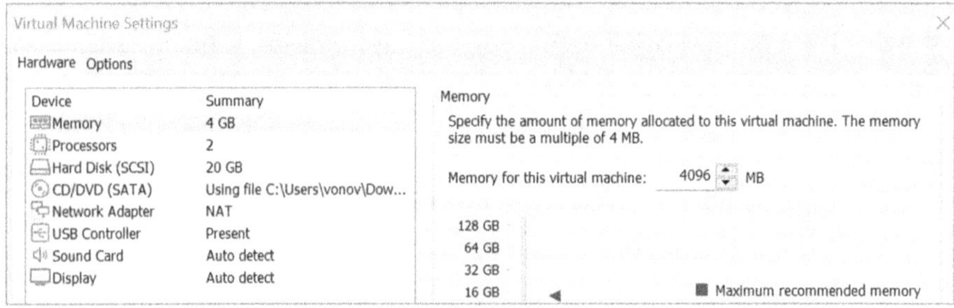

***Figure 5-2.** Virtual Machine Settings Screen*

5. From the tabs at the top, click the **Options** tab, and then from the options on the left, click Advanced as shown in Figure 5-3.

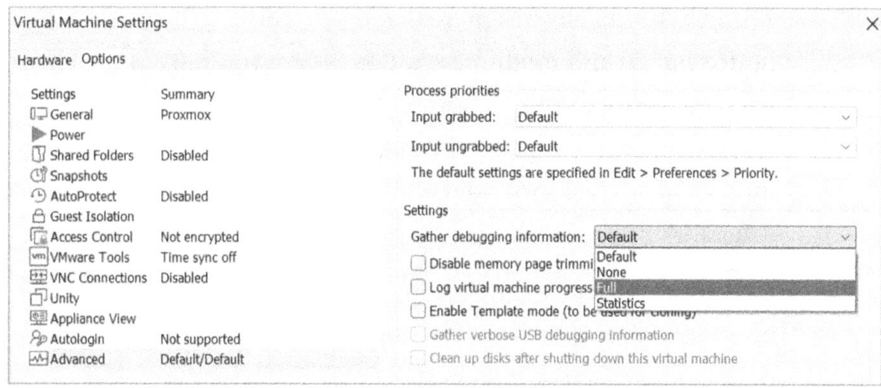

Figure 5-3. *Virtual Machine Advanced Settings Screen*

6. On the right-hand side, you will now see, in the lower part of the two boxes, a box called Settings.

7. The first option in this box is for Gather debugging information where you will see a drop-down menu where you can select the debugging level you want.

   As we are collecting log information for the purpose of troubleshooting, select the option for **Full** from the drop-down menu as shown in Figure 5-3 above.

You will also notice that under the debug options there are some other options, enabled by clicking the check box. Although not all of them relate directly to collecting log files, some might help with gathering more accurate information.

These options provide the following options:

- **Disable memory page trimming –** Workstation Pro uses a memory trimming to return unused virtual machine memory to the host machine so that the host machine can make use of this memory to run other apps and processes and not just for Workstation Pro and VMs.

Trimming typically has no real effect on the performance and might be required when you have low-memory situations; however, the I/O generated when using the memory trimming can sometimes interfere with disk-oriented workload performance in a guest.

Therefore, you have the option to disable this in order to gather more accurate logs when you have performance issues, but also to see if this feature is causing the issue in the first place.

- **Log virtual machine progress periodically** - Rather than create log files continuously, you can select this option to collect information periodically.

  Included in the log file that Workstation Pro generates is information about your virtual machine's virtual CPU state, instruction pointer, and code segment registers.

  This information is not only useful for troubleshooting, but it can also help you when optimizing the performance of your virtual machines.

  You cannot use this feature for remote virtual machines.

- **Gather verbose USB debugging information** - This is only available when you select the option for Full. It is used to collect more information about any USB issues you might be experiencing with USB devices connected to the virtual machine.

Now that you have configured the level of debugging that you want for collecting the data on your virtual machines, you can now power the virtual machines on, start using them, and therefore start collecting that data.

When you power on a virtual machine that has debugging enabled, you will see a warning message pop-up as shown in Figure 5-4.

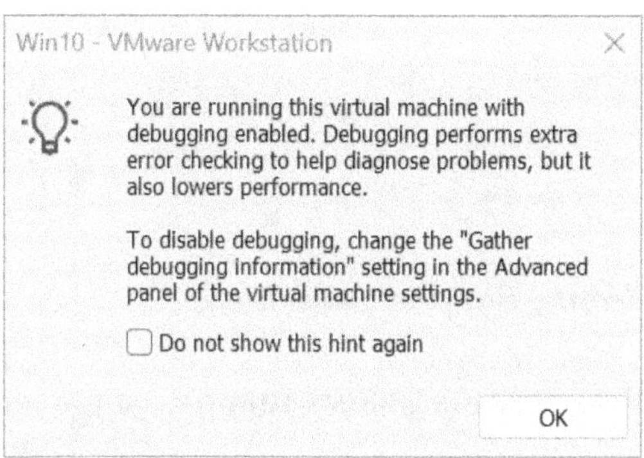

Figure 5-4. *Debug Warning Message*

With the debugging feature enabled and the virtual machine being used, you need to now try and reproduce the problem so that it is captured in the log file.

Therefore, continue to use the virtual machine until that problem materializes before collecting the log files.

To continue with this example, let's say you have now seen the problem with the virtual machine, so now would be the time to go and collect the log files. To do this for a virtual machine, follow the steps described:

1. From the Workstation Pro application, from the menu, click **Help**.

2. Then, from the Help menu, click to expand the option for **Support**.

3. Now click **Collect Support Data...** as shown in Figure 5-5.

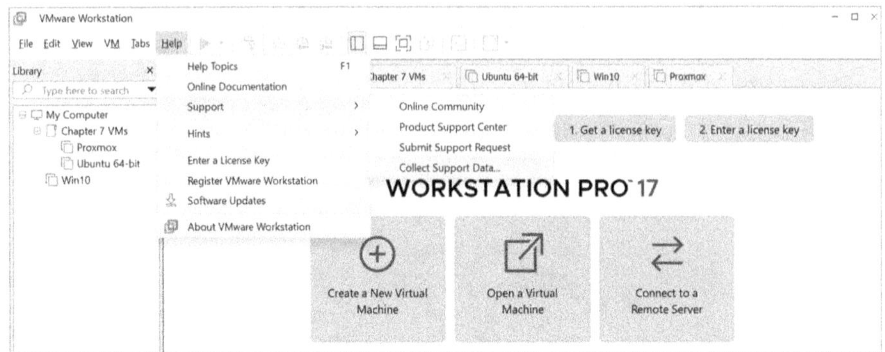

***Figure 5-5.** Collecting Support Data Menu*

4. You will now see the **Collect Support Data** screen.
5. You will see that all your virtual machines are listed and also whether they are powered on. It also reports on the status of VMware Tools which is key as this is what is going to collect the data from the virtual machine.
6. In this example, we have the Win10 virtual machine powered on, and VMware Tools is running so this is the virtual machine we are going to use to collect data from.
7. Check the box next to the Win10 virtual machine to select it as shown in Figure 5-6.

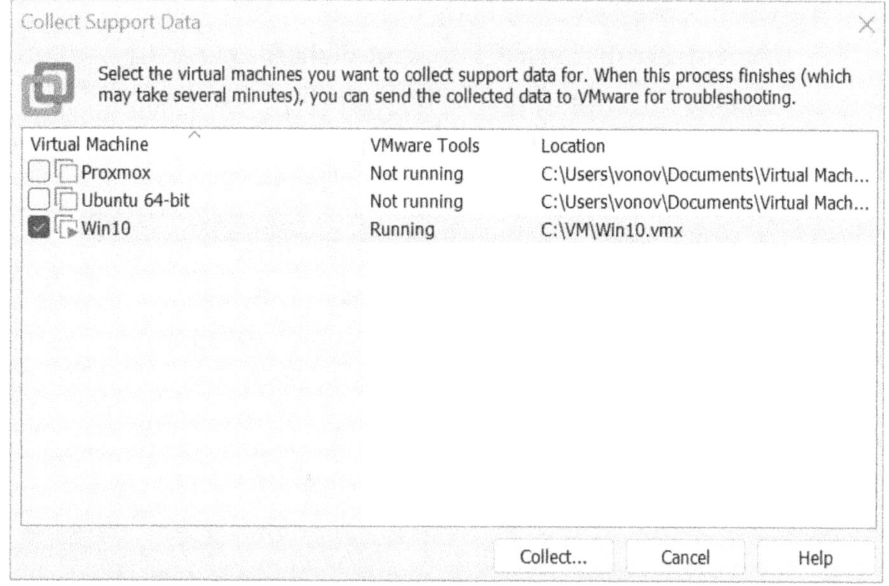

Figure 5-6. *Collecting Support Data Screen*

8. Now press the **Collect...** button. You will see the **Save As** screen as shown in Figure 5-7.

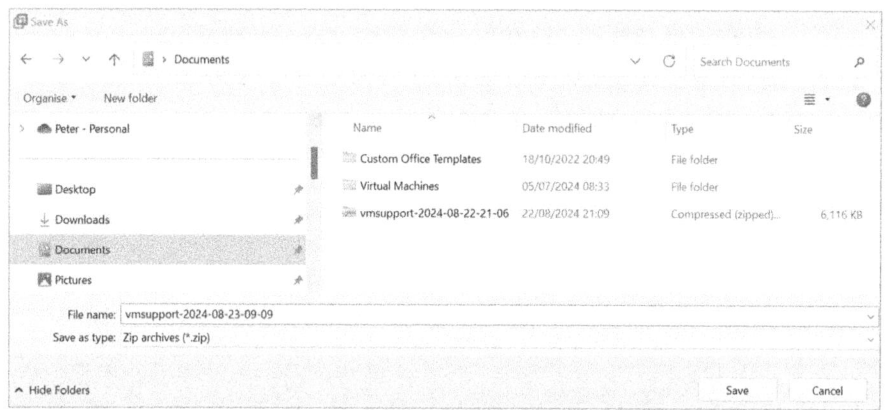

Figure 5-7. *Save As Screen for Data Capture*

9. On the **Save As** screen, navigate to the location you want to save the log file. The name of the file has also been populated in the **File name** field. It is best to leave it as is as this is the naming convention that VMware expects to see when you upload the file.

10. Now click **Save.**

11. You will see the collection process start with the first part being the collection of the guest operating system (virtual machine) data as shown in Figure 5-8.

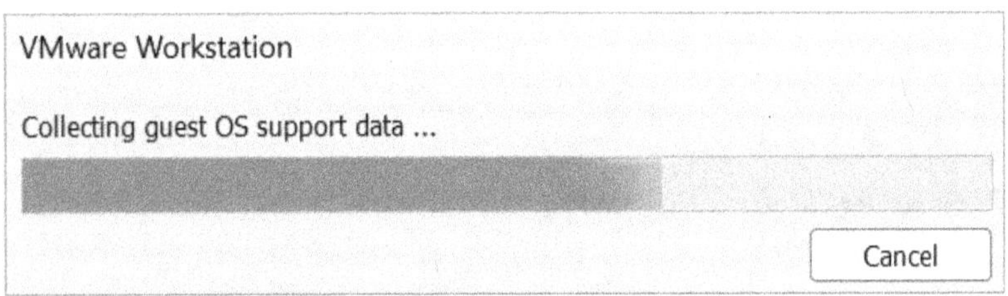

Figure 5-8. *Support data being collected*

12. Once this task has completed, then you will see the following **System Information** dialog box stating that the system information is being refreshed as shown in Figure 5-9.

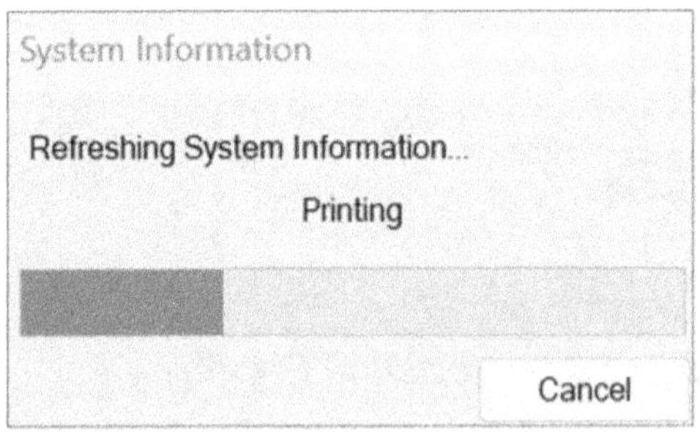

Figure 5-9. *System Information Dialog Box*

13. The next part of the process is to collect the host operating system data. This is the information relating to the operating system that is running on your host machine.

    As the process completes, you will see the following dialog box showing the status as shown in Figure 5-10.

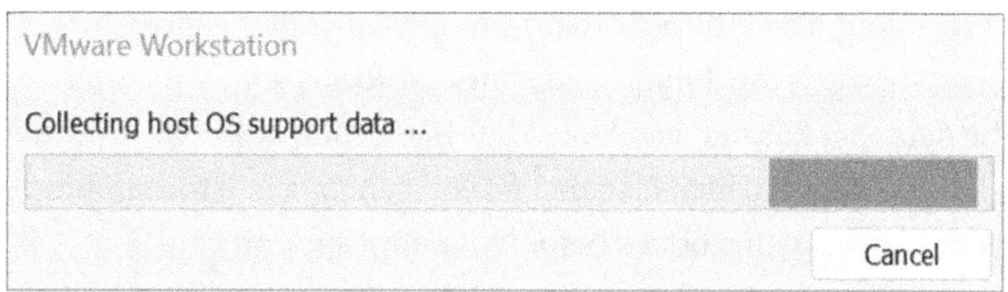

Figure 5-10. *Collecting Support Data Screen for Host OS*

14. Finally, once the collection process has successfully completed, you will see the following dialog box as shown in Figure 5-11.

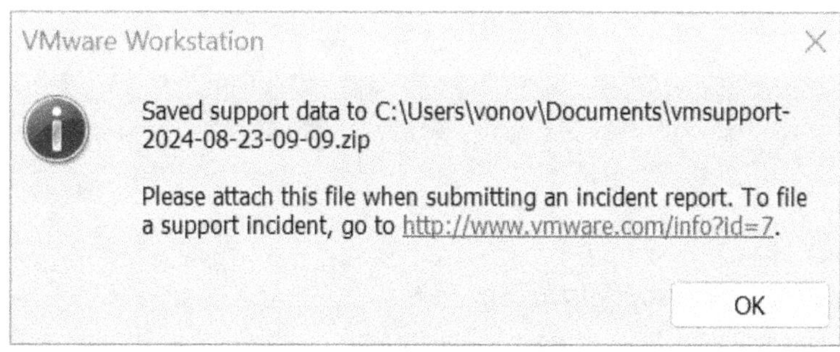

Figure 5-11. *Support Data Successfully Saved*

15. If you need to send the output of the data collected, the zip file in this instance, then navigate to the location stated in the dialog box.

16. Click the **OK** button to close the data collection process.

We have now successfully collected the support data for the Win10 virtual machine. The last thing to do would be to edit the virtual machine settings and switch the debug mode back to **None**.

The data that has been collected has been compressed into a single zip file to aid sending it, which also means you can look at it too should you want to understand any errors before making a support call.

If you navigate to the folder in which the data was collected, you will see the following as shown in Figure 5-12.

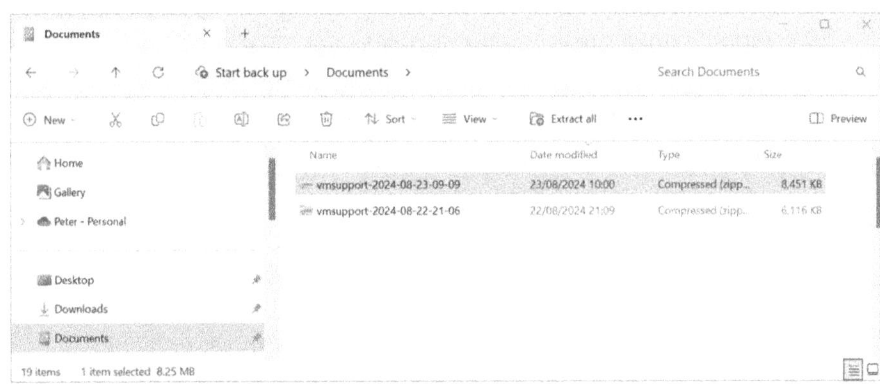

Figure 5-12. *Support Data .zip File*

If you double-click the support file and then navigate to where the actual data can be found. To do this, you will need to click through to the following:

```
\Users\vonov\AppData\Local\Temp\vmware-
support\vmsupport-2024-08-23-09-58
```

You will see the following as shown in Figure 5-13.

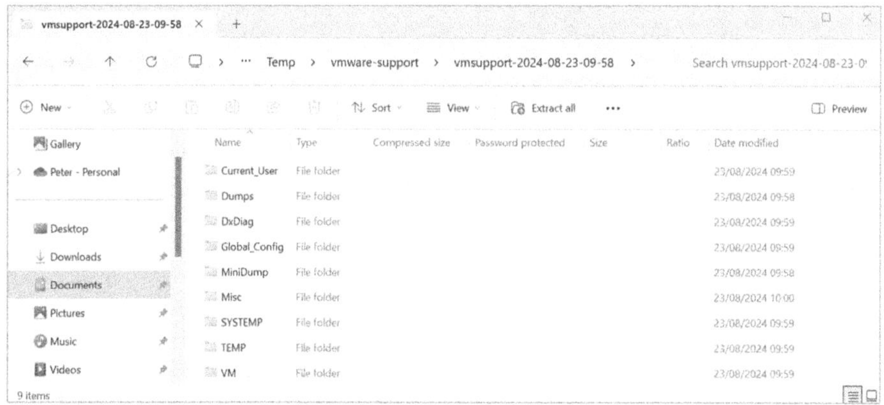

Figure 5-13. *Folders in the vmsupport.zip File*

As you can see, there are a number of folders that have been collected as part of the process, which contain the relevant data.

You can look through any of these folders and files to inspect the text files in the folders that contain the actual information for the log files.

For example, if you double-click and open the DxDiag folder and then open the DxDiag text file in Notepad, you will see something like the screenshots shown in Figure 5-14.

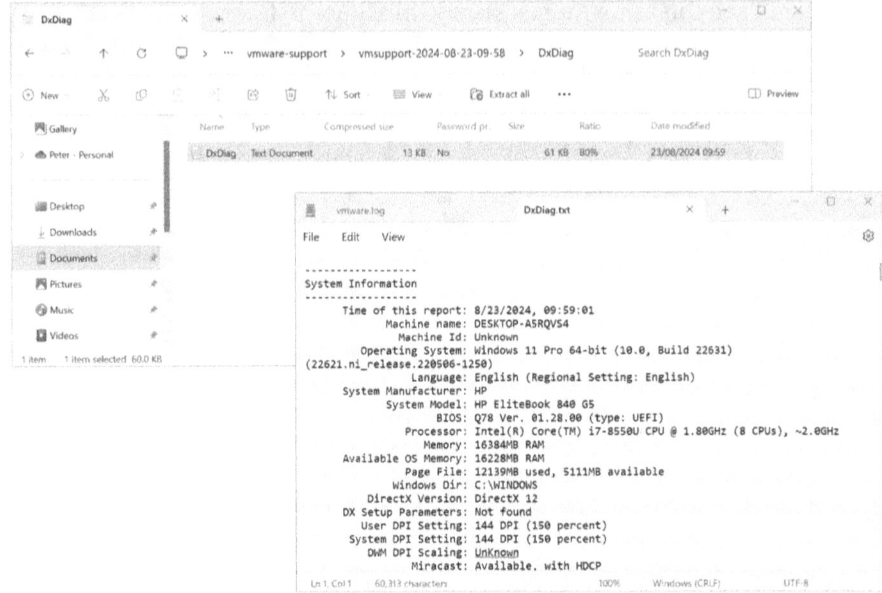

Figure 5-14. *Opening the DxDiag Data File*

Here, you can clearly see that the details of the host machine on which Workstation Pro is running have been captured.

Next, we are going to look at collecting support data for the host machine.

Gathering Debugging Information for the Host

The process for collecting support data for the host machine is pretty much the same process as we have just covered in the previous section.

The key difference is that you don't select any virtual machines from the **Collect Support Data** screen.

To do this, follow the steps described:

1. From the Workstation Pro application, from the main menu, click **Help**.

2. Then, from the **Help** menu, click to expand the option for **Support**.

3. Now click **Collect Support Data...** as shown in Figure 5-15.

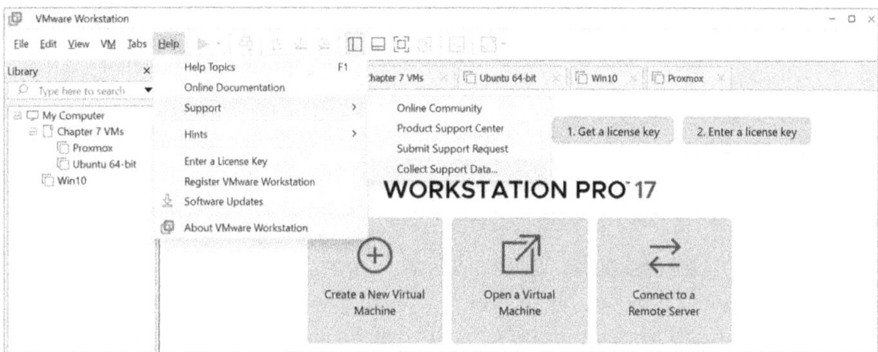

***Figure 5-15.** Collecting Support Data Menu*

4. You will now see the **Collect Support Data** screen.

5. Make sure that all the virtual machines listed are not selected by unchecking all the boxes next to them.

6. With all the virtual machine boxes deselected, click the **Collect...** button to start the capture process as shown in Figure 5-16.

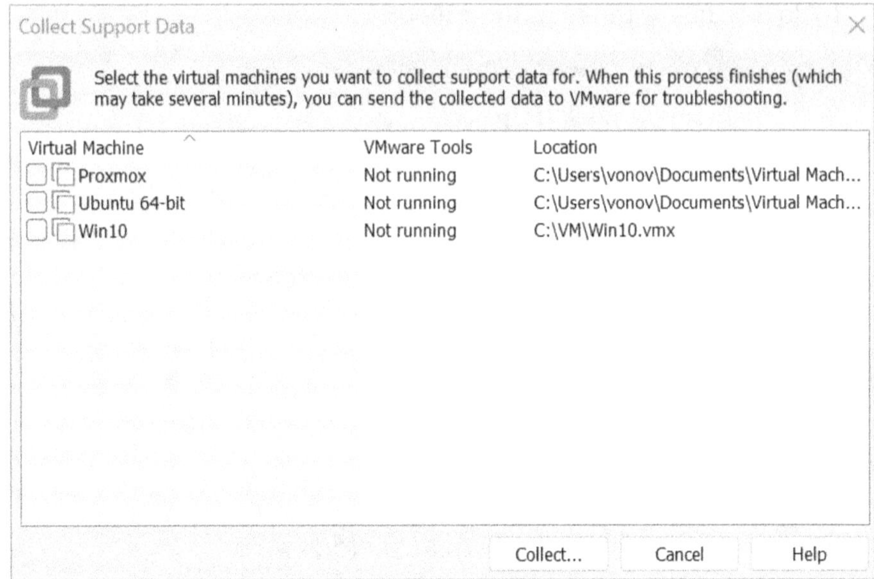

Figure 5-16. *Deselect the Virtual Machines*

7. Clicking the Collect... button will display the **Save As** screen as shown in Figure 5-17.

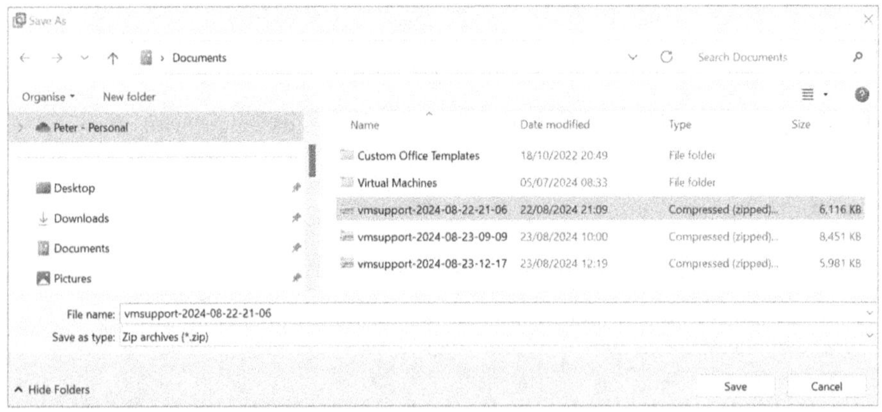

Figure 5-17. *Save As Screen for Data Capture*

8. Navigate to the location you want to save the log file. The name of the file has also been populated in the **File name** field. Again, it is best to leave it as is as this is the naming convention that VMware expects to see when you upload the file.

9. Now click **Save**.

10. You will see the collection process start with the collection of the host machine data as shown in Figure 5-18.

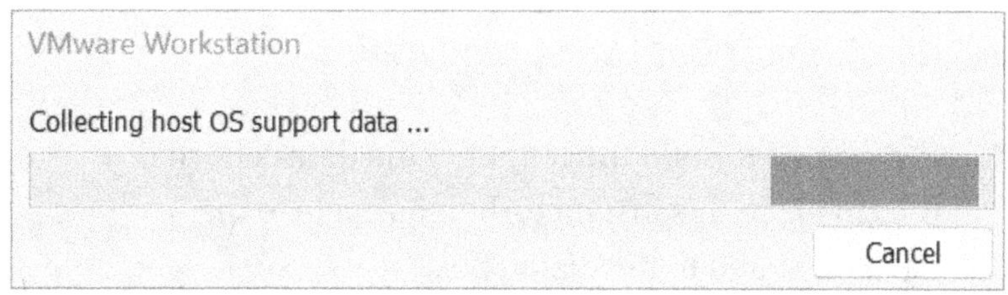

Figure 5-18. *Support data being collected*

11. You will also see the **System Information** box appear as the process continues to run as shown in Figure 5-19.

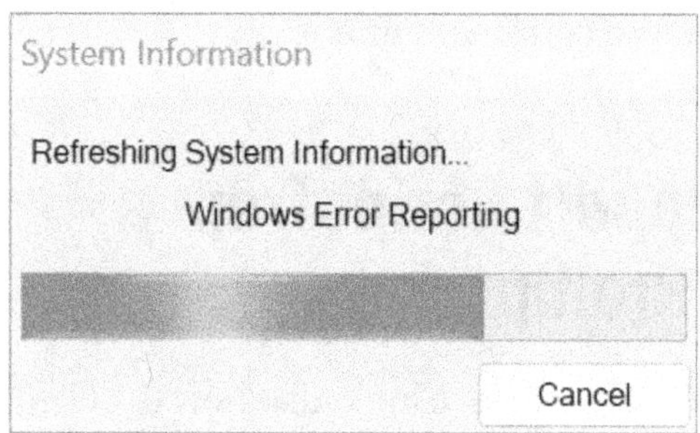

Figure 5-19. *System Information Dialog Box*

12. Finally, once the collection process has successfully completed, you will see the following dialog box as shown in Figure 5-20.

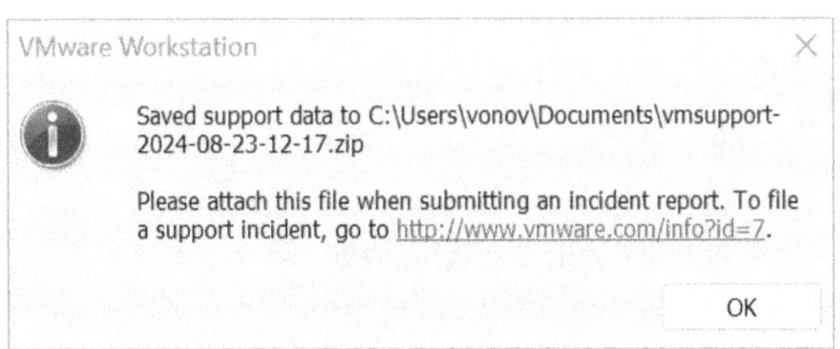

Figure 5-20. *Support Data Successfully Saved*

13. If you need to send the output of the data collected, the zip file in this instance, then navigate to the location stated in the dialog box.

14. Click the **OK** button to close the data collection process.

We have now successfully collected the support data for the host machine.

In the next section, we are going to look at how you can run the support script from the command line.

Run the Support Script from a Command Prompt

In the previous sections, we have looked at how to collect the support data by clicking the menu within the Workstation Pro application.

However, this can also be done from the command line which would facilitate running this remotely. The use case may be that your internal IT team wants to capture the support data automatically using a script.

To run the support script from the command line, follow the steps described:

1. Open a command prompt on the host machine that is running Workstation Pro and hosting the virtual machines you want to collect data for.

2. Navigate to the location of where the support script is located. By default, this can be found in the C:\Program Files (x86)\VMware\VMware Workstation folder.

3. Run the support script as follows: **`cscript vm-support.vbs`**.

4. You will see the script run as shown on Figure 5-21.

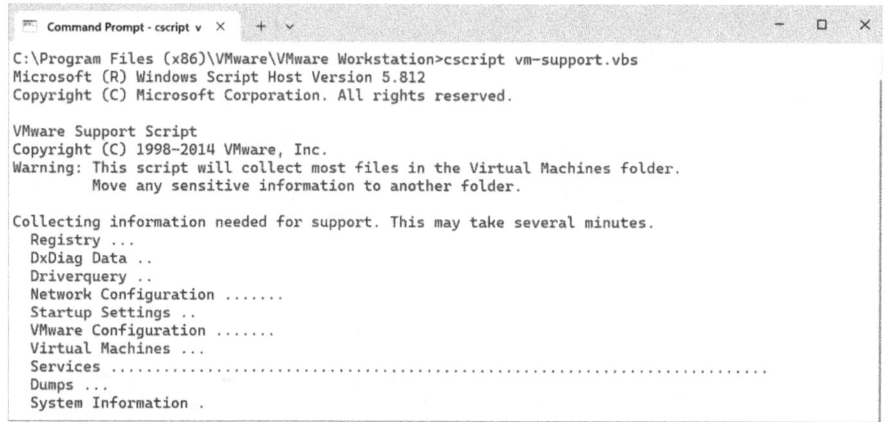

Figure 5-21. *Support Script Running from the Command Line*

5. You will also see the **System Information** dialog box appear as the system information gets refreshed as shown in Figure 5-22.

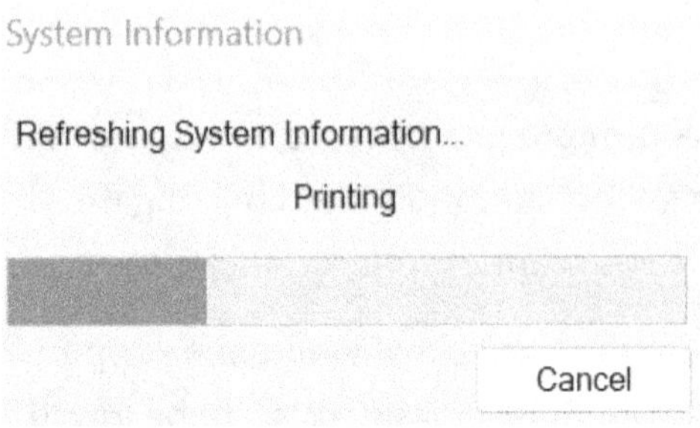

Figure 5-22. *Refreshing the System Information Dialog Box*

Once the script has finished running, which could take several minutes, the zip file is created, and you will see the **Done!** message appear in the command prompt.

You will also see that the path to where the support .zip file has been saved to is shown.

Unlike when running the collect support data feature from within the Workstation pro application, there is no option to select where this file is saved to, so by default, the command line script will save it to C:\Users\<current user>\AppData\Local\Temp\vmware-support folder.

You have now successfully run the support script from the command line of the host machine.

Register and Create a Support Request

If you need to log a support case with VMware support, you then will need to have a few prerequisites completed.

The first one is to have the support data already collected in case the support team asks for it. It's better to have it ready rather than go away and get it and then have to come back to the support team. It just speeds things up and allows you to go through the logs in real time with the support team.

You will also likely be asked for your license key. You will find this in the email that was sent to you when you registered your Workstation Pro instance with VMware. It isn't visible from the Workstation Pro application UI.

You can now submit your support case. To do this, from the Workstation Pro UI, click **Help** and then click to expand the **Support** options. Now click **Submit Support Request** as shown in Figure 5-23.

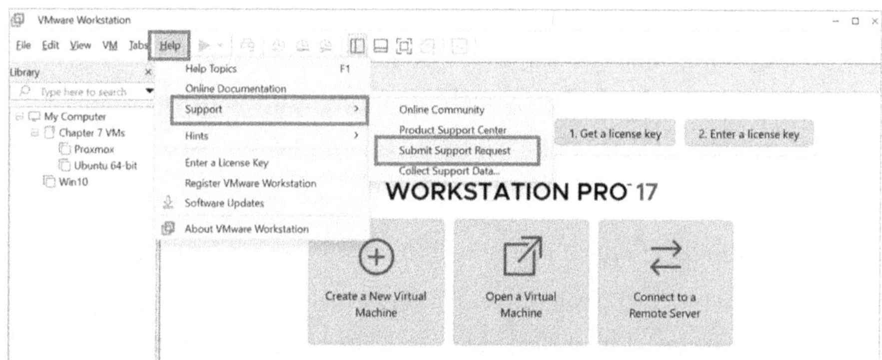

Figure 5-23. *Submitting a Support Request*

This will take you to the VMware/Broadcom support site.

You will need an account in order to login to submit your support case to VMware/Broadcom.

Troubleshooting VM Performance Issues

In this chapter, we have only really talked about collecting support data which is key to troubleshooting your environment whether it is an issue with the Workstation Pro app or one of the virtual machines that it is hosting.

This should be your first port of call when looking at issues, regardless of whether you are going to submit a support case to VMware. The log files captured will point out errors and issues that you can then look to resolve.

We are not going to look at troubleshooting virtual machines in any great depth as that could be an entire chapter in its own right, so for this section, we are going to highlight the top ten issues, in no particular order:

1. VM is performing poorly and running slowly – Start by verifying whether or not any reduced performance is unexpected behavior. Sometimes when you virtualize a machine, it is common to see some reduction in its overall performance due to the virtualization overhead.

   You might experience the following:

   - The virtual machine was previously working at an acceptable performance level but has now started running slowly.
   - The virtual machine performs significantly slower than a similar setup on a physical computer.
   - You want to optimize your virtual machines for the best performance possible.

   Troubleshoot a performance problem by looking at the CPU, memory, and disk usage if you experience these conditions. Also look at the log files and maybe consider increasing resources available to the virtual machine. It might be worth checking with the application vendor that they actually support their application running on a virtual machine and look at whether it is the app causing the issue or the underlying OS.

2. Verify that you are running the most recent version of the VMware Workstation Pro. For download information, see the VMware Download Center or you can check for updates from within the Workstation Pro application.

3. Check that VMware Tools is installed on the virtual machine and running the correct version. The version listed in the toolbox application must match the version of the product hosting the virtual machine. To access the toolbox, double-click the VMware icon in the notification area on the task bar, or run vmware-toolbox in Linux. Some VMware products indicate when the version does not match by displaying a message below the console view.

4. Review the virtual machine's virtual hardware settings and verify that you have provided enough resources to the virtual machine, including memory and CPU resources. Use the average hardware requirements typically used in a physical machine for that operating system as a guide. Adjustments to the settings are required to factor in the application load: higher for larger loads such as databases or multiuser services and lower for less intense usage such as casual single-user application like email or web clients. Consult your operating system and application documentation for more information.

5. Ensure that any antivirus software that is installed on the host machine is configured to exclude scanning the virtual machine files. Install antivirus software inside the virtual machine for proper virus protection.

6. Check the hosts storage is configured for optimal performance for the workloads being hosted. For example, when running containers, it is recommended to use SSD-based storage devices.

7. Verify that there are enough free resources on the host to satisfy the requirements of the virtual machine. In VMware-hosted products, resources must be shared by both the host operating system and all running guests.

8. Disable the CPU power management features on the host. In some cases, these features can cause CPU performance issue with virtual machines.

9. Verify that host networking issues are not impacting the performance of the virtual machine.

10. Verify that the host operating system is working properly and is in a healthy state. When the host is not working correctly, it may draw excessive resources from the guests.

We have now discussed the most popular areas of concern when troubleshooting virtual machine and host machine performance issues. Next, we are going to look at a couple of other sources of information that can help troubleshoot or provide information to help you solve any issues.

Other Support Sources

There are a couple of other sources of information that can help when looking at troubleshooting issues with Workstation Pro. The first of these is the Workstation Pro online community as shown in Figure 5-24.

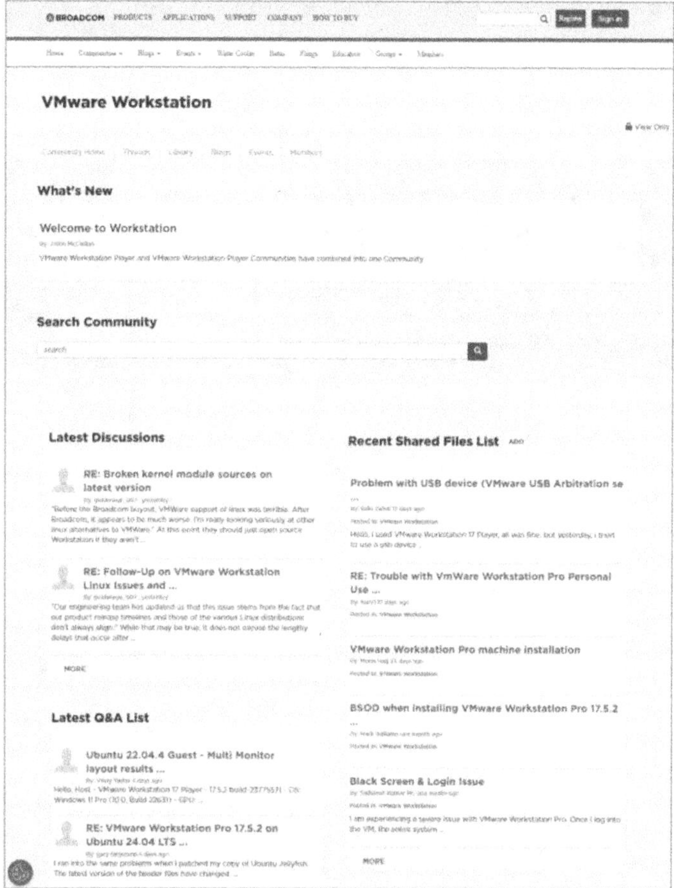

***Figure 5-24.** Workstation Online Community*

The online community can be accessed from the **Help** menu in the Workstation Pro application and selecting the **Support** option and then clicking the option for **Online Community**.

Alternatively, you can use the following link:

`https://community.broadcom.com/vmware-cloud-foundation/communities/communityhomeblogs?CommunityKey=fb707ac3-9412-4fad-b7af-018f5da56d9f`

Also available from the Help and Support menu from within Workstation Pro is access to the Product Support Center as shown in Figure 5-25.

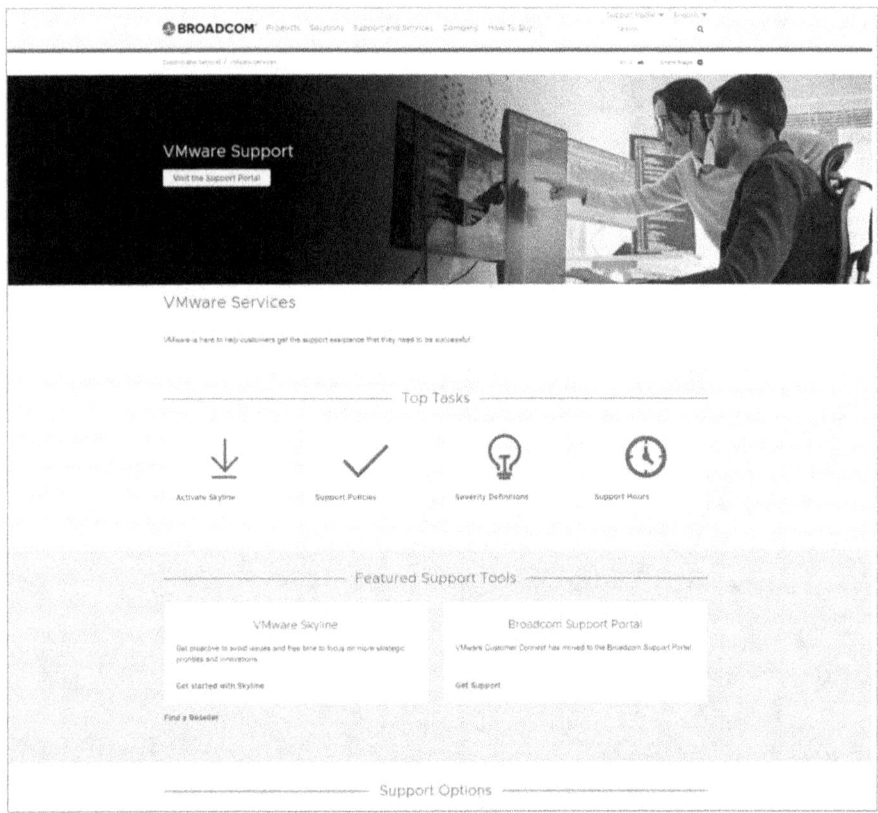

***Figure 5-25.** Support Services Website*

Alternatively, you can use the following link:

`https://www.broadcom.com/support/vmware-services`

Summary

In this chapter, we have looked at some tips for troubleshooting your VMware Workstation environment.

We started by looking at the different debugging levels that can be configured to collect different levels of support information and data.

Next, we looked at ways of collecting that information using the Workstation Pro application and then using a script that can be run from the command line.

Armed with the support data, we then looked at how to log a support case or how to navigate through the log files that have been collected.

We finished the chapter by looking at some of the more common issues you may encounter when troubleshooting and what to look for when working through the issues before highlighting a few other useful sources of information.

In the next chapter, we are going to look at the VMware Workstation Pro application.

CHAPTER 6

Workstation Player

In this book and the previous Workstation book, we focused on the Workstation Pro solution; however, there is another version of the Workstation available, other than the Fusion for the Apple Mac. The product in question is Workstation Player, and we are going to discuss that solution in this chapter.

What Is a Workstation Player?

Workstation Player has been designed to run virtual machines on a Windows or Linux host machine. This book focuses on the Windows version.

The key use case here is to deliver prebuilt virtual machines for people to run where they don't need to edit virtual machine settings or have the advanced features that Workstation Pro delivers.

For example, it could be used to deliver a corporate desktop image as a virtual machine where the end user is using their own personal (BYOD) machine. Corporate IT can manage the virtual machine running in a secure and isolated sandbox environment and not have to worry about the underlying host machine, its hardware, or its operating system.

You still can create virtual machines with VMware Player and open existing virtual machines, but you won't have features such as being able to clone a virtual machine or take a snapshot of a virtual machine or be able to edit network settings such as the Virtual Network Editor. Those features and others can only be found in the full-blown Workstation Pro solution.

P. von Oven, *Learning VMware Workstation Pro for Windows: Volume 2*,
https://doi.org/10.1007/979-8-8688-0864-7_6

In this chapter, we are going to look at the requirements for running Workstation Player, how to download it, how to install it, and then a brief overview of how it works.

Workstation Player Requirements

To run Workstation Player, your host system should have the following minimum requirements:

- 1GHz or faster processor (2GHz recommended)
- 1GB RAM minimum (2GB RAM recommended)
- 150GB disk space for the installation

These minimum requirements are what is required just to run the Workstation Player application. You will also need to ensure that you have enough CPU, memory, and disk requirements to host and run the guest operating system and applications that the guest virtual machine will be running.

Just as a point to note, these are in addition to the minimum requirements to run the Workstation Player application.

Downloading Workstation Player

Workstation Player is available to download free of charge for personal and home use; however, if you want to use it within your organization, then you will need a commercial license.

To start the download, head over to the Workstation Player product page on the VMware website as shown in Figure 6-1.

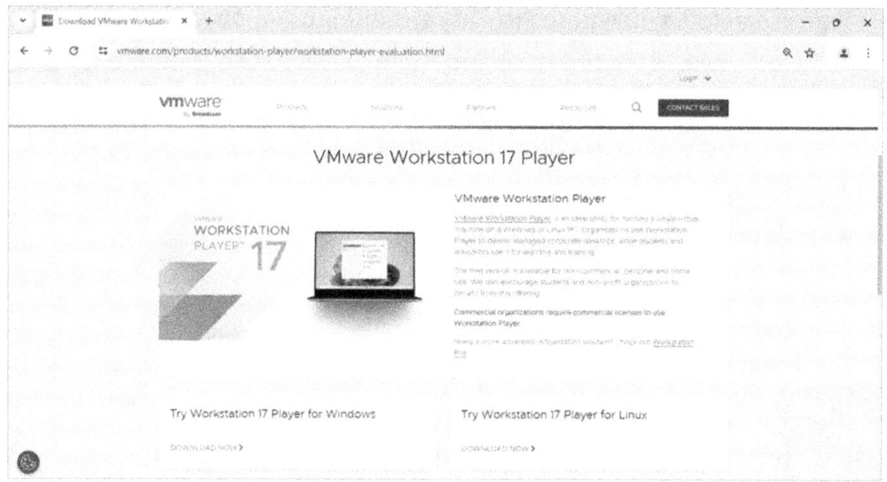

Figure 6-1. *VMware Workstation Player Page*

Click **DOWNLOAD NOW** >.

You will be taken to the Broadcom support website login page where you will need to login with an appropriate account.

Once logged in, navigate to the **VMware Cloud Foundation** section by clicking the drop-down menu next to where your login name is displayed as shown in Figure 6-2.

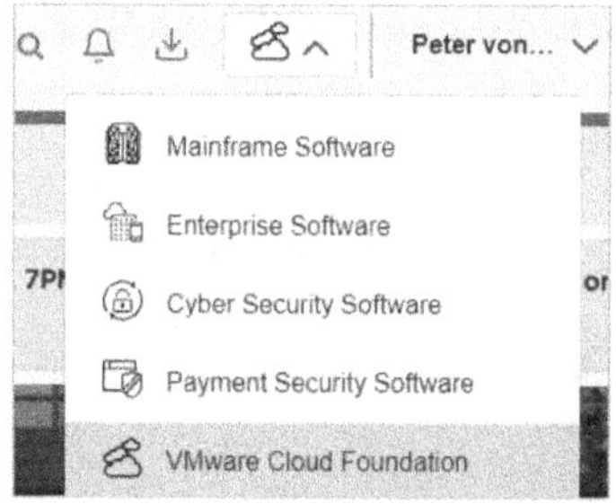

Figure 6-2. *Selecting VMware Cloud Foundation*

Once selected, you will see the **My Downloads - VMware Cloud Foundation** page. From the left-hand menu, select the option for **My Downloads**.

You will now see all the downloads that fall under the heading of VMware Cloud Foundation. Scroll down until you find the entry for **VMware Workstation Player** as shown in Figure 6-3.

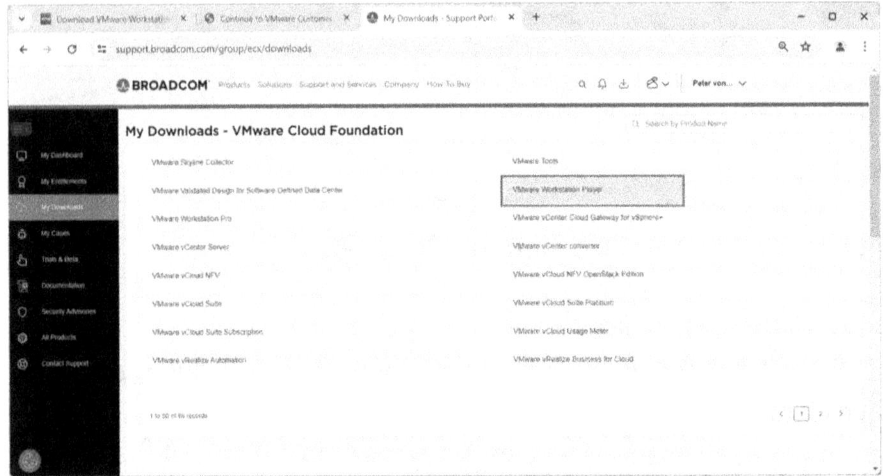

Figure 6-3. *Selecting VMware Workstation Player*

You will see the download page as shown in Figure 6-4.

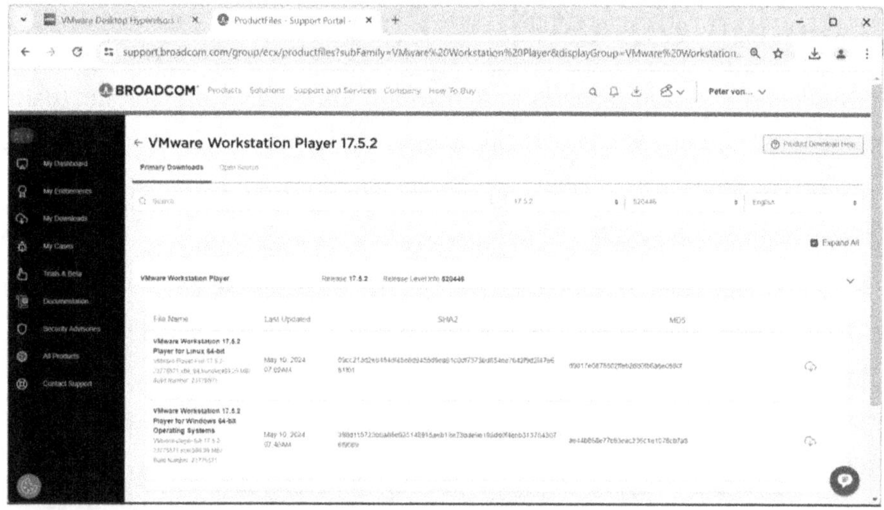

Figure 6-4. VMware Workstation Player Download Page

Click the cloud icon to download. In this example, we are downloading the Windows 64-bit version. You will download a zip file containing the installer which you will need to unzip as shown in Figure 6-5.

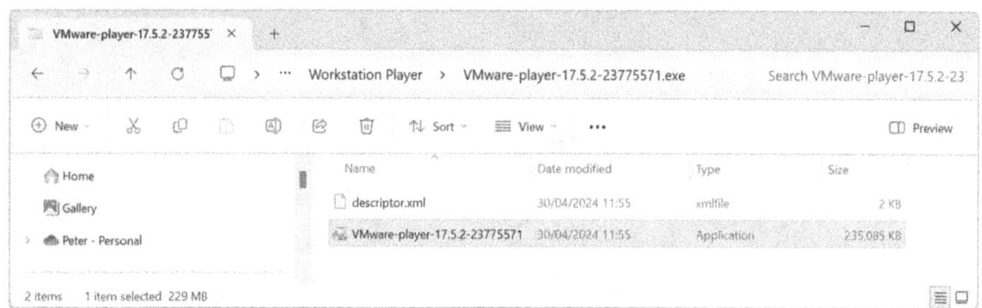

Figure 6-5. VMware Workstation Player Installer Unzipped

You are now ready to install Workstation Player.

Note You cannot install Workstation Player and Workstation Pro on the same host machine.

Installing Workstation Player

In this section, we are going to walk through the process, step by step using actual screenshots, for installing Workstation Player.

1. On the host machine you are installing Workstation Player, navigate to the location of the Workstation Player installer file that you downloaded in the previous section, **VMware-player-17.5.2-23775571**, and double-click to launch it.

2. You will see the installer load as shown in Figure 6-6.

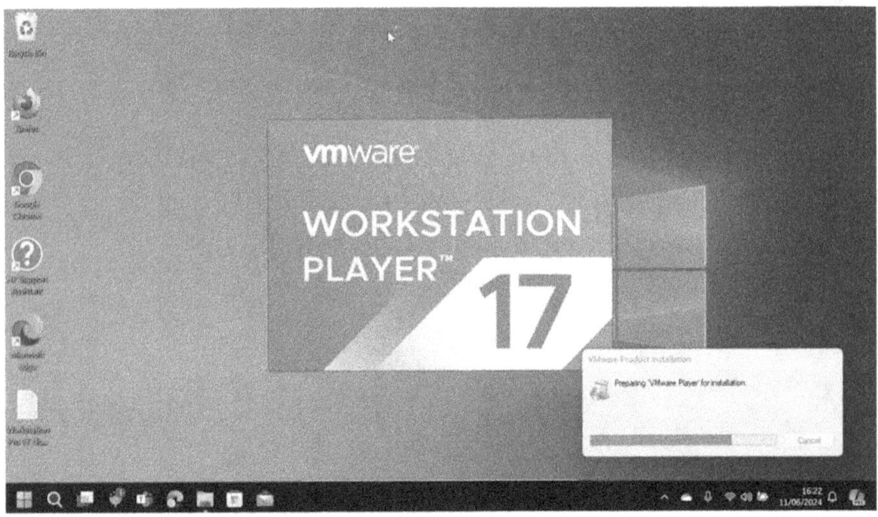

Figure 6-6. *VMware Workstation Player Installer Loading*

3. Once the installer has loaded, you will see the **Welcome to the VMware Workstation 17 Player Setup Wizard** dialog box as shown in Figure 6-7.

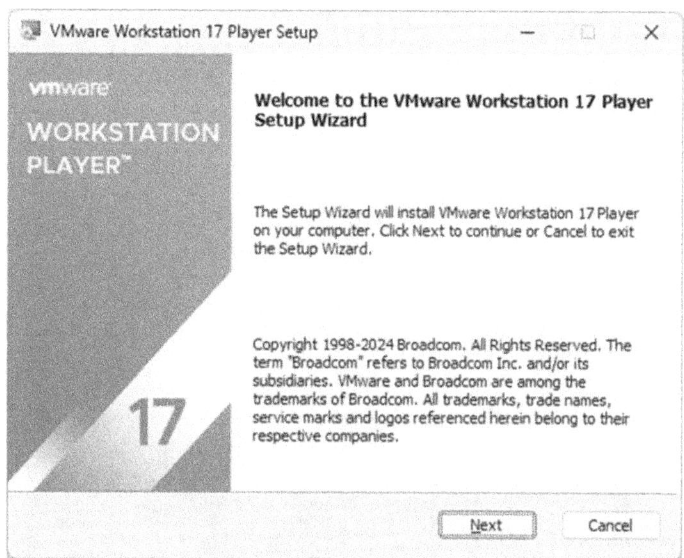

Figure 6-7. *Welcome to VMware Workstation Player Setup Wizard Dialog Box*

4. Click the **Next** button to continue.

5. You will see the **End User License Agreement** dialog box as shown in Figure 6-8.

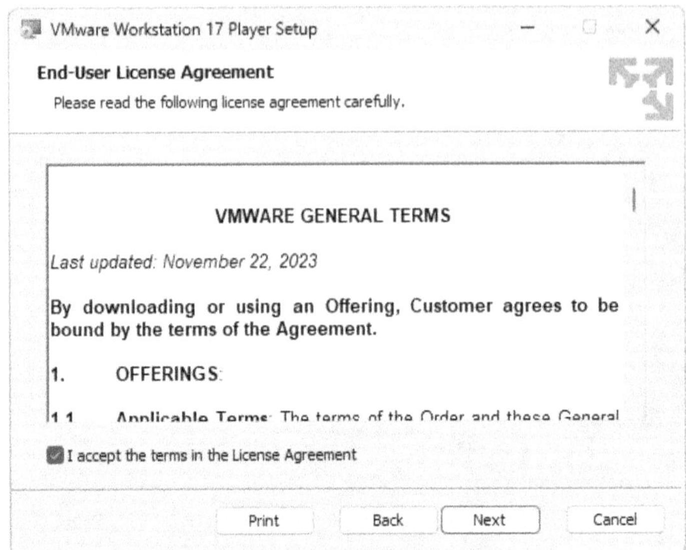

***Figure 6-8.** End-User License Agreement screen*

6. Check the **I accept the terms of the License Agreement** box and then click **Next** to continue.
7. You will see the **Custom Setup** dialog box as shown in Figure 6-9.

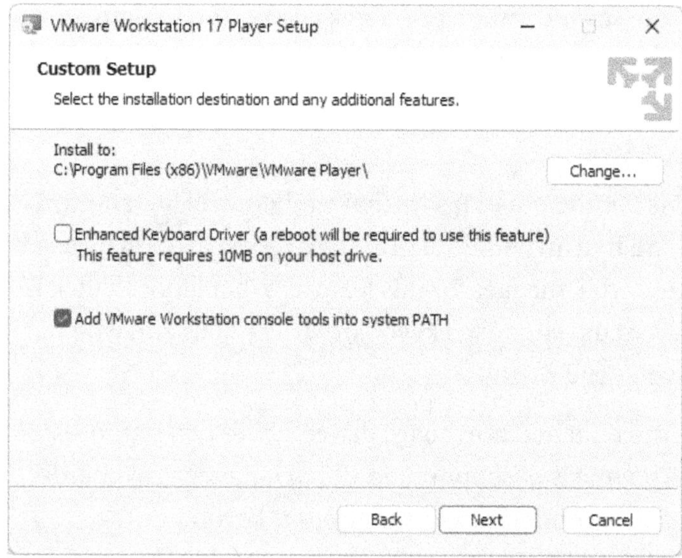

Figure 6-9. *Custom Setup Configuration Dialog Box*

The first option on this screen is to configure the destination folder for where the installation files will be copied to.

By default, it is **C:\Program Files(x86)\VMware\VMware Player**\, but if you want to change the default location, click the **Change...** button. This will open another dialog box (not shown) for **Change destination folder**.

In this box, you can browse to the folder location you want to use (existing folder) or create a new folder. Click **OK** when you have selected the new folder. For this example, we are going to stick with the default folder location which is the recommended option unless there is a good reason why you need to change the location.

The second option is a check box for the **Enhanced Keyboard Driver**. This is not selected by default, and to install the enhanced keyboard driver, simply check the box.

As per the notes, it says that a reboot will be required and that an additional 10MB of disk space will be used to install the files for this feature. What it doesn't tell is what the enhanced keyboard driver does and whether you need it.

The enhanced keyboard driver serves two purposes. The first is to support additional language keyboards. The second purpose is to support keyboards that have additional capabilities such as additional keys for multimedia functions or shortcut keys that launch things like calculator. Typically, these keyboards tend to work fine without the enhanced keyboard driver, but if you find you are having issues, you can always enable this feature later. For now, we are going to leave this option unchecked.

Finally, you have the option to **Add VMware Workstation console tools into system PATH**. This enables you to directly run console tools or command line tools as they are now added to the system path. The tools we are talking about are some of the automation commands such as **vmrun**. In this installation, we are going to leave this set as default which means this is enabled.

8. Once you have configured any custom setup features, click **Next** to continue.

9. You will now see the **User Experience Settings** dialog box as shown in Figure 6-10.

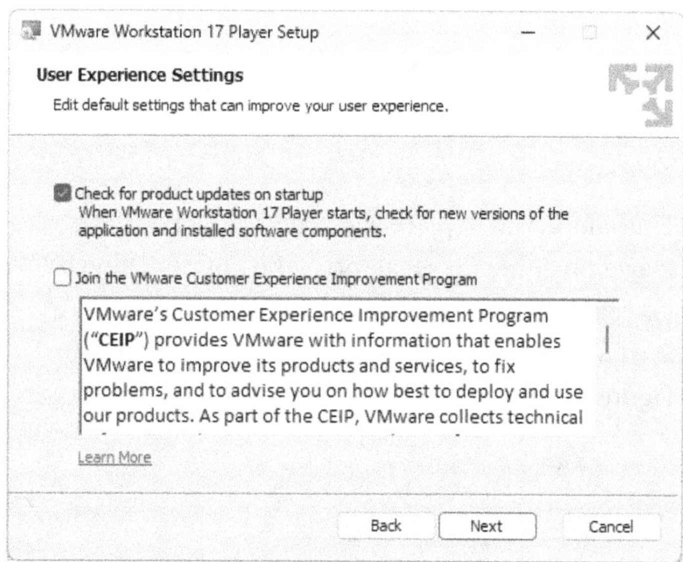

Figure 6-10. *User Experience Settings Dialog Box*

If you don't want to check for updates each time you start Workstation Player, then uncheck the box for **Check for product updates on startup**.

The second option is to **Join the VMware Customer Improvement Program**, or CEIP.

This allows VMware to collect technical information about the VMware solutions that you are using, in this case Workstation Player.

It is not a licensing check!

In this example, we are going to disable this by unchecking the box. You can always reenable it later should you wish to.

10. Click **Next** to continue.

    The next configuration screen is to configure **Shortcuts**.

    This allows you to place shortcuts for Workstation Player on either the **Desktop** of the host machine or to create a shortcut in the Programs Folder on the Start Menu of the host machine. This is shown in Figure 6-11.

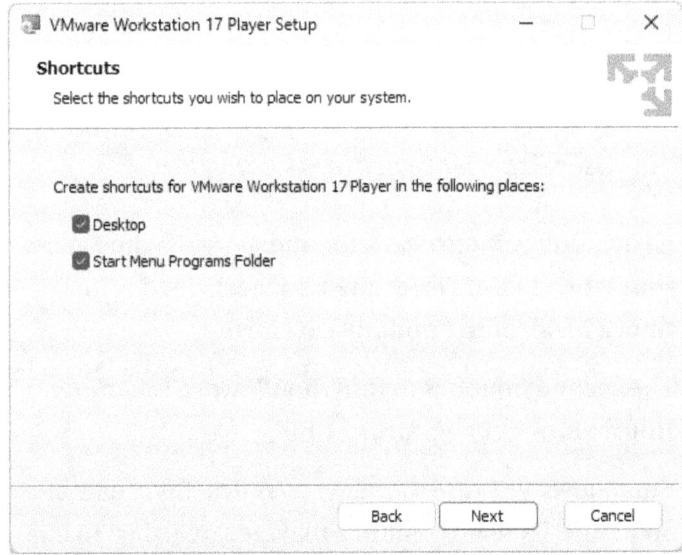

Figure 6-11. *Shortcuts Dialog Box*

By default, both options are selected.

In this installation example, we are going to keep the default settings and leave boxes checked.

11. Click **Next** to continue.

12. You will see the **Ready to install VMware Workstation 17 Player** screen as shown in Figure 6-12.

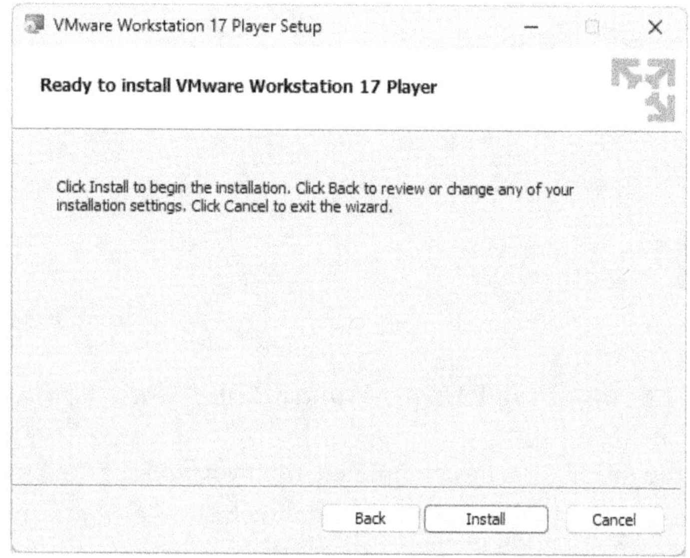

Figure 6-12. *Ready to install VMware Workstation 17 Player*

If you are happy that you have made all the selected and the required configuration options for installation, then click the **Install** button.

If you need to go back and change any of the configured options, simply click the **Back** button to review the previous screen.

The installation will now start, and you will see the following screenshots as registry keys are set, files copied, and network drivers installed.

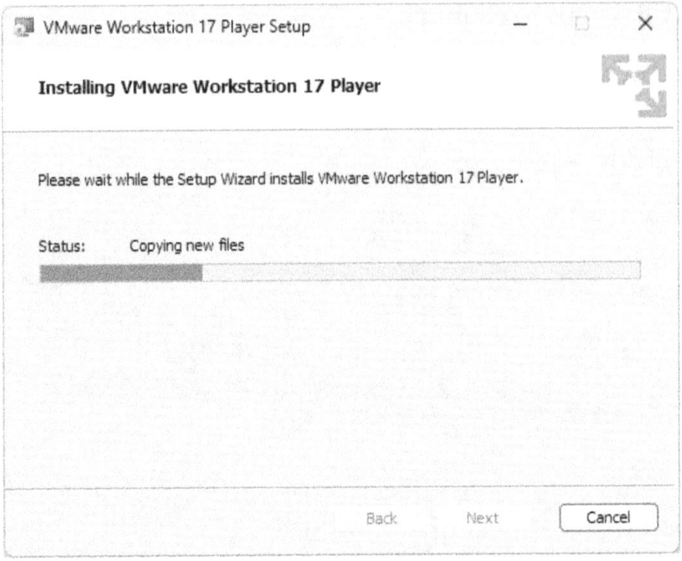

Figure 6-13. Installing VMware Workstation 17 Player

Once the installation has completed, then you will see the **Enter License Key** dialog box as shown in the following screenshot:

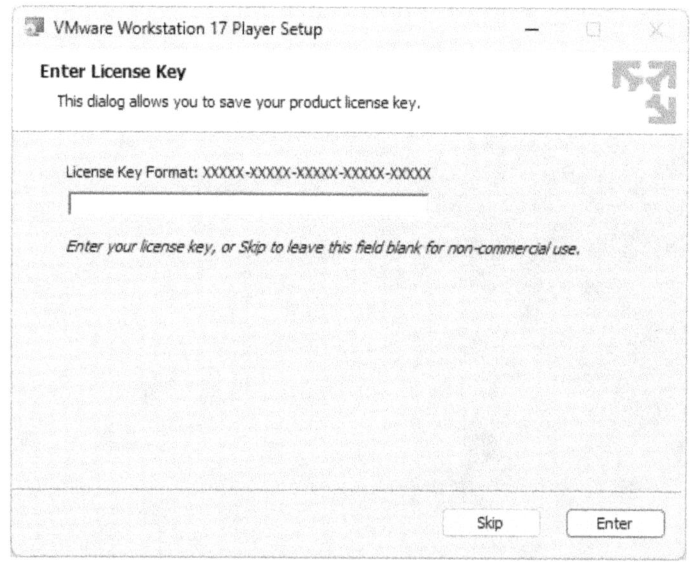

***Figure 6-14.** Entering a License Key*

You can either click the **Skip** button and not enter a license key or you can type in a license key and then click the **Enter** button.

If you skip license key entry at this stage, you can come back to it and add a license key later.

With either option, you will now see the **Completed the VMware Workstation 17 Player Setup Wizard** as shown in Figure 6-15.

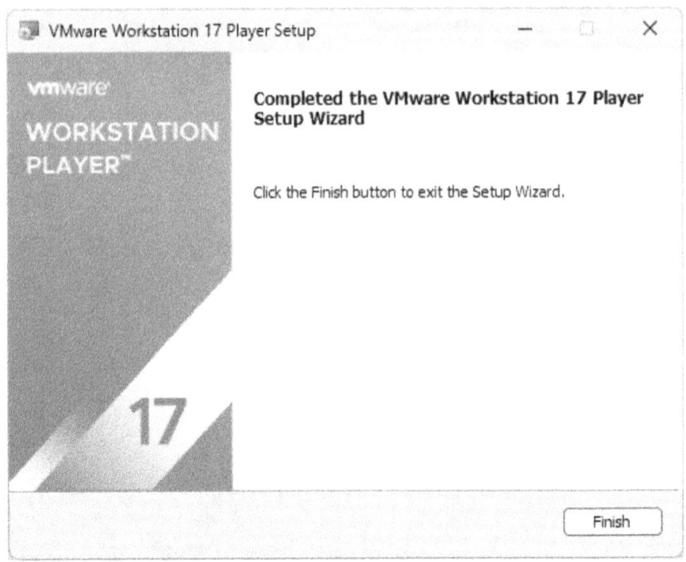

Figure 6-15. *Installation Completed*

Click the **Finish** button to complete the installation and close the installer.

VMware Workstation Player has now been successfully installed and is ready to be used.

To check this, press the Windows key on the host device and in the search box type **VMware**. You will see **VMware Workstation 17 Player** appear in the **Best Match** section as shown in Figure 6-16.

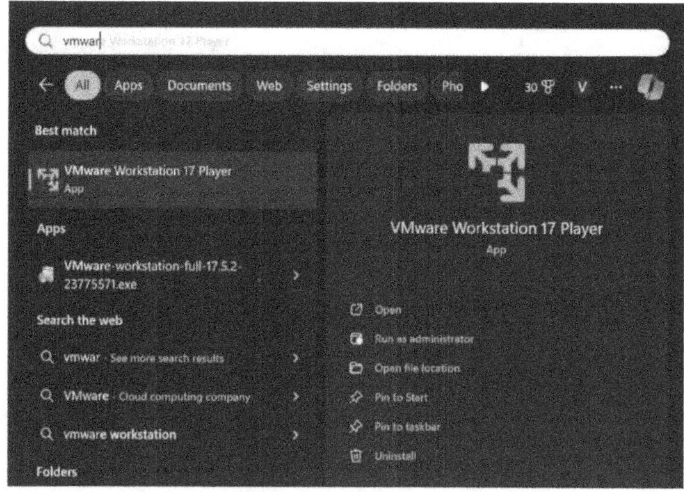

Figure 6-16. *VMware Workstation Player Installed*

If you click the app icon to launch Workstation Player, you will now see it running as shown in Figure 6-17.

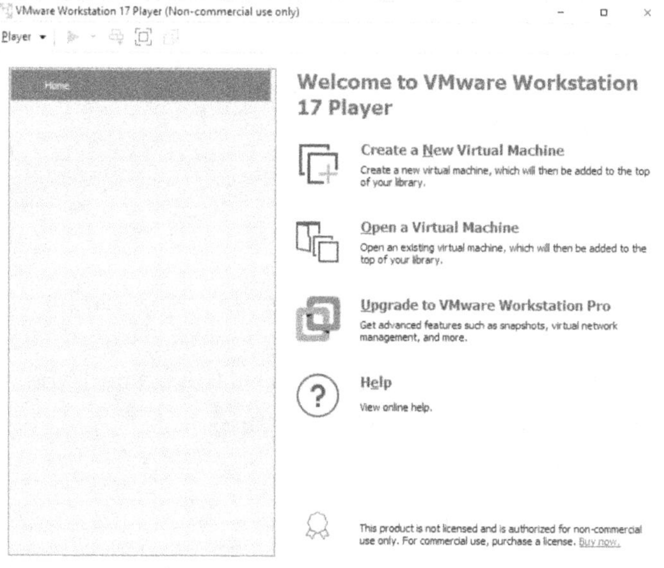

Figure 6-17. *VMware Workstation Player Running*

With Workstation Player now installed and running, in the next chapter, we are going to take a brief look at the user interface and the features available.

We will then look at how to create virtual machines and how to import an existing virtual machine.

Workstation Player User Interface

As you have seen in Figure 6-17, the Workstation Player user interface has far fewer options and menu drop-downs than Workstation Pro. In fact, there is only one drop-down menu which is **Player** as shown in Figure 6-18.

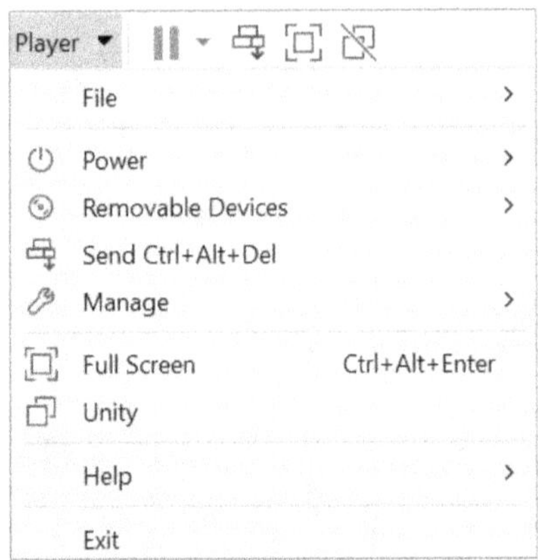

Figure 6-18. *VMware Workstation "Player" Drop-Down Menu*

The first option is for **File** which, if you click to expand, you will see a few different options as shown in Figure 6-19.

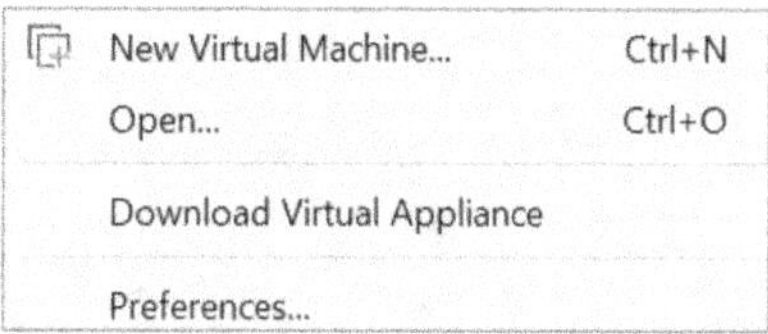

***Figure 6-19.** File Menu Options*

- **New Virtual Machine** - Starts the new virtual machine wizard to guide you through the process of creating and configuring a new virtual machine. You can also select the New Virtual Machine option by right-clicking the **Library** pane under **My Computer**.
- **Open** - Allows you to open an existing virtual machine. When selected, a Windows Explorer box will open to allow you to browse to an existing VM configuration file or an OVF template.
- **Download Virtual Appliance** - Takes you to the Bitnami by VMware website where you can download packages of virtual appliances as shown in Figure 6-20.

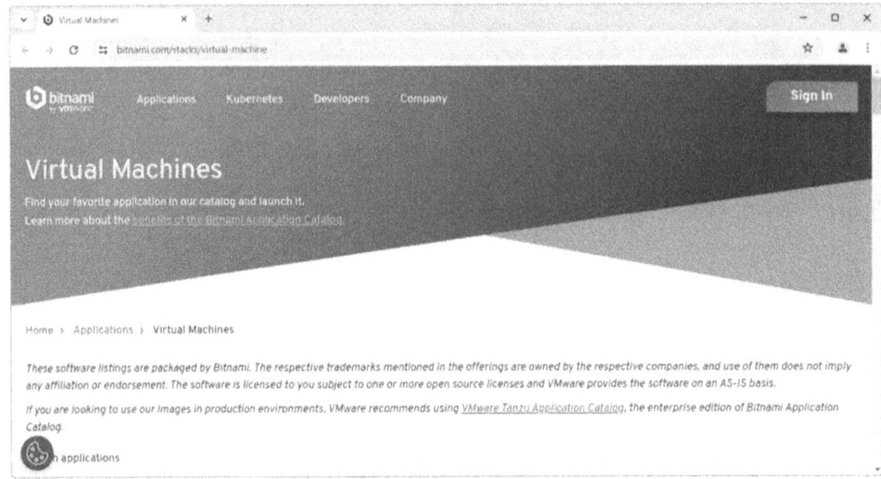

***Figure 6-20.** Bitnami by VMware Website*

- **Preferences** – Launches the preferences configuration screen. The preferences screen allows you to configure the behavior of Workstation Player, configuring options such as the following:
  - **Close behavior** – Configures what happens when you close a virtual machine
  - **Software updates** – Checks for updated when you launch Workstation Player, or check for software components as and when required
  - **Customer Experience Improvement Program** – Allows you to join or leave the program that collects statistics on Workstation Player
  - **USB** – Allows you to define what happens when you plug in a USB device which is detected by Workstation Player
  - **Color theme** – Allows you to select either light or dark mode

The preferences configuration screen is shown in Figure 6-21.

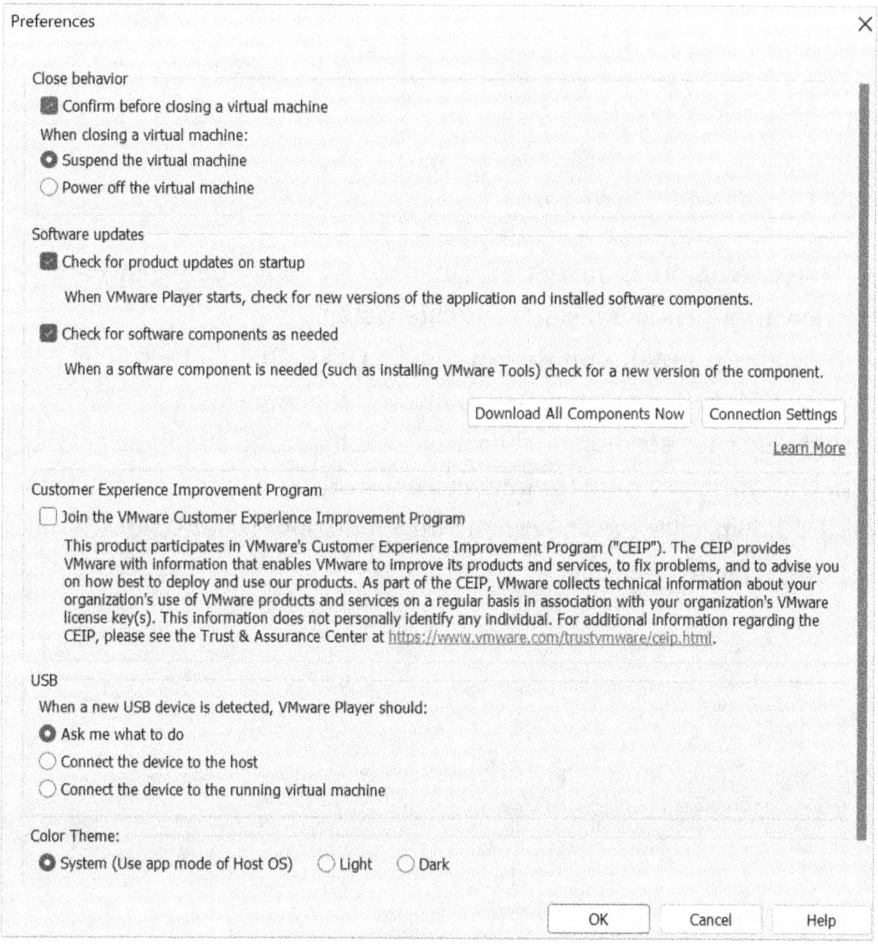

Preferences

Close behavior

Confirm before closing a virtual machine

When closing a virtual machine:

Suspend the virtual machine

Power off the virtual machine

Software updates

Check for product updates on startup

When VMware Player starts, check for new versions of the application and installed software components.

Check for software components as needed

When a software component is needed (such as installing VMware Tools) check for a new version of the component.

Download All Components Now | Connection Settings

Learn More

Customer Experience Improvement Program

Join the VMware Customer Experience Improvement Program

This product participates in VMware's Customer Experience Improvement Program ("CEIP"). The CEIP provides VMware with information that enables VMware to improve its products and services, to fix problems, and to advise you on how best to deploy and use our products. As part of the CEIP, VMware collects technical information about your organization's use of VMware products and services on a regular basis in association with your organization's VMware license key(s). This information does not personally identify any individual. For additional information regarding the CEIP, please see the Trust & Assurance Center at https://www.vmware.com/trustvmware/ceip.html.

USB

When a new USB device is detected, VMware Player should:

Ask me what to do

Connect the device to the host

Connect the device to the running virtual machine

Color Theme:

System (Use app mode of Host OS) Light Dark

OK | Cancel | Help

Figure 6-21. *Preferences Configuration Screen*

Next are the **Power** options as shown in Figure 6-22.

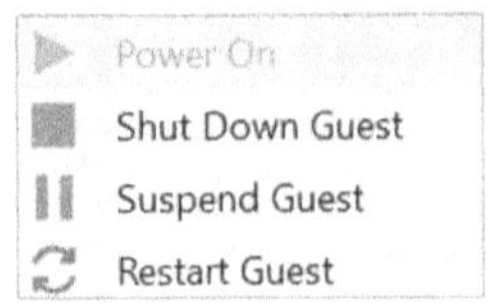

Figure 6-22. *Power Options*

The power options are self-explanatory and allow you to power on, shut down, suspend, or restart a virtual machine.

Next are the options for **Removable Devices**. This allows you to connect devices that are attached to the host machine and pass them through and connect them to the virtual machine. You simply select the virtual machine you want to connect a device to, and then from the list of devices shown, click the > to expand the menu options and click Connect as shown if Figure 6-23.

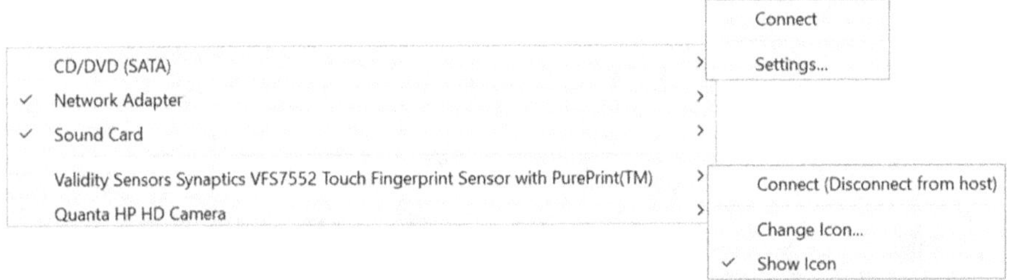

Figure 6-23. *Removable Devices Menu*

Equally, if you want to disconnect a device from the virtual machine and return it the host machine, then again click virtual machine you want to disconnect the device from, and then from the list of devices shown, click the > to expand the menu options and click **Disconnect**.

You also have the option to edit the hardware settings by clicking the **Settings...** option.

You can only edit settings for the core hardware devices such as CD drives, network, or sound cards, basically only those devices that appear by default on the hardware configuration screen. Plug-in devices such as USB memory sticks or USB web cams cannot be reconfigured. These devices are shown in the bottom of the device list, separated by a line from those that are configurable.

Next is the Send Ctrl+Alt+Del option which sends the Ctrl+Alt+Del command or keystroke to the virtual machine selected to either logon, lock, switch user, sign out, change password, or launch the task manager.

With the **Manage** option, you can either install VMware Tools, view the Message Log, or you have the option to open the configuration page for the selected virtual machine. This is shown in Figure 6-24.

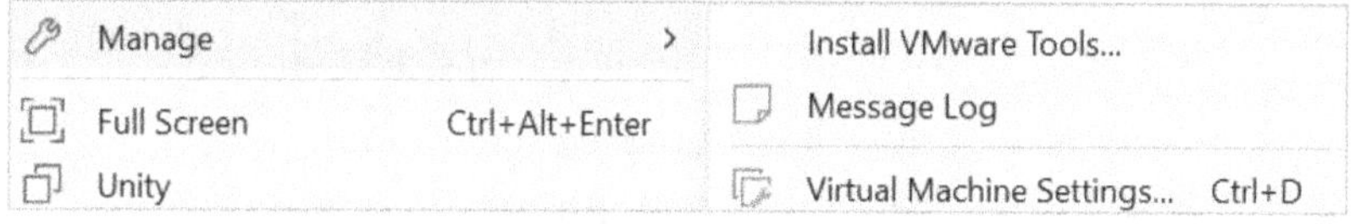

Figure 6-24. *Manage Menu Options*

The next two options relate to how the screen of the virtual machine is displayed on the host machine. You can see these two menu options in the previous screenshot, Figure 6-24.

- **Full screen** – This option switches the currently selected virtual machine, when running, to full screen mode, meaning the virtual machine will use the entire screen real estate of the host machine.

If you select full screen for a virtual machine that is not running, then the Workstation Pro application will switch to full screen which hides the menu and toolbars of the application along with the Windows taskbar.

- **Unity** - In Unity mode, the application running on virtual machines will appear on the desktop of the host machine. This means that you can launch this application from the host machine.

  When launched, the virtual machine console view is hidden.

  Applications from the virtual machine will appear on the host machine's taskbar the same way as other host applications.

  Once running in Unity mode, you can use keyboard shortcuts to copy, cut, and paste images, plain text, formatted text, and email attachments between applications. You are also able to drag and drop as well as copy and paste files between the host machine and the virtual machine.

  When you save a file or open a file when running an application in Unity mode, the file system displayed for opening and saving that file is the virtual machines file system.

  It is not the host machine's file system, and therefore, you will not be able to open a file from the host machine or save a file to the host machine.

The next option comes under the heading of **Help** and is made up of several different options and is shown in Figure 6-25.

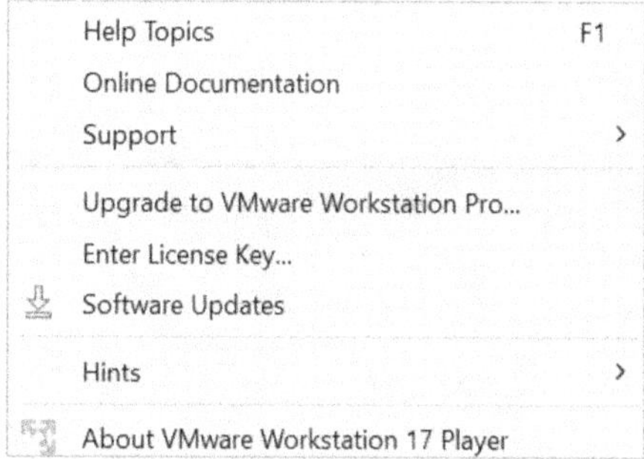

***Figure 6-25.** Help Menu Options*

The first one is **Help Topics** which is also accessible by pressing the F1 key on the keyboard of the host machine.

Selecting this option takes you to the VMware Docs website and the **Using VMware Workstation Player for Windows** page as shown in Figure 6-26.

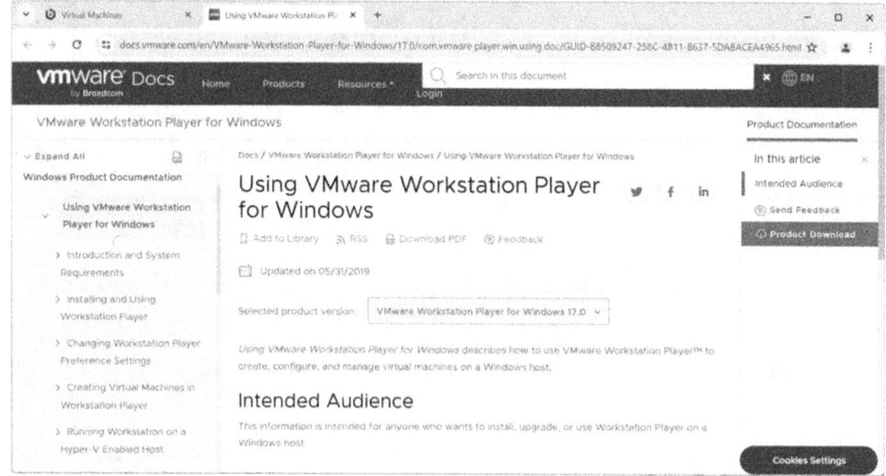

***Figure 6-26.** VMware Workstation Player Help Page*

The next option, **Online Documentation**, also takes you to the VMware website, but this time to a different page – the **VMware Workstation Player for Windows Documentation** page in Figure 6-27.

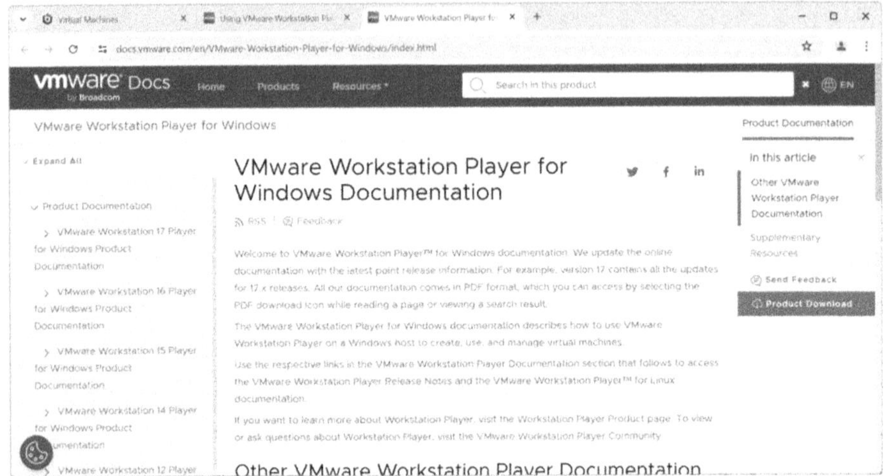

Figure 6-27. *VMware Workstation Player Documentation Page*

The next option in the **Help** menu is for **Support**. Under the Support menu, there are two different options as shown in Figure 6-28.

Figure 6-28. *Support Menu Options*

Clicking the **Online Community** option takes you to the Broadcom website for the VMware Workstation Player and VMware Workstation Player Community pages where you can ask the community any questions that you may have about the product.

You can also search to see if others have experienced that same issue and whether there is a solution or workaround.

The page is shown in Figure 6-29, but for reference, the URL to the site is detailed below:

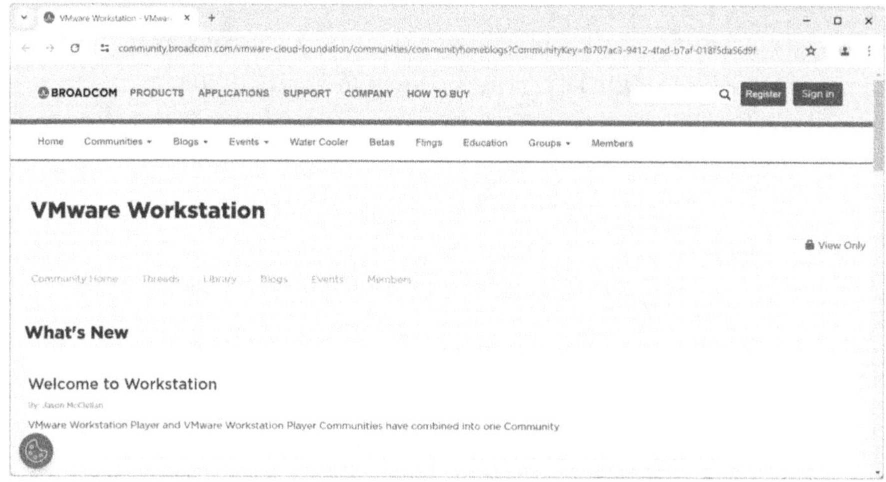

Figure 6-29. *Workstation Online Community Pages*

`https://community.broadcom.com/vmware-cloud-foundation/communities/communityhomeblogs?CommunityKey=fb707ac3-9412-4fad-b7af-018f5da56d9f`

The other option under support is the **Request a Product Feature** option.

Clicking this will take you to a **Contact Sales** online form on the VMware Broadcom website. It is a generic contact us style form, so there isn't a particular way of highlighting that you are requesting a product feature. A better option would be to raise something on the community pages or seek out a vExpert and engage with them.

Next in the help menus is the option for **Upgrade to VMware Workstation Pro....** Clicking this will take you to the VMware website where you can download the "full" Workstation Pro version. Ultimately, this will take you to the Broadcom support website, and so you will require a login to gain access to the site.

With the **Enter License Key** option, you can add a license key for Workstation Player to allow it to be used for commercial use instead of personal use.

If you click this option, you will see the **Enter License Key** dialog box to enable you to enter the key. This is shown in Figure 6-30.

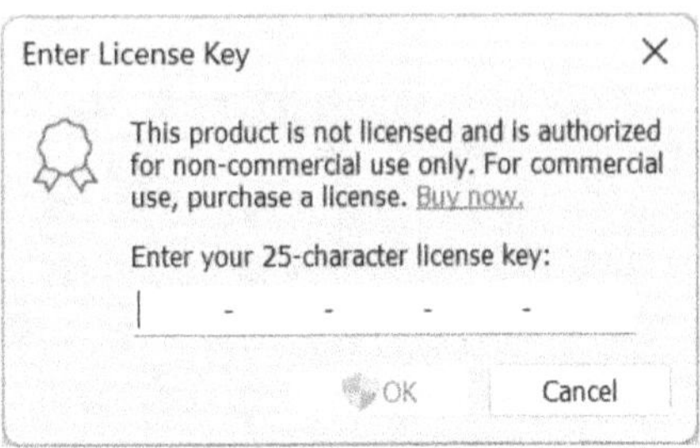

Figure 6-30. *Enter License Key Dialog Box*

Next, you can check to see that you are running the latest version of Workstation Player by clicking the **Software Updates** option from the help menu.

Clicking this option will open the **Software Updates** dialog box where you can click the **Check for Updates** button. This will connect to the update server and check to see if there is a newer version available for download. This is shown in Figure 6-31.

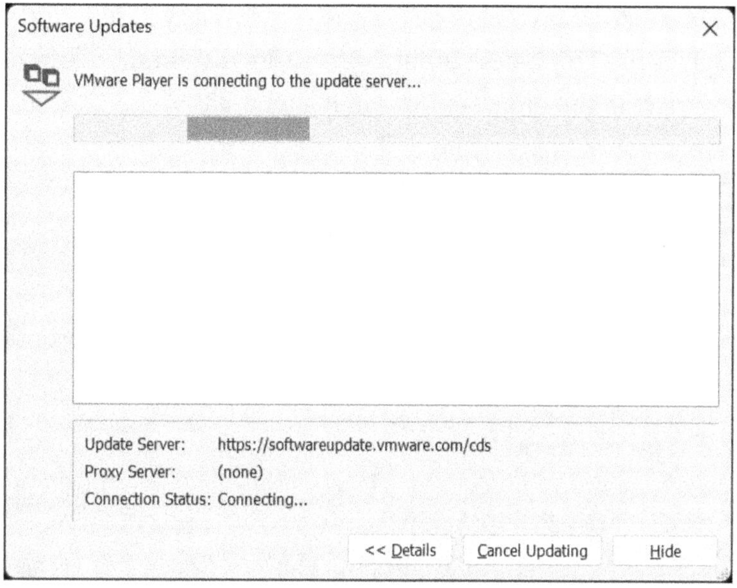

Figure 6-31. *Checking for Software Updates*

If there is a new version available, then it will appear in the dialog box and allow you to select is and download it.

If there are no new version available for download, then you will see the following message appear as shown in Figure 6-32.

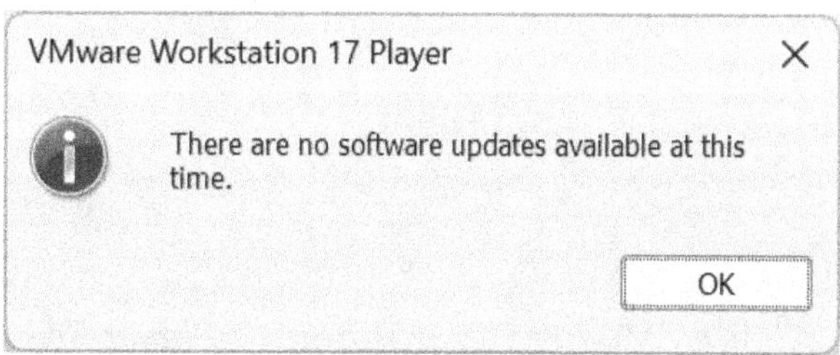

Figure 6-32. *No Software Updates Available*

With the **Hints** option, which is next in the help menu, you can either switch the hints on or off.

The hints feature is used to display helpful tips as you use Workstation Player such as the "To release input, press Ctrl + Alt" hint.

An example of the hints is shown in Figure 6-33.

Figure 6-33. *Hints*

Finally, there is the **About VMware Workstation 17 Player** option as shown in Figure 6-34.

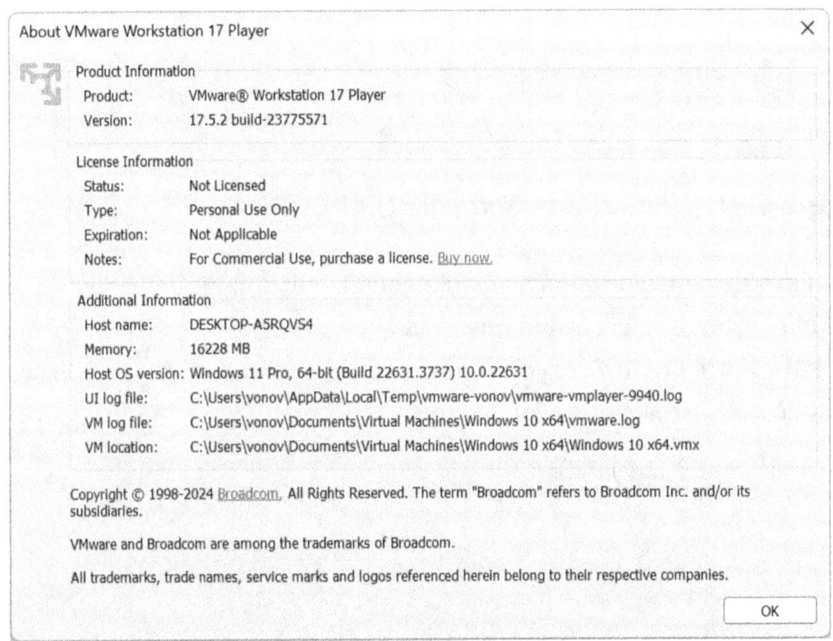

Figure 6-34. *About VMware Workstation 17 Player Screen*

This provides you with information such as product information, license information, and information about the host machine.

The only other option under the Player drop-down menu is **Exit** which closes the Workstation Player application.

Now we have covered the menu options in Workstation Player; the last part to cover with the user interface is the four icons that you will find next to the Player drop-down menu. These are shown in Figure 6-35.

***Figure 6-35.** Option Buttons*

The first of these buttons is for controlling the power of the virtual machines and has a drop-down menu from which you can select other power options as shown in Figure 6-36.

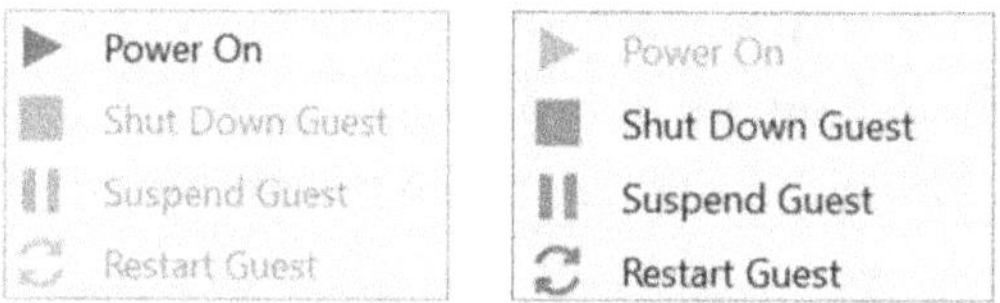

***Figure 6-36.** Power Option Buttons*

The power options provide the following functionality:

- **Power on** – Classified as a hard option, this essentially turns on a virtual machine.
- **Shut down guest** – This initiates a graceful shutdown of a virtual machine by sending a power off command to the operating system running in the virtual machine. The virtual machine will then power off using the correct procedure depending on the operating system it is running. It is worth noting that not all guest operating systems will support a graceful shutdown.
- **Suspend guest** – The suspend feature saves the current state of a virtual machine. When the virtual machine is resumed, it continues from the exact point where

it was suspended, including any applications that were running at the time the virtual machine was suspended.

When you initiate a suspend action, then a virtual machine suspended state or vmss or .vmem file is created in the same folder as the virtual machine is stored.

The virtual machine is also disconnected from the network, and if the IP address was acquired using DHCP, then the IP address will be released. Once resumed, the virtual machine will continue to work from where it left off and you cannot return to the same state as when the virtual machine was first suspended.

- **Restart guest** – Another soft option which first gracefully shuts down the virtual machine and then performs a startup guest action. To do this, VMware Tools runs scripts both before the virtual machine shuts down and then again when the virtual machine starts up.

The next button is for sending Ctrl+Alt+Del to the virtual machine selected to either logon, lock, switch user, sign out, change password, or launch the task manager.

Next to that button you will find the button for entering full screen mode. This option switches the currently selected virtual machine, when running, to full screen mode, meaning the virtual machine will use the entire screen real estate of the host machine.

If you select full screen for a virtual machine that is not running, then the Workstation Pro application will switch to full screen which hides the menu and toolbars of the application along with the Windows taskbar.

The final button is for entering Unity mode.

You will also notice on the toolbar, to the far right-hand side, another icon that looks like two arrows. This is highlighted in red in Figure 6-37.

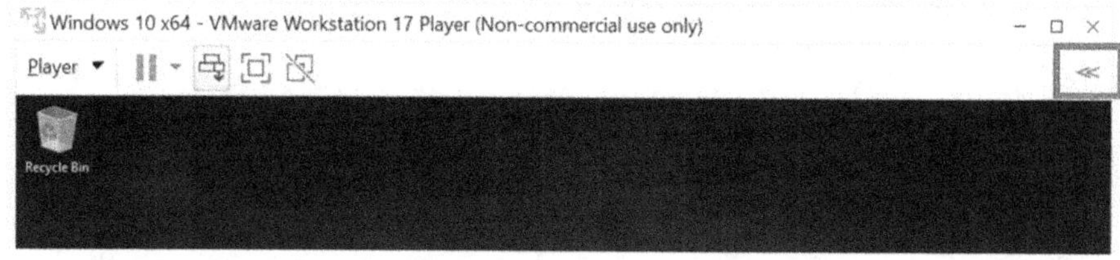

Figure 6-37. *Display the Status Bar*

If you click this icon, then the status bar will now be visible. It shows information about the currently selected virtual machine such as hard disk activity, network activity, and devices connected.

This is only displayed for virtual machines that are powered on.

Figure 6-38 shows the status bar for the selected virtual machine.

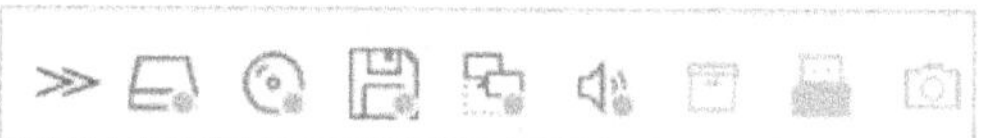

Figure 6-38. *Status Bar*

The icons shown represent the following hardware (from left to right):

- Hard disk
- CD ROM driver
- Floppy disk drive
- Network adapter
- Sound card

- External USB disk (grayed out as this is connected to the host)
- Fingerprint reader (grayed out as this is connected to the host)
- Web camera (grayed out as this is connected to the host)

The final part of the user interface that we are going to cover is the main screen which includes the home page and the details of the existing virtual machines.

Figure 6-39 shows the home screen, selected by clicking **Home** in the left-hand side of the screen.

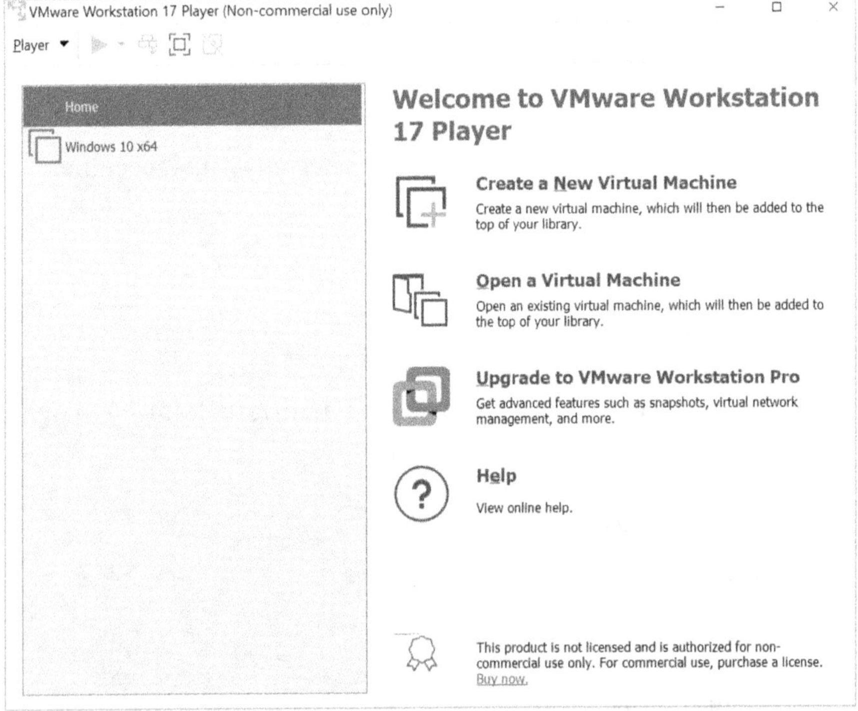

Figure 6-39. *Home Page*

On this screen, you have several options to select from shown on the right-hand side of the screen:

- **Create a new virtual machine** - Allows you to create a new virtual machine from scratch
- **Open a virtual machine** - Opens Windows Explorer to allow you to navigate to an existing virtual machine you want to use in Workstation Player
- **Upgrade to VMware Workstation Pro** - Takes you to the VMware website where you can download Workstation Pro
- **Help** - Takes you to the VMware Docs website

You will also see a note at the bottom of the screen stating the current method in which the product has been licensed.

If you already have virtual machines created, then they will appear listed under the home icon in the left-hand window. If you click the virtual machine, then you will see the status of that virtual machine as well as being able to power it on if it is powered off or edit the virtual machine settings. This is shown in Figure 6-40.

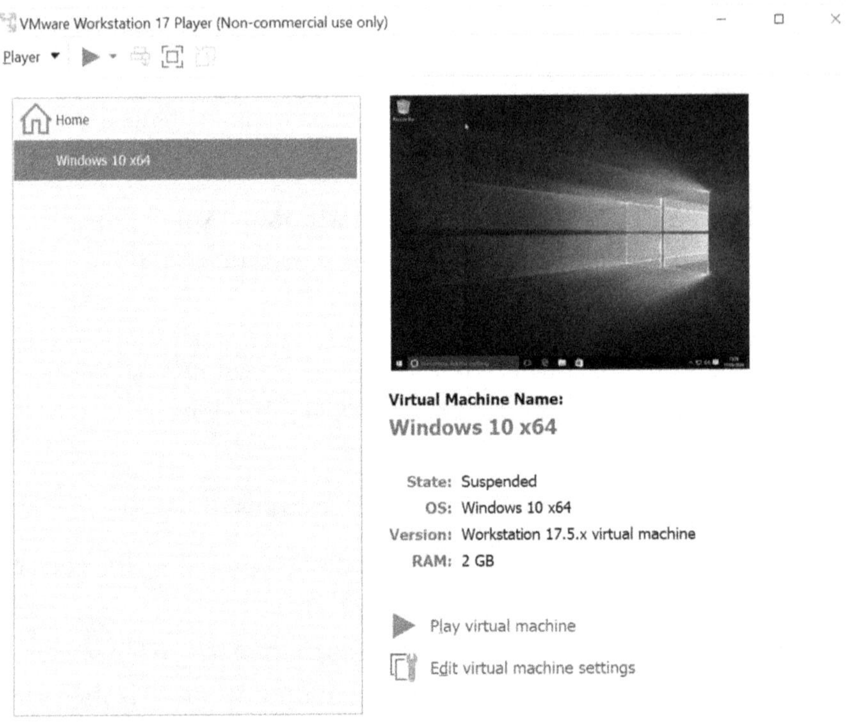

Figure 6-40. *Virtual Machine Details Screen*

Now that we have completed a tour of the Workstation Player user interface, in the next section, we are going to look at how to create and configure a new virtual machine.

Creating a New Virtual Machine

VMware Workstation Player does allow you to create virtual machines. I just wanted to make this point as a popular misconception is that you cannot create a new virtual machine in Workstation Player and that you can only power on and use existing virtual machines.

However, it is worth pointing out that Workstation Player doesn't offer all the features and capabilities found in Workstation Pro.

In this section, we are going to create a Windows 10 virtual machine.

1. Click **Create a New Virtual Machine**.
2. **You will see the New Virtual Machine Wizard** as shown in Figure 6-41.

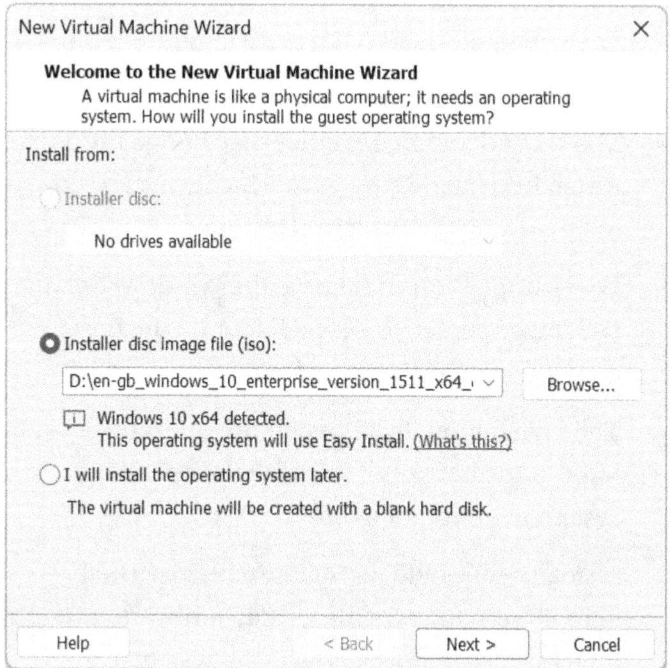

Figure 6-41. *New Virtual Machine Wizard*

You don't get the custom advanced option for creating a new virtual machine in Workstation Player like you do in Workstation Pro.

---

3. On this screen, you have the option of selecting the source of the installation. You have the following choices:

    - The first option, **Installer disc**, is for installing the operating system from an installation disk, whereby the installation disk is inserted into a CD ROM drive for example.
    - You would then select the drive letter from the drop-down menu.
    - The second option, **Installer disc image file**, is to install from an ISO image to which you can browse to by clicking the **Browse...** button.
    - For example, you could have the Windows Server ISO image copied to a local folder on the host machine to which you navigate to.
    - The final option, **I will install the operating system later**, is to choose not to install the operating system at this point in time.

      Instead, you would just create a blank virtual hard drive, configure the virtual hardware, and then install the chosen operating system at a later date.

      Essentially, you are just creating a blank and empty VM container for future use.

4. In this example, click the radio button for **Installer disc image file (iso)** and then click **Browse...**.

   You will see a File Explorer window open to allow you to browse to the location of the ISO file required. In this example, we have navigated to and selected a Windows 10 ISO image.

5. Now click **Next** >. You will now see the **Easy Install Information** screen.

6. In the **Windows product key** box, type in the product/license key for the operating system being installed.

   You can miss this step out and enter the key once the OS has been installed or if you have an alternative way, such as KMS, to activate and register the operating system. You will see a pop-up warning box saying that you didn't add a license key and that you will need to add one manually at a later stage.

7. In the **Version of Windows to install**, click the drop-down box and select the version of the operating system you want to install.

8. Next you have the option to personalize Windows by adding your **Full name**, **Password**, and **Confirm** password. These are optional and if selected will then allow you to check the box for **Log on automatically**. The **Easy Install Information** screen is shown in Figure 6-42.

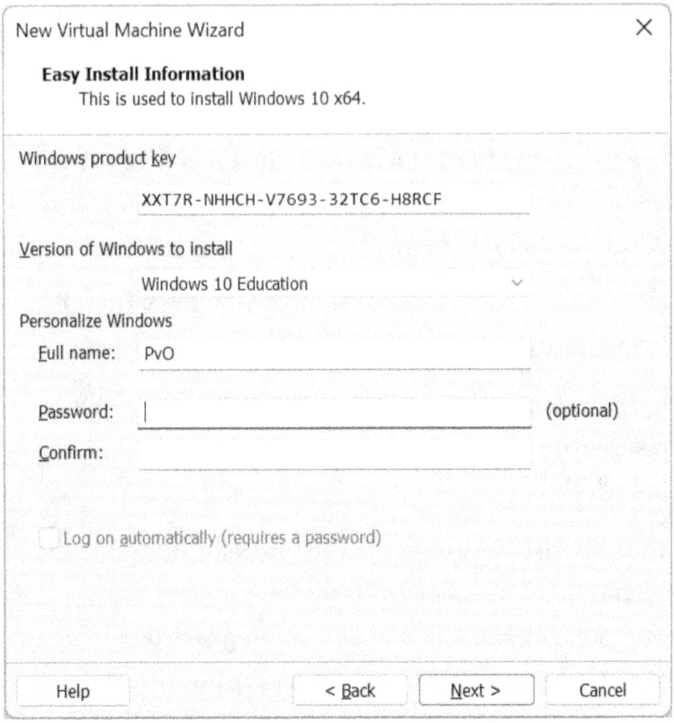

Figure 6-42. *Easy Install Information Screen*

9. Now click **Next** >. You will now see the **Name the Virtual Machine** screen.

10. In the **Virtual machine name** box, type in a unique name for the virtual machine. Don't forget that the virtual machine name doesn't just appear in the library; it is also used as the filenames for the virtual machine configuration file and virtual hard disk files. In this example, we have called it Windows 10 desktop image as shown in Figure 6-43.

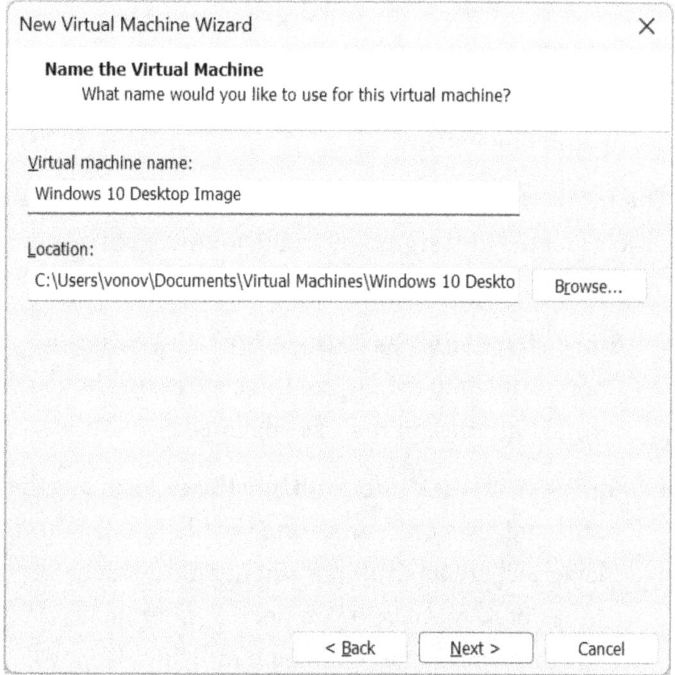

Figure 6-43. *Naming the New Virtual Machine*

11. In the **Location** box, you will see that the default folder location is used to store the virtual machine files. This is the documents folder on the host machine. If you want to change this, then click the **Browse...** button and select a new folder location.

12. Now click **Next >**. You will now see the **Specify Disk Capacity** screen.

13. The first option is for **Maximum disk size (GB)** which allows you to specify the size of the virtual hard disk that will be created for the operating system of this virtual machine.

In this case, the recommended size of 60GB has already been entered. You can change this if required by typing in a new size value or by using the up and down arrows.

14. The next two options define how the virtual hard disk is created and stored, with the following two options available:

    - **Store virtual disk as a single file** - This basically does as the name suggests and creates one large virtual hard disk of the size specified.
    - **Split virtual disk into multiple files** - Again, as the name suggests, instead of one big file, Workstation Player will create multiple smaller files which are easier to manage if you need to migrate or copy the virtual machine. Each individual file will grow sequentially as the virtual hard disk fills. We will show this once the virtual machine has been created when we look at the different files Workstation Pro creates when creating a new virtual machine. The **Specify Disk Capacity** screen is shown in Figure 6-44.

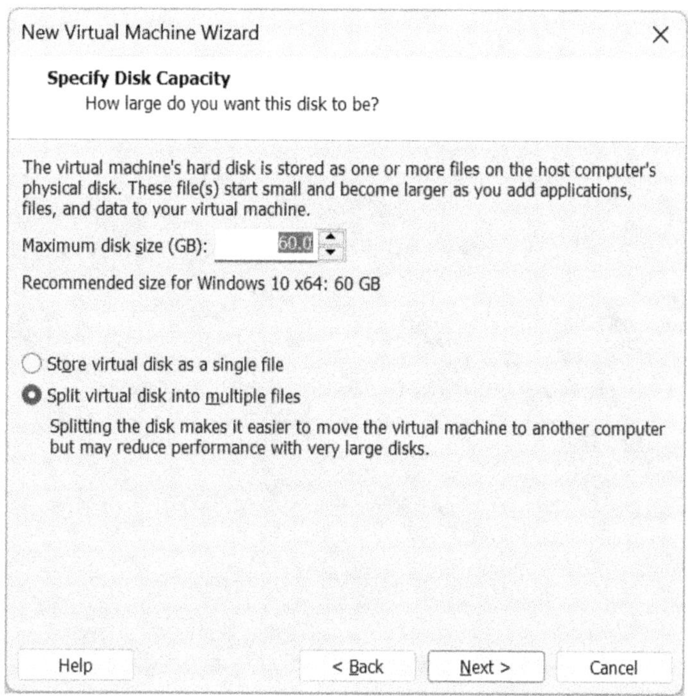

Figure 6-44. *Specifying the Disk Capacity*

15. In this example, click the radio button for **Split virtual disk into multiple files** and then click **Next >**.

16. You will now see the **Ready to Create Virtual Machine** screen as shown in Figure 6-45.

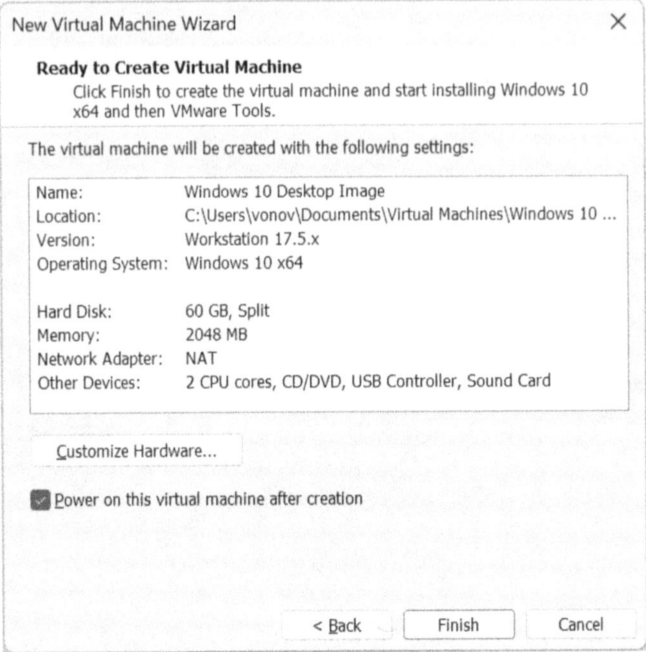

Figure 6-45. *Ready to Create Virtual Machine*

17. This screen displays the selected configuration of how the virtual machine will be created. You also have the option to customize the hardware by adding additional hardware to the virtual machine.

    You can do this by clicking the **Customize Hardware...** button which will enable you to change the configuration of memory, processors, CD ROM drives, network adapters, USB controllers, sound cards, and display settings.

    There is also the option to add any new hardware that is required by clicking the **Add...** button. We covered this in greater detail in Volume 1 of the *Workstation Pro* book.

In this example, we are going to stick with the default options as shown in Figure 6-46.

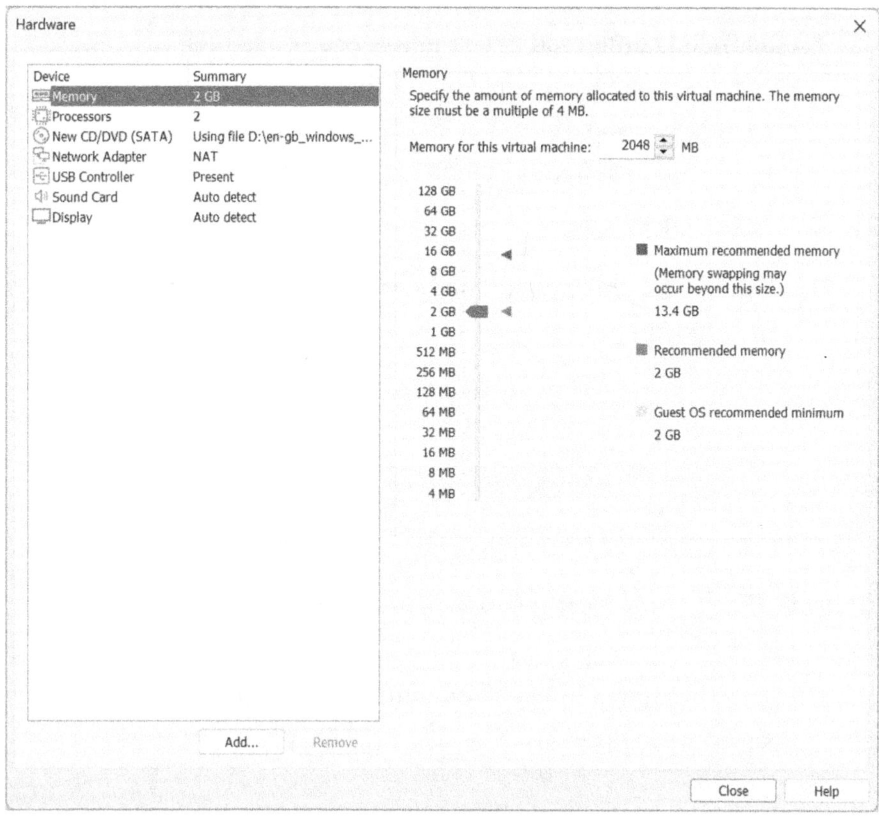

Figure 6-46. *Customizing Hardware Screen*

18. Click **Close** on the customize hardware screen, if you clicked it, to return to the **Ready to Crete Virtual Machine** screen to complete the configuration.

19. The final option is the check box for **Power on this virtual machine after creation**. Selecting this option means that as soon as the virtual machine has been configured, it will power on, and in this case, as we have attached an ISO image of Windows 10, this will boot from that ISO to the Windows 10 setup and installation screens.

20. Now click **Finish**.

21. You will see the creation of the virtual hard disk and the following message as shown in Figure 6-47.

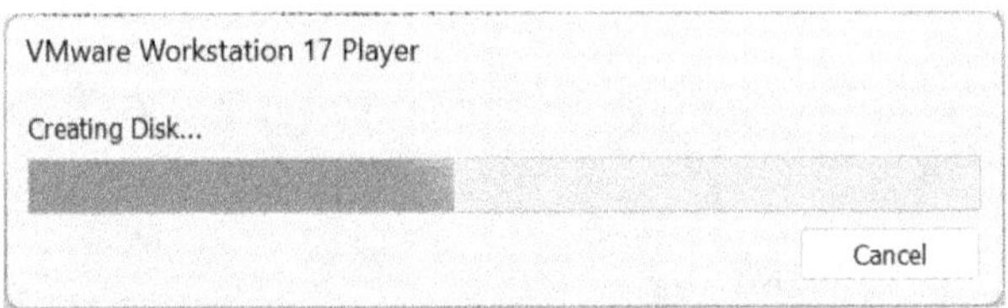

Figure 6-47. *Virtual Hard Disk Being Created*

22. The virtual machine will boot to **Windows Setup** as shown in Figure 6-48.

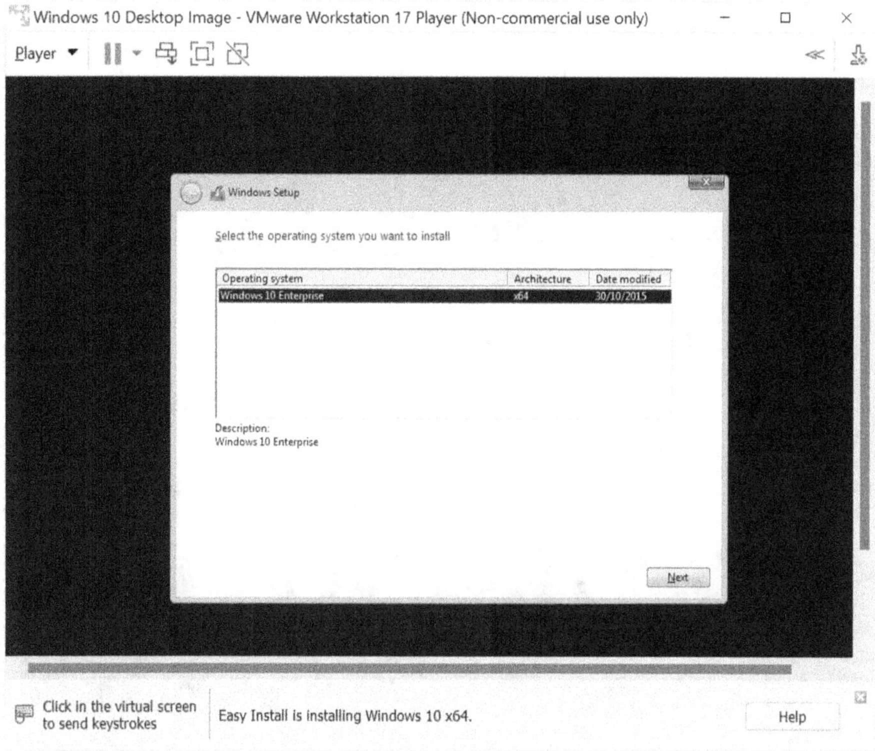

Figure 6-48. *New Virtual Machine Booted to Windows Setup*

The next steps are not VMware Workstation related and are the standard tasks you would complete to install Windows 10 regardless of this being a virtual machine.

As such, one of the most important tasks is to install VMware Tools which in this case was completed automatically as we are using the Easy Install option for installing the OS.

Once installation has successfully completed, you will see the desktop of the virtual machine and that it is ready to use as shown in Figure 6-49.

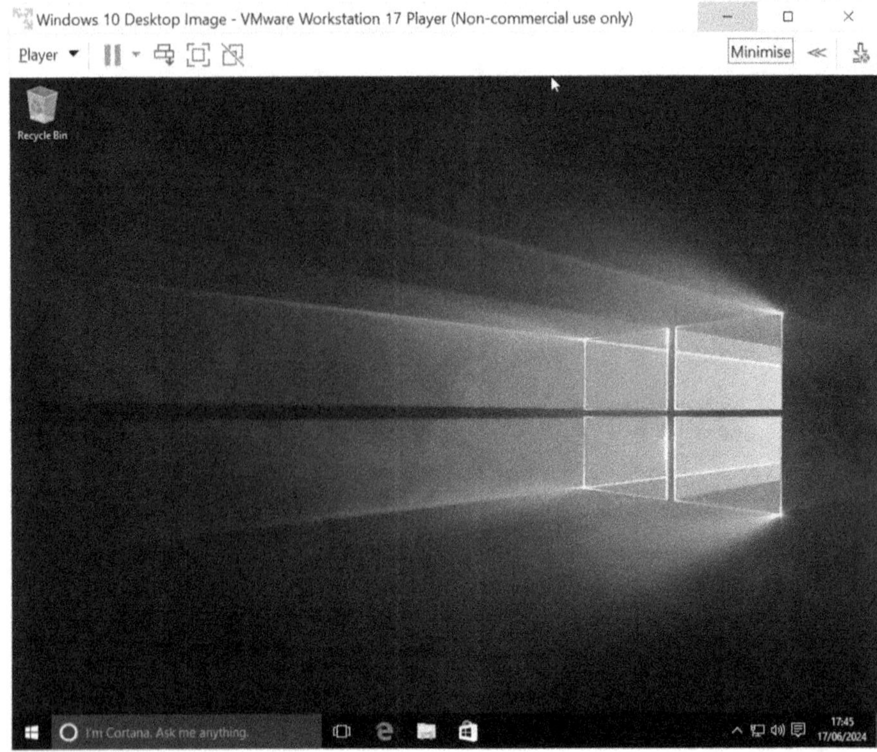

Figure 6-49. *New Windows 10 Virtual Machine Completed Build*

We have now successfully built a virtual machine in Workstation Player. In the next section, we are going to look at adding an existing virtual machine.

Adding an Existing Virtual Machine

Previously, we walked through the steps required to build a brand-new virtual machine from scratch.

In this section, we are going to look at adding an existing virtual machine to Workstation Player. This could be a machine that has been created using Workstation Player, Workstation Pro, or another VMware solution. In the use case of BYOD, this could be a corporate desktop machine that you use in Workstation Player to have access to a corporate desktop environment on your own device.

To add an existing virtual machine to Workstation Player, follow the steps described:

1. Click **Home** from the left-hand library pane.
2. Now click **Open a Virtual Machine**.
3. You will see the **Open Virtual Machine** screen open which is a Windows Explorer window open that allows you to navigate to the location of the virtual machine files for the virtual machine you want to add to the Workstation Player library as shown in Figure 6-50.

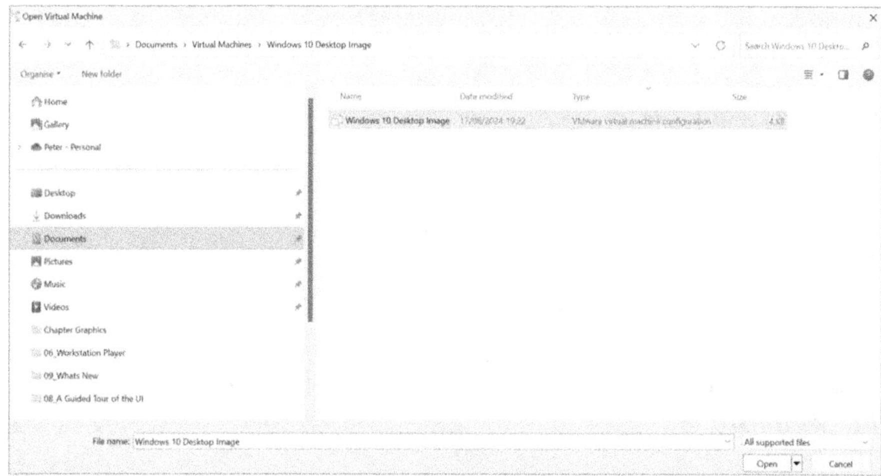

Figure 6-50. *Navigating to the Virtual Machine to Open*

4. Now click the **Open** button.

5. The virtual machine, in this example the Windows 10 desktop image, has now been added to the library whereupon you can now power it on and use it as shown in Figure 6-51.

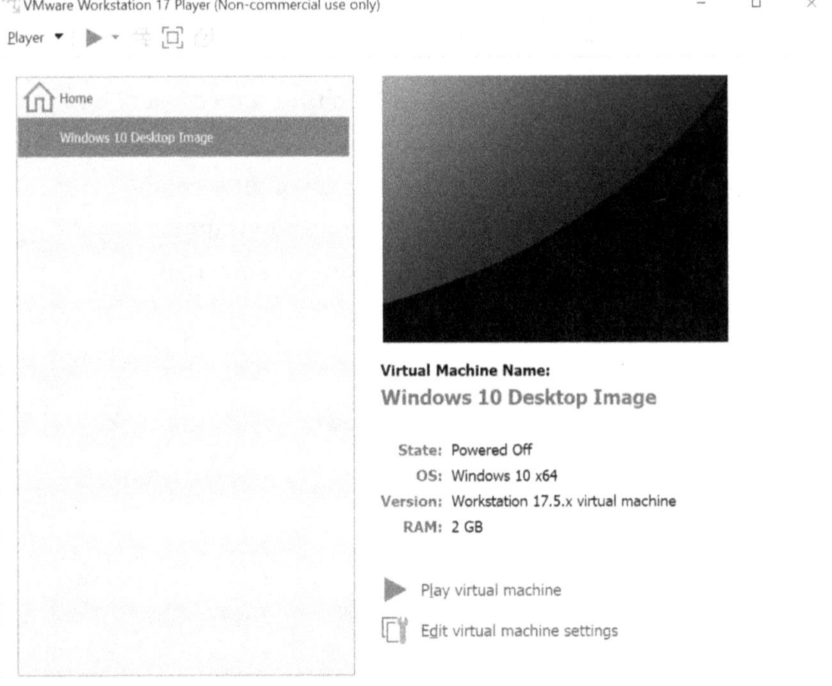

Figure 6-51. *Virtual Machine Added to the Workstation Player Library*

We have now successfully demonstrated the process for adding an already existing virtual machine to the Workstation Player library.

In the next section, we are going to take a brief look at a couple of management or housekeeping tasks you can perform on virtual machines in the library.

Managing an Existing Virtual Machine

With virtual machines in the library, there are a few options available for managing these virtual machines.

If you right-click the virtual machine in the library pane, you will see that a contextual menu appears with a few additional menu options.

This is shown in Figure 6-52.

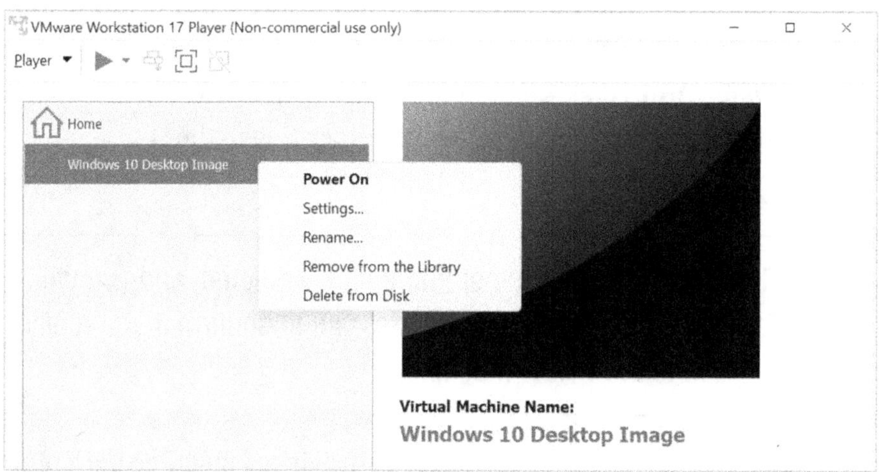

***Figure 6-52.** Additional Menu Options*

These options are as follows:

- **Power on** - Powers on the virtual machine.
- **Settings** - Launches the configuration page where you can configure the virtual hardware settings and options.
- **Rename** - Allows you to rename the virtual machine. This is the name in the library pane, and any new name is not reflected in the filenames of the files that make up the virtual machine.

- **Remove from the library** – Removes the virtual machine from the library view but does not delete any of the virtual machine's files or virtual disks.

Note You won't see any form of warning, and the virtual machine will immediately be deleted from the inventory and no longer appear in the library.

- **Delete from disk** – Removes the virtual machine from the library view and deletes all files relating to the virtual machine.

Note The virtual machine is not immediately deleted, and you will see the following warning box pop-up for you to confirm if you really did want to delete the virtual machine.

Once deleted, there is no way of getting the virtual machine back other than if you had a backup that you could restore from. The warning box is shown in Figure 6-53.

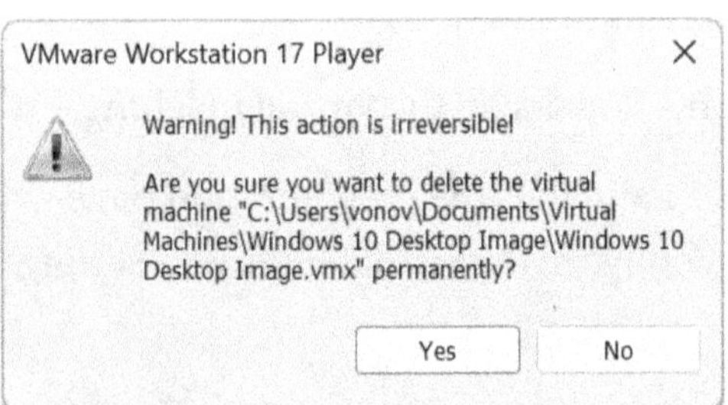

Figure 6-53. *Warning Box for Deleting a Virtual Machine*

Speaking of contextual menus, if you right-click the **Home** entry in the library view, you will see that there are two options there too as shown in Figure 6-54.

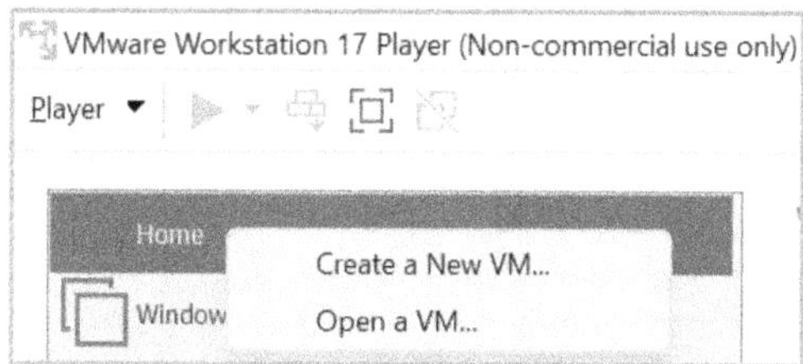

Figure 6-54. *Contextual Menu Options for the Library Home*

These options are for creating a new virtual machine or opening an existing virtual machine.

We have now completed our overview of Workstation Player.

Summary

In this chapter, we have introduced you to VMware Workstation Player and its use cases in enabling end users to run virtual machines on their Windows endpoint devices.

We then went on to show you how to download the software and then how to install and configure it ready for creating or using existing virtual machines.

Once installed, we took a brief look at the user interface and the menu options and how to navigate the product.

Finally, we walked through the steps of how to build and configure a new virtual machine, using a Windows 10 desktop as an example, and then how to add and open an already existing virtual machine.

In the next chapter, we are going to look at how to install additional operating systems on Workstation Pro. In Volume 1 of the *Workstation Pro* book, we installed ESXi and vCenter Server as well as Windows desktop and server operating systems as examples, but in the next chapter, we are going to look at a Linux operating system as well as an alternative hypervisor solution.

CHAPTER 7

Creating Alternative OS VMs

In this chapter, we are going to build on what we covered in Volume 1 of this book and create and configure some more virtual machines but this time running alternative operating systems.

The alternative OS's we are going to cover are for Ubuntu Linux, and given the current climate of people looking at alternative hypervisors, we are going to install one of the solutions that is becoming more popular: Proxmox.

Building an Ubuntu Virtual Machine

To build and configure a new virtual machine, follow the steps described:

1. Launch Workstation Pro.
2. Click the **File** option from the menu and then select the option for **New Virtual Machine** as shown in Figure 7-1. We also have a folder called **Chapter 7 VMs** in which we are going to create the virtual machines for this chapter.

P. von Oven, *Learning VMware Workstation Pro for Windows: Volume 2*,
https://doi.org/10.1007/979-8-8688-0864-7_7

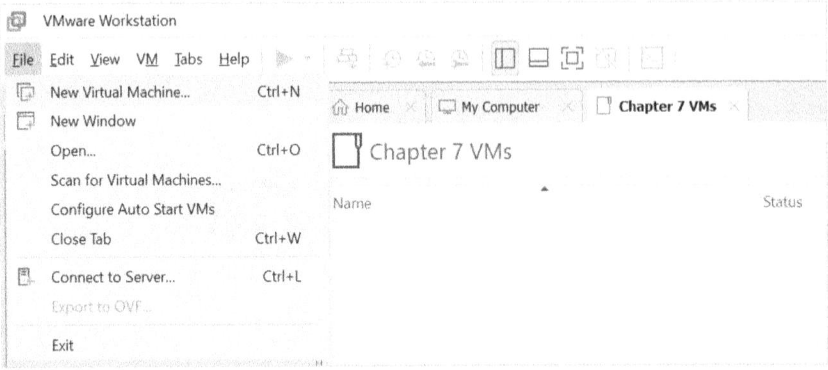

Figure 7-1. Creating a New Virtual Machine

3. You will now see the **Welcome to the New Virtual Machine Wizard** screen as shown in Figure 7-2.

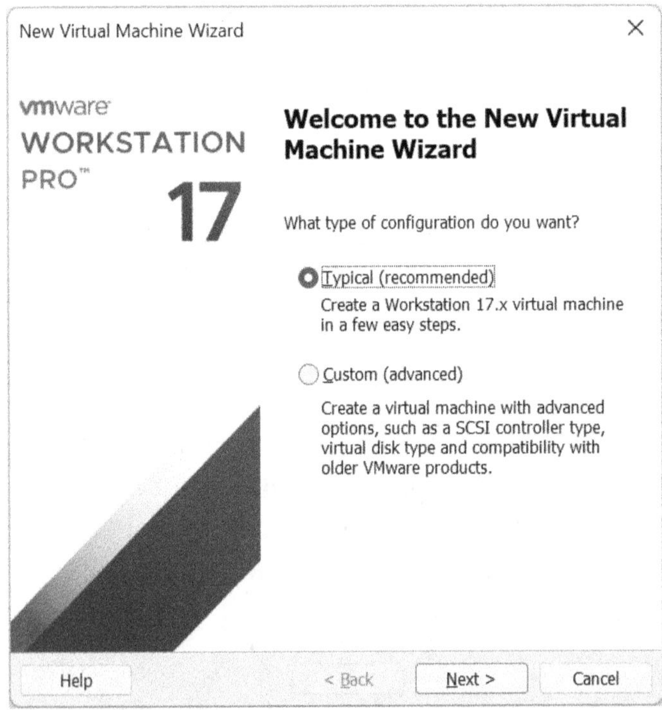

Figure 7-2. Welcome to the New Virtual Machine Wizard Screen

4. Click the radio button for **Typical (recommended)**.
5. Now click the **Next** > button.
6. You will see the **Guest Operating System Installation** screen.
7. On this screen, you have the option of selecting the source of the installation. You have the following choices:
    - The first option is for installing the operating system from an installation disk with that installation disk inserted into a CD ROM drive for example. You would then select the drive letter from the drop-down menu.
    - The second option is to install from an ISO image to which you can browse to.
    - The final option is to choose not to install the OS and just create a blank virtual hard drive and then install the chosen operating system at a later date.

The Guest Operating System Installation screen is shown in Figure 7-3.

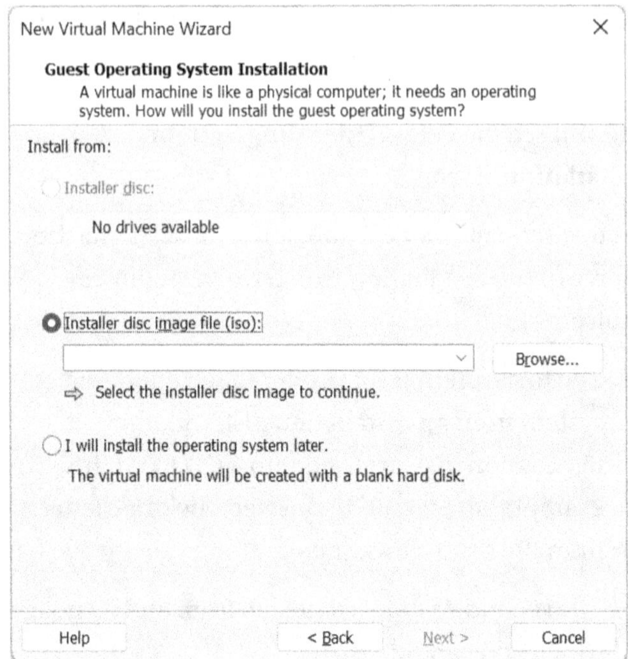

Figure 7-3. *Guest Operating System Installation Screen*

8. In this example, click the radio button for **Installer disc image file (iso)** and then click **Browse...**. You will see a **Browse for ISO Image** window open as shown in Figure 7-4.

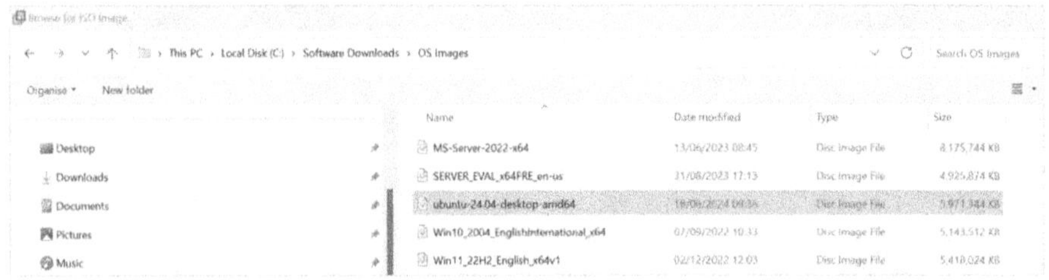

Figure 7-4. *Browse for ISO Image Screen*

9. Navigate to the location of the ISO file required; click to select it, in this case the Ubuntu Desktop ISO image; and then click **Open**.

10. You will return to the **Guest Operating System Installation** screen where in the **Installer disc image file (iso)** box, you will now see the full path to the selected ISO image entered as shown in Figure 7-5.

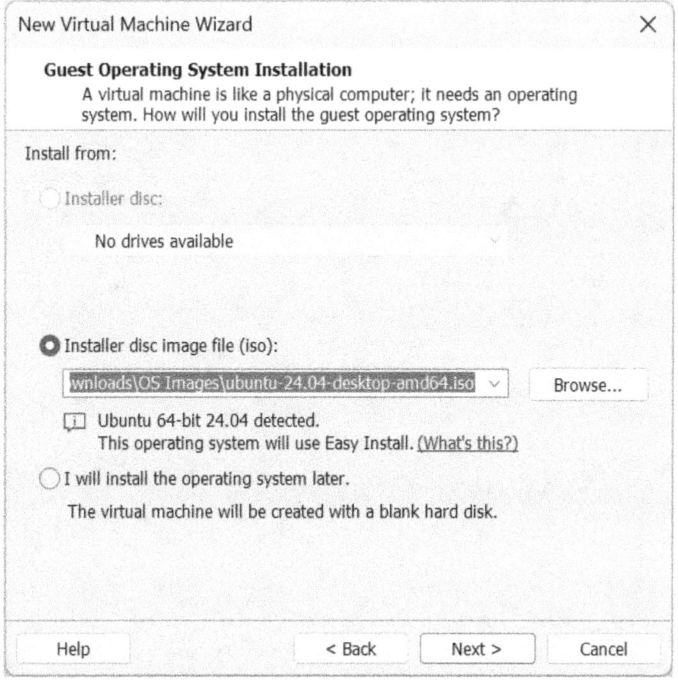

Figure 7-5. *ISO Image Selected*

11. Now click **Next** >.

12. You will now see the **Easy Install Information** screen where you can personalize the Linux installation.

13. In the **Full name** field, type in your name.
14. In the **User name** field, type in the username you want for your login.
15. Then, in the **Password** field, type in the password you want to use for this user account.
16. Finally, in the **Confirm** field, type the password in again. This is shown in Figure 7-6.

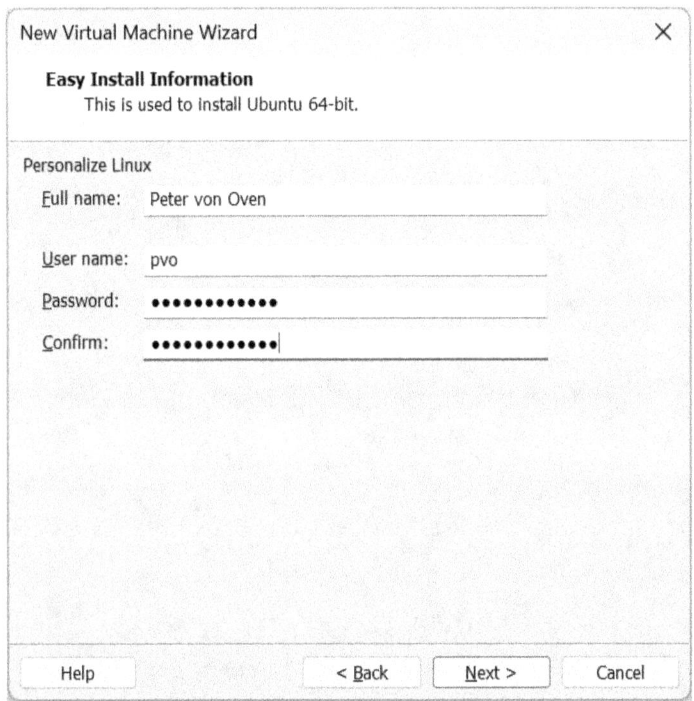

Figure 7-6. *Easy Install Information*

17. Once you have completed the details, click **Next** >.
18. You will now see the **Name the Virtual Machine** screen.
19. In the **Virtual machine name** box, type in a unique name for the virtual machine. Don't forget that the virtual machine name doesn't just appear in the library; it is also used as the file names for the virtual machine configuration file and virtual hard disk files. In this example, we have called it **Ubuntu 64-bit**.
20. In the **Location** box, you will see that the default folder location is used to store the virtual machine files. If you want to change this, then click the **Browse...** button and select a new folder location.

    The **Name the Virtual Machine** screen is shown in Figure 7-7.

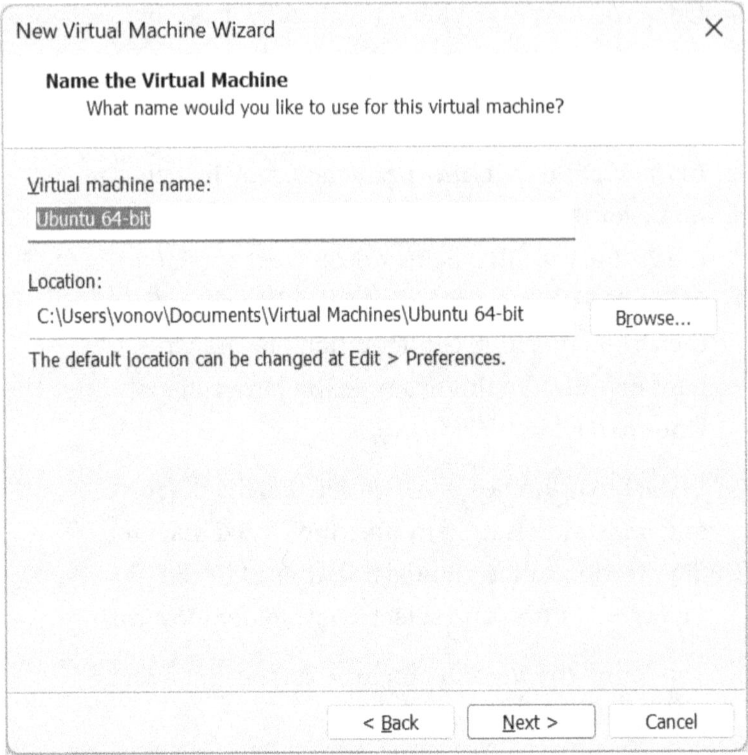

Figure 7-7. *Naming the Virtual Machine*

21. Now click **Next** >.
22. You will now see the **Specify Disk Capacity** screen.
23. The first option is for **Maximum disk size (GB)** which allows you to specify the size of the virtual hard disk that will be created for the operating system of this virtual machine. In this case, the recommended size of 60GB has already been entered. You can change this if required by typing in a new size value or by using the up and down arrows.

24. The next two options define how the virtual hard disk is created and stored, with the following two options available:

    - **Store virtual disk as a single file** - This basically does as the name suggests and creates one large virtual hard disk of the size specified.

    - **Split virtual disk into multiple files** - Again, as the name suggests, instead of one big file, Workstation Pro will create multiple smaller files which are easier to manage if you need to migrate or copy the virtual machine. Each individual file will grow sequentially as the virtual hard disk fills. We will show this once the virtual machine has been created when we look at the different files Workstation Pro creates when creating a new virtual machine. The **Specify Disk Capacity** screen is shown in Figure 7-8.

Figure 7-8. *Specify Disk Capacity Screen*

25. In this example, click the radio button for **Split virtual disk into multiple files** and then click **Next >**.

26. You will now see the **Ready to Create Virtual Machine** screen. This screen displays the selected configuration of how the virtual machine will be created. You also have the option to customize the hardware by adding additional hardware to the virtual machine.

27. The final option is the check box for **Power on this virtual machine after creation**.

    Selecting this option means that as soon as the virtual machine has been configured, it will power on and, in this case, as we have attached an ISO image of Ubuntu, this will boot from that ISO to the Ubuntu setup and installation screens.

28. The **Ready to Create Virtual Machine** screen is shown in Figure 7-9.

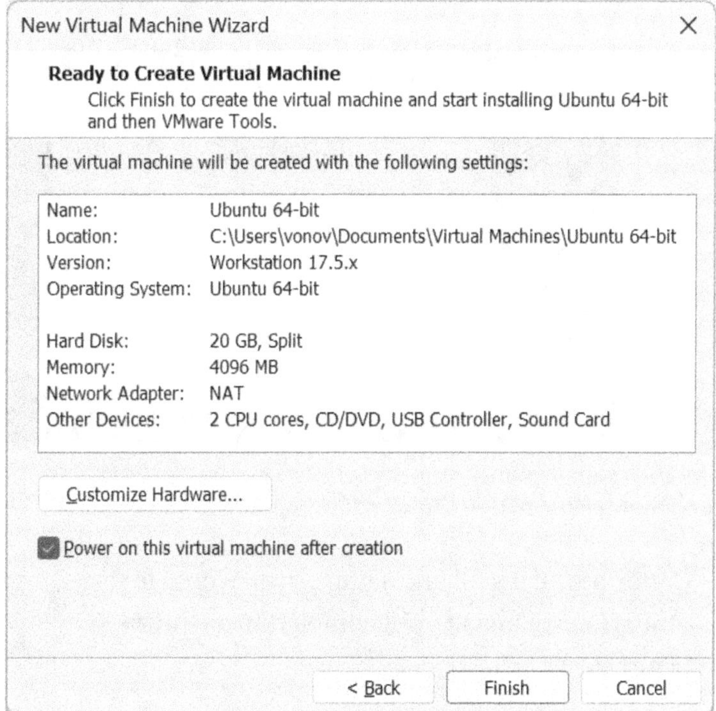

Figure 7-9. *Ready to Create Virtual Machine*

29. Now click the **Finish button**. You will see the creation of the virtual hard disk message appear as the disk is created ready for the installation of the operating system.

30. Next, as the ISO image was attached as part of the configuration, it will be mounted, and the virtual machine will boot from it displaying the OS installation screen. In this case for Ubuntu as shown in Figure 7-10.

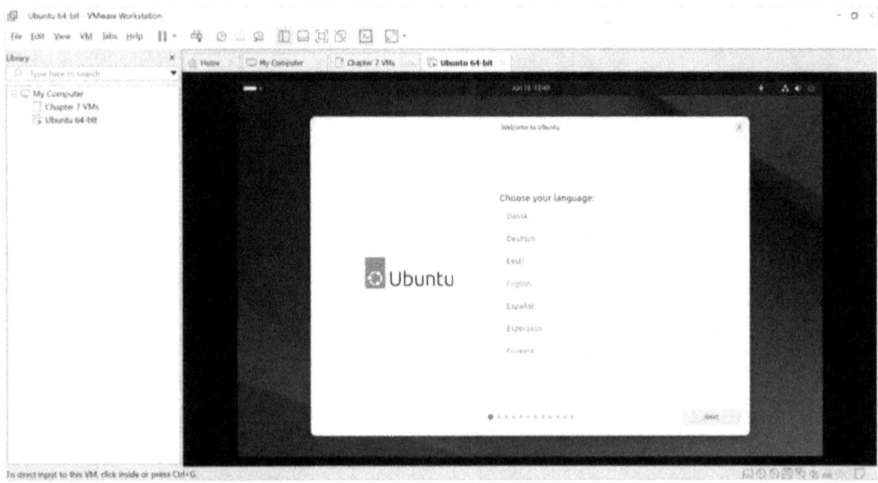

Figure 7-10. *Virtual Machine Booted to Ubuntu Setup*

31. Continue the install and setup as you would for any other Ubuntu install until completion as shown in Figure 7-11.

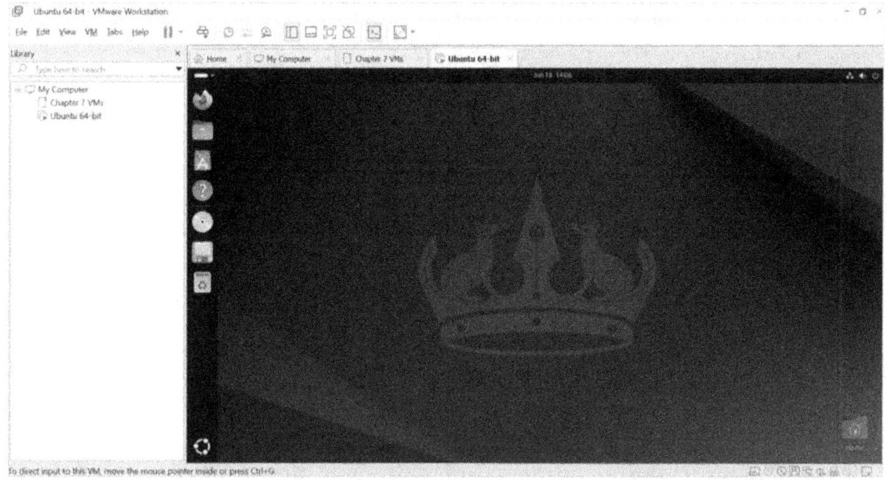

Figure 7-11. *Ubuntu Virtual Machine Setup Complete*

You have now successfully built and configured an Ubuntu Desktop virtual machine.

In the next section, we are going to look at creating an alternative hypervisor host machine using Proxmox as the hypervisor.

Building a Proxmox Virtual Machine

The second operating system that we are going to look at is actually a hypervisor, and so we will be building a nested environment. This demonstrates another great use case for Workstation Pro in enabling you to test new solutions without the need for building out infrastructure platforms.

For this example, given its rise in popularity, we are going to look at installing Proxmox.

To build and configure a new virtual machine for running Proxmox, follow the steps described:

1. Launch Workstation Pro.
2. Click the **File** option from the menu and then select the option for **New Virtual Machine** as shown in Figure 7-12. Again, we are using the folder called **Chapter 7 VMs** in which we are going to create the virtual machines for this chapter.

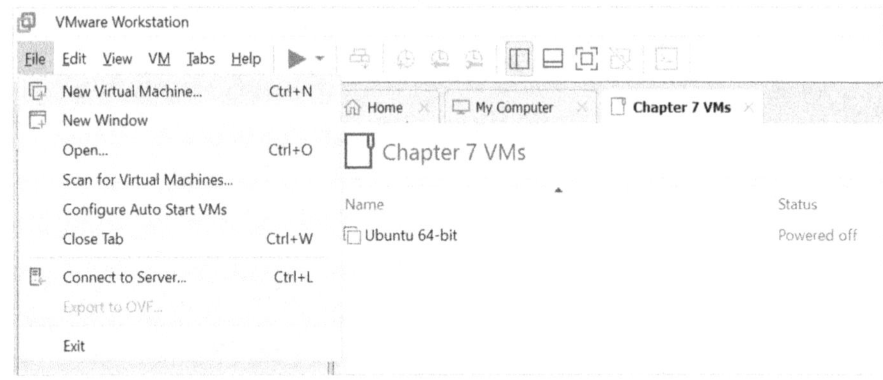

***Figure 7-12.** Creating a New Virtual Machine for Proxmox*

3. You will now see the **Welcome to the New Virtual Machine Wizard** screen as shown in Figure 7-13.

Figure 7-13. *Welcome to the New Virtual Machine Wizard Screen*

4. Click the radio button for **Typical (recommended)**.
5. Now click the **Next** > button.
6. You will see the **Guest Operating System Installation** screen.
7. As before, you have the option of selecting the source of the installation. You have the following choices:
   - The first option is for installing the operating system from an installation disk with that installation disk inserted into a CD ROM drive for example. You would then select the drive letter from the drop-down menu.

- The second option is to install from an ISO image to which you can browse to.
- The final option is to choose not to install the OS and just create a blank virtual hard drive and then install the chosen operating system at a later date.

The Guest Operating System Installation screen is shown in Figure 7-14.

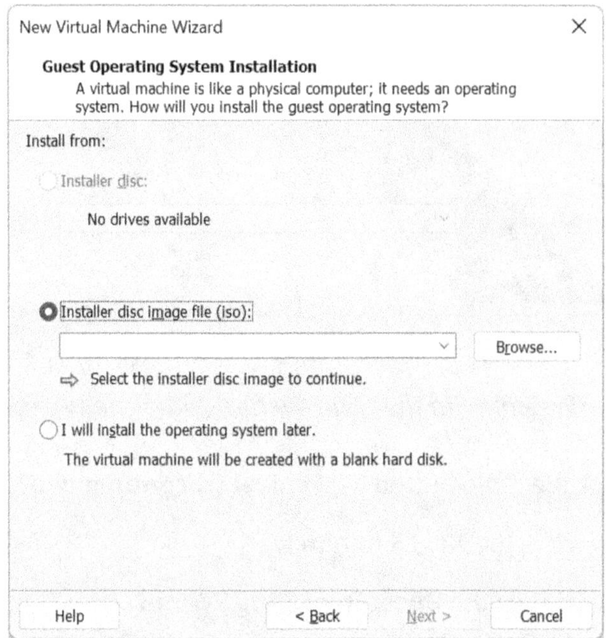

***Figure 7-14.** Guest Operating System Installation screen*

8. Click the radio button for **Installer disc image file (iso)** and then click **Browse....** You will see a **Browse for ISO Image** window open as shown in Figure 7-15.

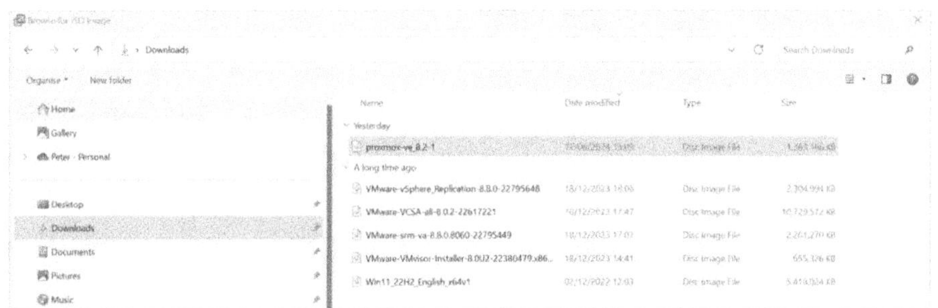

Figure 7-15. *Browse for ISO Image Screen*

9. Navigate to the location of the ISO file required, click to select it, in this case the Proxmox-VE ISO image, and then click **Open**.

10. You will return to the **Guest Operating System Installation** screen.

11. In the **Installer disc image file (iso)** box you will now see the full path to the selected ISO image entered as shown in Figure 7-16.

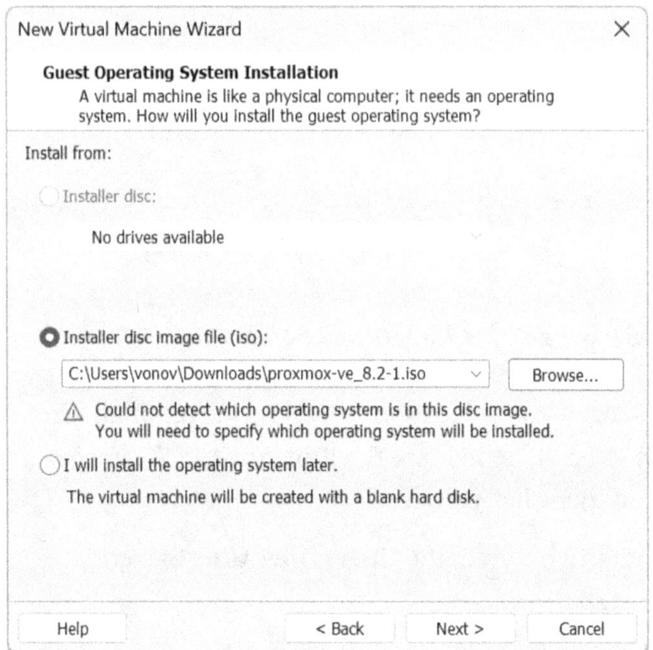

Figure 7-16. *ISO Image Selected*

You will see that Workstation Pro was unable to automatically detect which operating system the disc image file relates to, and so you will need to specify that in the next configuration screen.

---

12. Now click **Next >**.
13. You will now see the **Select a Guest Operating System** screen as shown in Figure 7-17.

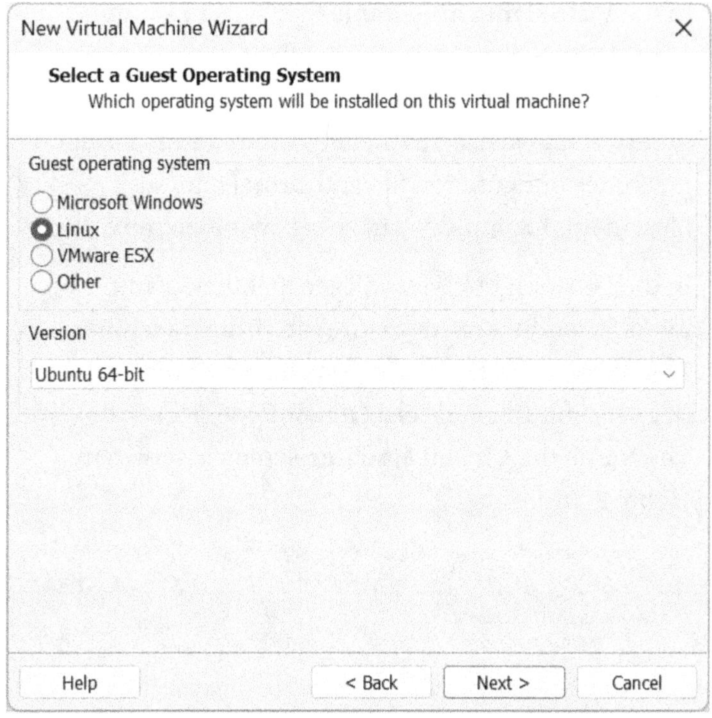

***Figure 7-17.** Select an Operating System for the New VM*

14. Under **Guest operating system**, click the radio button for **Linux.**

15. Now under the **Version** heading, click the drop-down menu and select the option for **Ubuntu 64-bit.**

16. Now click **Next >**.

17. You will now see the **Name the Virtual Machine** screen.

18. In the **Virtual machine name** box, type in a unique name for the virtual machine. Don't forget that the virtual machine name doesn't just appear in the library; it is also used as the file names for the virtual machine configuration file and virtual hard disk files. In this example, we have called it **Proxmox**.

19. In the Location box, you will see that the default folder location is used to store the virtual machine files. If you want to change this, then click the Browse... button and select a new folder location. The **Name the Virtual Machine** screen is shown in Figure 7-18.

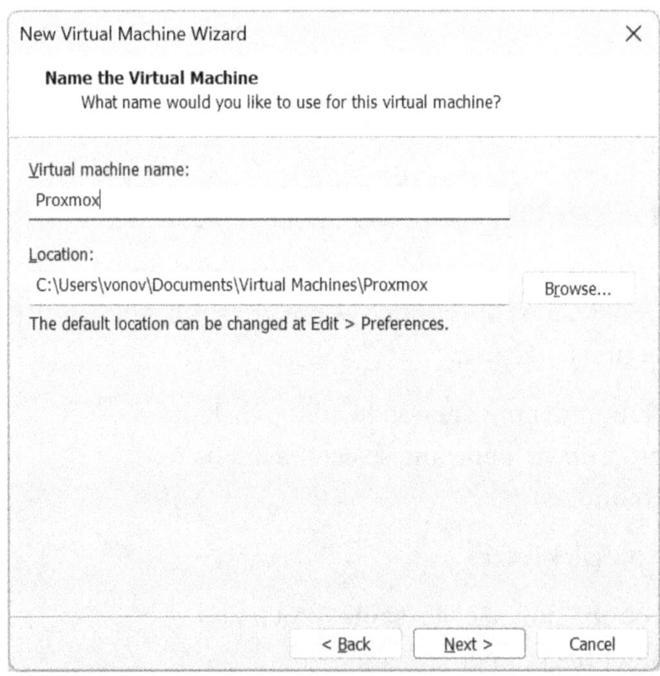

Figure 7-18. *Naming the Virtual Machine*

20. Now click **Next** >. You will now see the **Specify Disk Capacity** screen.

21. The first option is for **Maximum disk size (GB)** which allows you to specify the size of the virtual hard disk that will be created for the operating system of this virtual machine. In this case, the recommended size of 60GB has already been entered. You can change this if required by typing in a new size value or by using the up and down arrows.

22. The next two options define how the virtual hard disk is created and stored, with the following two options available:

    - **Store virtual disk as a single file** - This basically does as the name suggests and creates one large virtual hard disk of the size specified.

    - **Split virtual disk into multiple files** - Again, as the name suggests, instead of one big file, Workstation Pro will create multiple smaller files which are easier to manage if you need to migrate or copy the virtual machine. Each individual file will grow sequentially as the virtual hard disk fills. We will show this once the virtual machine has been created when we look at the different files Workstation Pro creates when creating a new virtual machine. The **Specify Disk Capacity** screen is shown in Figure 7-19.

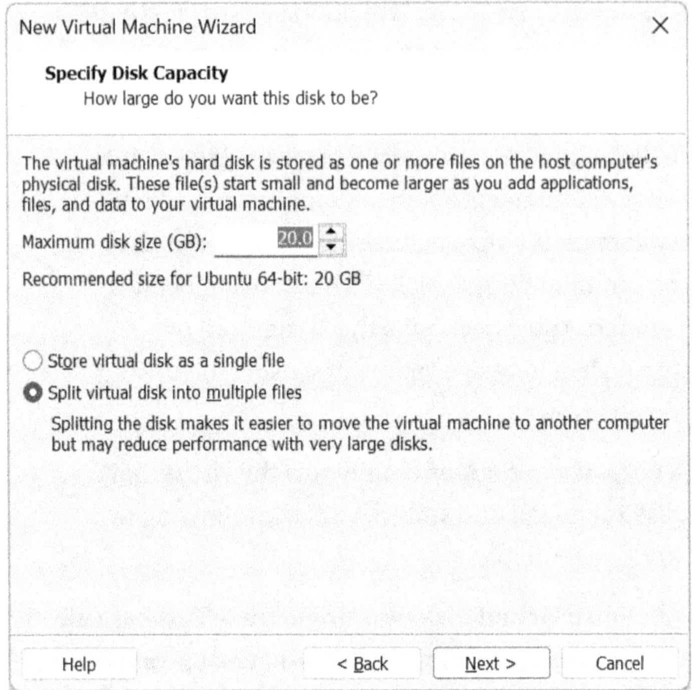

Figure 7-19. *Specify Disk Capacity Screen*

23. In this example, click the radio button for **Split virtual disk into multiple files**.
24. Now click **Next >**.
25. You will now see the **Ready to Create Virtual Machine** screen.
26. This screen displays the selected configuration of how the virtual machine will be created. You also have the option to customize the hardware by adding additional hardware to the virtual machine.
27. This is shown in Figure 7-20.

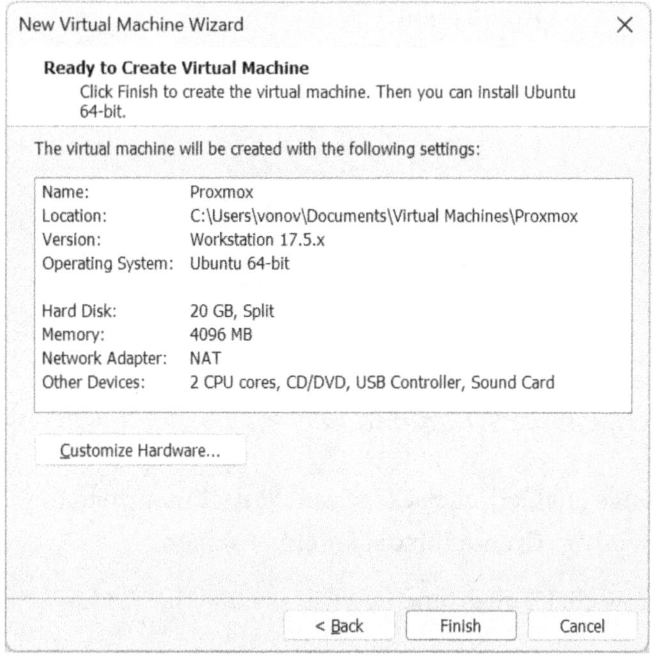

Figure 7-20. *Ready to Create Virtual Machine*

As we are installing another hypervisor, in this example Proxmox, it has a requirement for Intel VT to be enabled on the CPU, so therefore, we need to customize the hardware which we will do in the following steps:

28. Click the **Customize Hardware...** button.
29. From the **Hardware** tab, click the option for **Processors**.
30. Under the **Virtualization engine** option on the right-hand side, check the box for **Virtualize Intel VT-x/EPT or AMD-V/RVI**.

31. This is shown in Figure 7-21.

Virtual Machine Settings

Hardware Options

Device	Summary
Memory	4 GB
Processors	2
Hard Disk (SCSI)	20 GB
CD/DVD (SATA)	Using file C:\Users\vonov\Dow...
Network Adapter	NAT
USB Controller	Present
Sound Card	Auto detect
Display	Auto detect

Processors

Number of processors: 2

Number of cores per processor: 1

Total processor cores: 2

Virtualization engine

- [x] Virtualize Intel VT-x/EPT or AMD-V/RVI
- [ ] Virtualize CPU performance counters
- [ ] Virtualize IOMMU (IO memory management unit)

***Figure 7-21.** Enable Virtualized Intel VT-x*

32. Once enabled, click **Close and you will** return to the **Ready to Create Virtual Machine** screen.

33. Now click Finish, and you will see that the VM has been created as shown in Figure 7-22.

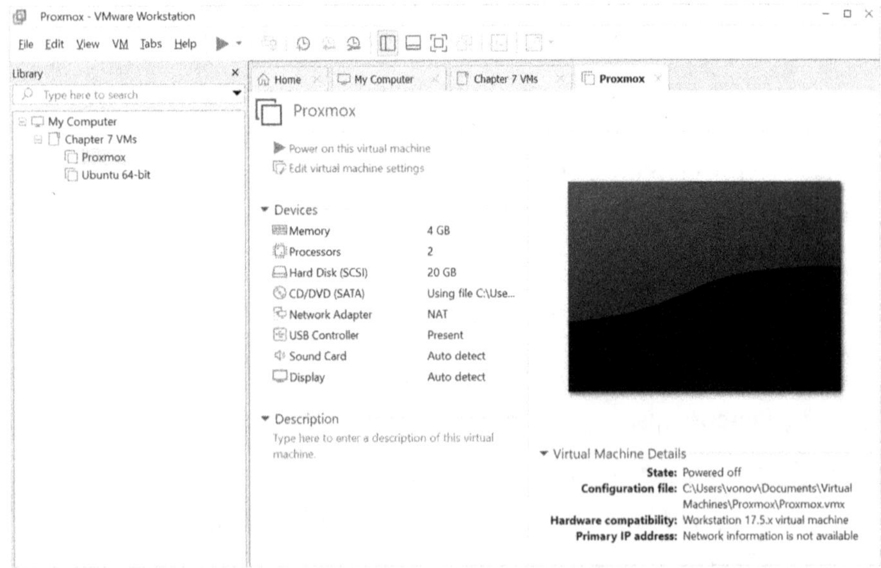

***Figure 7-22.** VM Successfully Created*

You will also see, unlike other VMs created with Easy Install, that there was no check box to power the virtual machine on automatically when you complete the configuration and the VM is built.

You will need to power on the VM manually by clicking the green "play" button and the **Power on this virtual machine** option which is also shown in Figure 7-22.

Once powered on, you will see the **Proxmox VE Installer** as shown in Figure 7-23.

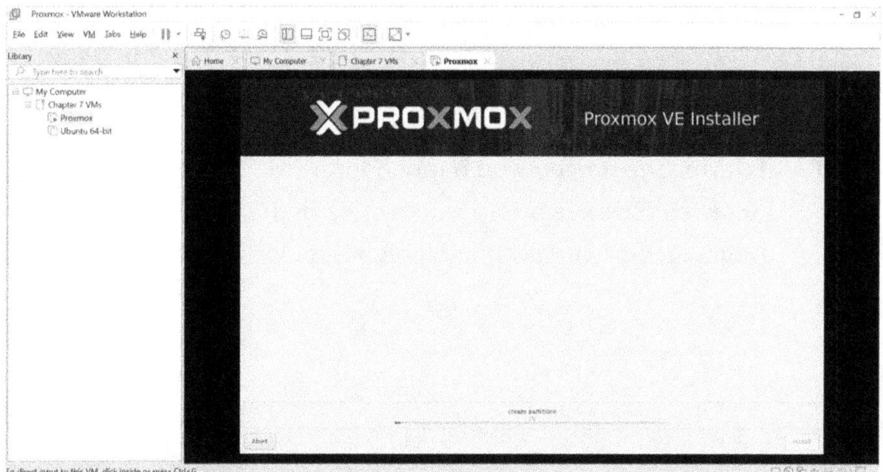

***Figure 7-23.** Proxmox VE Installer*

34. Continue the installation as you would for any other Proxmox installation.

35. The process is shown in Figure 7-24.

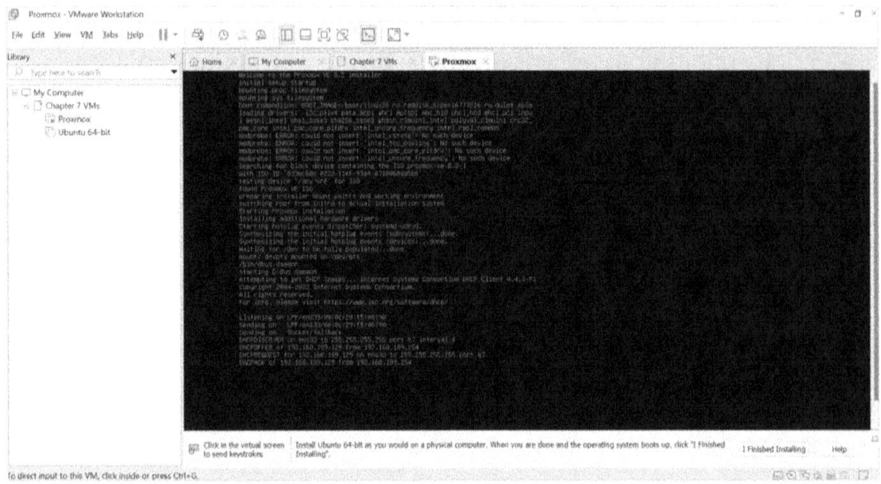

Figure 7-24. *Proxmox Installation Process*

36. If during the process you happen to see the following message pop-up, shown in Figure 7-25, then it means you haven't enabled Intel VT.

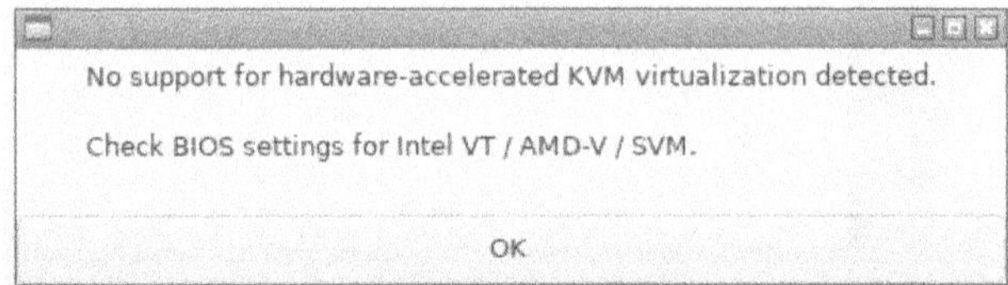

Figure 7-25. *Intel VT Not Enabled Warning*

You will need to power off the VM and enable Intel VT in the hardware settings and then power it back on again to complete the installation.

Once the installation has completed and the VM has rebooted, you will see the console as shown in Figure 7-26.

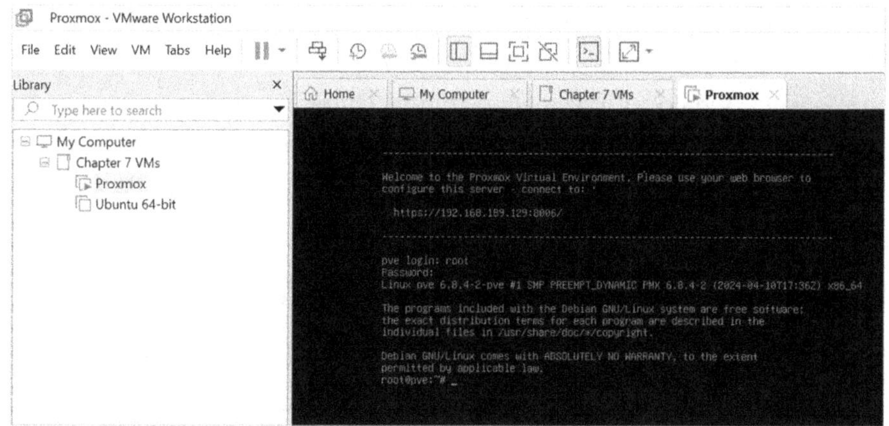

Figure 7-26. *Proxmox Successfully Installed and Running*

As a further check, login and access the console via a web browser to configure it as shown in Figure 7-27.

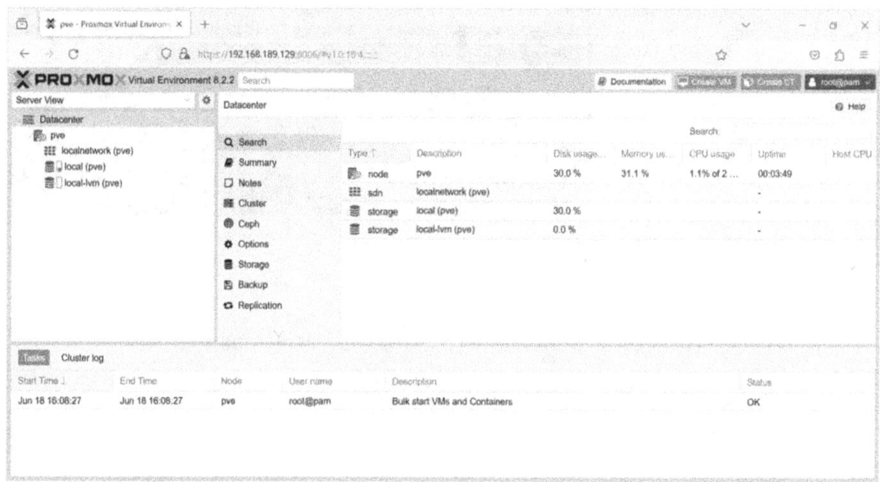

Figure 7-27. *Proxmox Web Console for Management*

Although Proxmox is installed and running, as it was an undetected OS from the start, then VMware Tools will not have been installed and so the VM will not be running at its optimum. Therefore, in the next section, we are going to install VMware Tools to ensure the correct drivers are installed.

Installing VMware Tools for Proxmox

To finish the installation of Proxmox on VMware Workstation Pro, we are going to install VMware Tools as this has not been done automatically.

1. Ensure the Proxmox VM is powered on as shown in Figure 7-28.

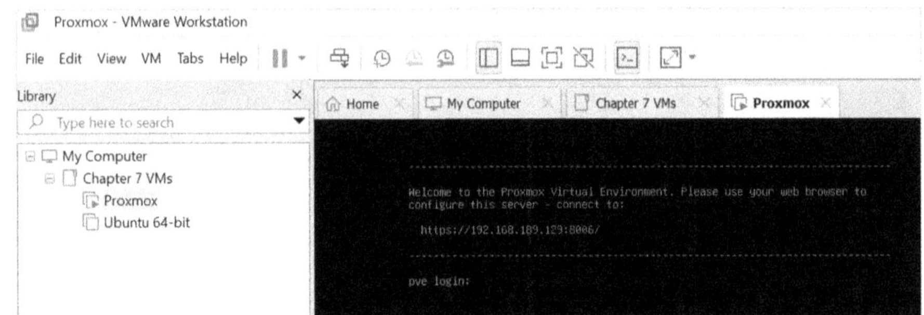

***Figure 7-28.** Proxmox VM Powered On*

2. From the console of the Proxmox VM, login as the root user. Once logged in, you will see the following (Figure 7-29).

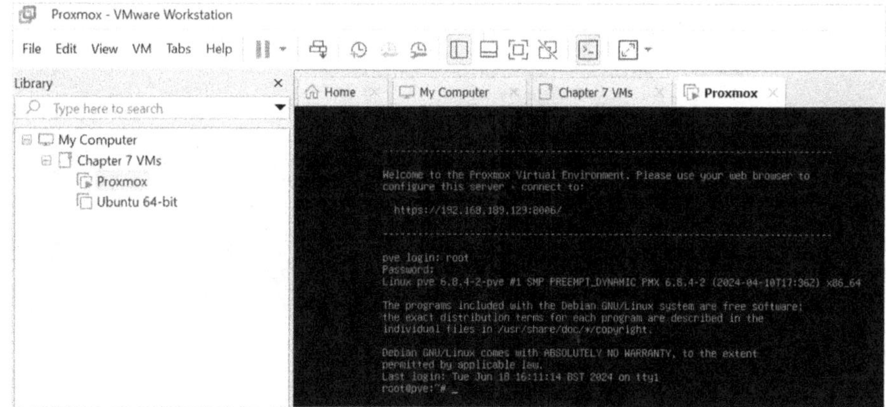

Figure 7-29. Proxmox VM Logged on as Root User

3. At the command line, run the **apt update** command.
4. The command will run as shown as shown in Figure 7-30.

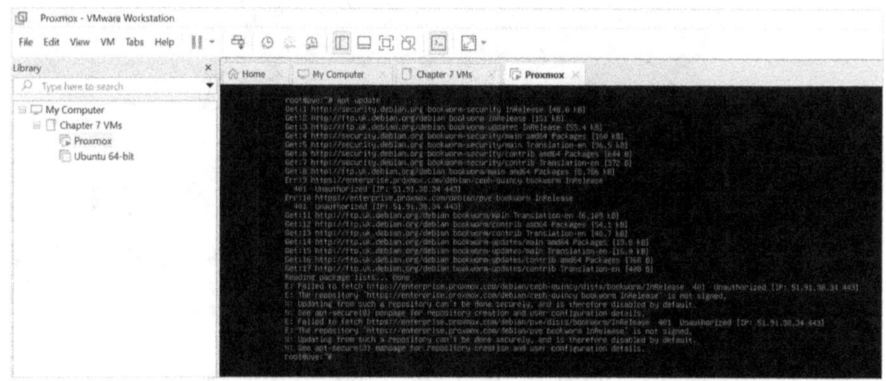

Figure 7-30. Results of Running the apt update Command

5. Now run the **apt install open-vm-tools** command as shown in Figure 7-31, pressing **Y** when prompted to continue. This will install the VMware Tools.

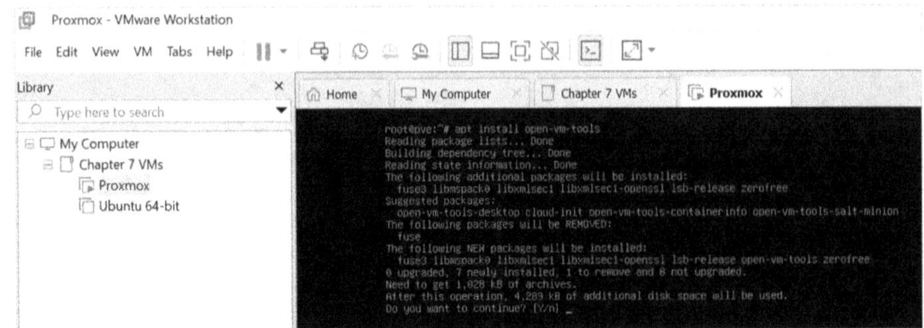

***Figure 7-31.** Running the apt install open-vm-tools Command*

6. The command will run as shown in Figure 7-32. It will take a few minutes to complete.

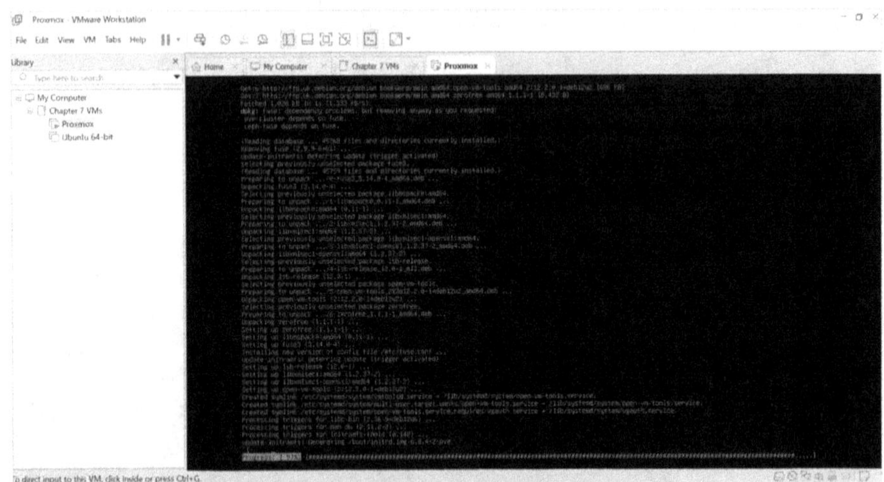

***Figure 7-32.** Results of Running the apt install open-vm-tools Command*

7. Once the installation has completed, run the **systemctl status open-vm-tools.service** command to check that VMware Tools has been successfully installed and is actively running as shown in Figure 7-33.

8. Finally run the **hostnamectl** command to show the details of the system and ensuring that it "knows" it is running on a VMware platform.

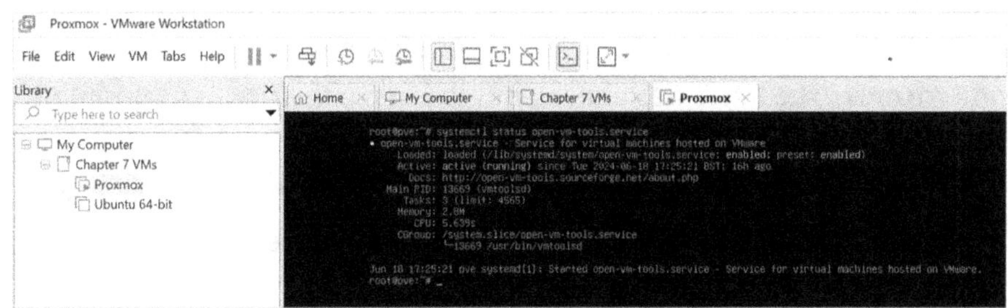

Figure 7-33. *VMware Tools Installed and Running*

9. This output of this command is shown in Figure 7-34.

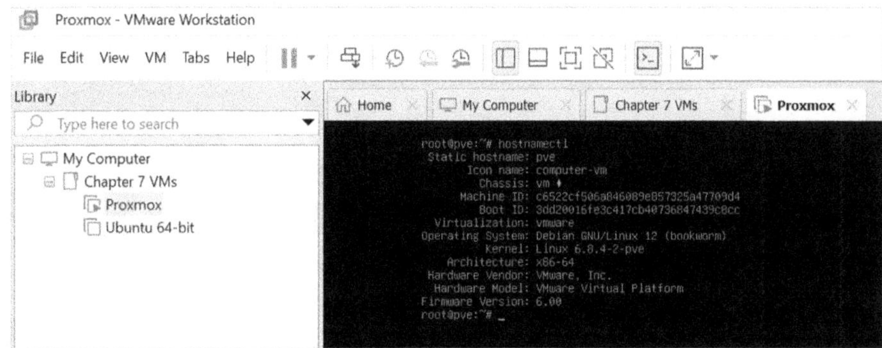

Figure 7-34. *Output of the hostnamectl Command*

You have now successfully installed Proxmox on the VMware Workstation Pro platform and installed the VMware Tools to enable the VM to run at its optimum performance.

Summary

In this chapter, we have looked at a couple of additional virtual machines running non-Windows operating systems.

We focused on just two of the more popular options, Ubuntu Desktop and Proxmox. The latter was chosen purely due to the rise in its popularity showing you how to test it using Workstation Pro.

Next, we looked at how to create the virtual machines and then how to install the operating system. In the case of Proxmox, we also looked at how to install VMware Tools.

In the next chapter, we are going to look at how to install Workstation Pro using the unattended option.

CHAPTER 8

Unattended Installation

In previous chapters of this book and in Volume 1 of the *Workstation Pro* book, we discussed the installation of Workstation Pro and how to install the software; however, that was done using a manual process.

We worked through each of the setup wizard screens manually inputting the required details as we worked through the installation.

In this chapter, we are going to look at how you can perform unattended installations using the command line and the Workstation Pro installer (MSI), covering all the different command line switches available. On the flip side, we will also look at how to uninstall Workstation Pro using the same command line methodology.

As well as using the command line and the Windows Installer, we will also look at how to extract that MSI Windows Installer so that you can also install Workstation Pro in an enterprise environment using Microsoft MECM or Intune.

We will start with the command line using the Workstation installer file and the various switch options.

P. von Oven, *Learning VMware Workstation Pro for Windows: Volume 2*,
https://doi.org/10.1007/979-8-8688-0864-7_8

Installing Workstation Pro Using the Command Line

In this section, we are going to look at how to perform an unattended installation using the Workstation Pro installer (MSI) and the command line options.

Before we look at the unattended installation itself, there are a couple of prerequisites you need to make sure are in place. Especially if you plan to remotely install Workstation Pro using something like SCCM.

Prerequisites

In this section, we are going to look at the prerequisites that you need to make sure are in place before you start the installation.

- Ensure that the host machine onto which you are installing Workstation Pro meets the host system requirements:

  https://docs.vmware.com/en/VMware-Workstation-Pro/17/com.vmware.ws.using.doc/GUID-47896F7A-2C4F-457E-8ED1-6E5AEFDDD64A.html#GUID-47896F7A-2C4F-457E-8ED1-6E5AEFDDD64A

- Ensure that there are no incompatible VMware products already installed on the host machine that might cause a conflict and prevent Workstation Pro from installing. You can check the list of incompatible products using the following link:

  https://docs.vmware.com/en/VMware-Workstation-Pro/17/com.vmware.ws.using.doc/GUID-105FF68B-D0AA-424C-8F4D-7B25845604C5.html#GUID-105FF68B-D0AA-424C-8F4D-7B25845604C5

- You will need the Workstation Pro software downloaded and a valid license key.
- Ensure that the host machine has version 2.0 or later of the MSI runtime engine. This version is available in Windows XP or newer and can be downloaded from Microsoft.

Once the prerequisites have been met, then you can start the installation.

Uninstalling Using the Command Line

In this section, we are going to install Workstation Pro using the MSI installer and the command line switches.

1. Log on to the target host machine as either an administrator account, local administrator, or other account that has permission to install software on the host machine.
2. Open a command line as an administrator shown in Figure 8-1.

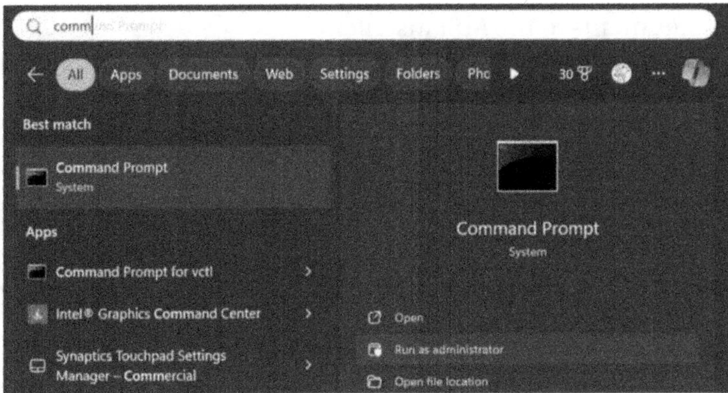

Figure 8-1. *Open Command Prompt As Administrator*

3. If you see the User Account Control warning box pop-up, click **Yes to continue**.

4. In the command line, type the following: `VMware-workstation-full-17.5.2-23775571.exe /s /v"/qn EULAS_AGREED=1 SERIALNUMBER="xxxxx-xxxxx-xxxxx-xxxxx-xxxxx" AUTOSOFTWAREUPDATE=1"` as shown in Figure 8-2.

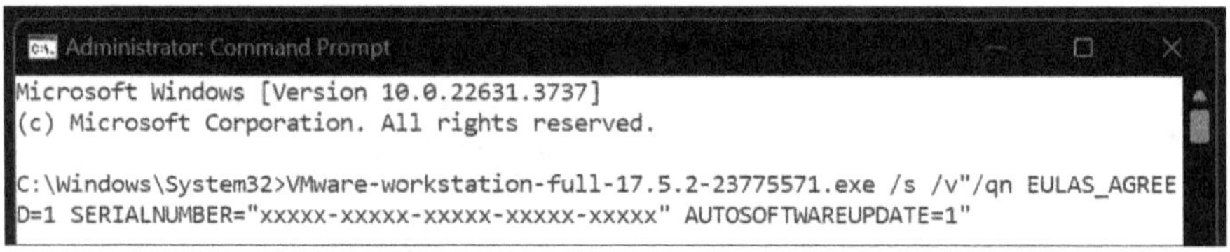

```
Administrator: Command Prompt
Microsoft Windows [Version 10.0.22631.3737]
(c) Microsoft Corporation. All rights reserved.

C:\Windows\System32>VMware-workstation-full-17.5.2-23775571.exe /s /v"/qn EULAS_AGREE
D=1 SERIALNUMBER="xxxxx-xxxxx-xxxxx-xxxxx-xxxxx" AUTOSOFTWAREUPDATE=1"
```

Figure 8-2. *Running the Installer from the Command Line*

It's worth noting that the version number you are installing may be different to the one shown in the example. Also, the build number will potentially be different too.

In this example, we have used a couple of switch options:

- **/s** - Used for silent install
- **/v** - Allows you to pass additional commands and arguments to the MSI installer
- **/qn** - MSIEXEC switch that allows you to run the installer with no user interface

---

Note Double quotes around the file path are important. All the MSI arguments are passed with the /v option. The outer quotes group the MSI arguments, and the double quotes put a quote in that argument.

The arguments passed in this example are for accepting the license agreement, entering the serial number, and switching on the auto update feature for Workstation Pro.

We will cover the options in the next section.

Command Line Switch Options

As you have seen in the previous section, we used a couple of additional command line options for specifying things like the serial number or accepting the license agreement.

In this section, we are going to cover these command line options and what they are used for. In addition to the command itself, additional parameters can also be used.

These are, in some cases, a simple enabled or disabled which is configured by adding either **=1** for enabled or **=0** for disabled to the end of the command. For other commands, specific values will need to be entered which are described in the following:

- **AUTOSOFTWAREUPDATE=1** - Enables automatic upgrades for Workstation Pro when a new build becomes available. This is the default setting.
- **AUTOSOFTWAREUPDATE=0** - Disables automatic upgrades for Workstation Pro when a new build becomes available.
- **DATACOLLECTION=1** - Sends the customer experience information program data to VMware. This is the default setting.
- **DATACOLLECTION=0** - Disables the sending of the customer experience information program data to Vmware.

- **DESKTOP_SHORTCUT=1** – Creates the shortcut on the desktop of the host machine when you install Workstation Pro. This is the default setting.
- **DESKTOP_SHORTCUT=0** – No desktop shortcut is created on the host machine when you install Workstation Pro.
- **EULAS_AGREED=1** – Allows you to silently accept the end user license agreement. Setting to 1 allows you to complete the installation or upgrade.
- **EULAS_AGREED=0** – Allows you to silently accept the end user license agreement. This is the default setting.
- **INSTALLDIR** – Allows you to specify a different directory for the Workstation Pro installation. By default, Workstation Pro is installed into C:\Program Files (86)\VMware\VMware. For example, INSTALLDIR=C:\PVO would install Workstation Pro into a directory called PVO.
- **KEEP_LICENSE=1** – Keeps the license keys when Workstation Pro is uninstalled. This is the default setting.
- **KEEP_LICENSE=0** – Removes the license keys when Workstation Pro is uninstalled.
- **KEEP_SETTINGFILES=1** – Keeps the settings files when Workstation Pro is uninstalled. This is the default setting.
- **KEEP_SETTINGFILES=0** – Removes the settings files when Workstation Pro is uninstalled.

- **SERIALNUMBER** - Allows you to enter a valid license key when Workstation Pro is installed. Type in the license key including the hyphens in the following format: "xxxxx-xxxxx-xxxxx-xxxxx-xxxxx".
- **SOFTWAREUPDATEURL** - Allows you to specify your own custom URL for managing any software updates. You can point to an internal URL rather than the VMware website so you can effectively control what new versions get installed. By default, updates come via the VMware sites.
- **STARTMENU_SHORTCUT=1** - Creates a start menu item when Workstation Pro is installed. This is the default setting.
- **STARTMENU_SHORTCUT=0** - No start menu item is created when Workstation Pro is installed.
- **SUPPORTURL** - Allows you to set a support URL or email alias so that end users can contact support with product issues through the Workstation Pro Help menu. This could be an internal support site within your organization.

In the next section, we are going to look at the MSI file.

Extracting the MSI File for Installation

In this section, we are going to look at how to get access to the core MSI file that is used by the Workstation Pro installer.

This can then be used by an endpoint management solution for delivering the installation at scale throughout an enterprise environment.

We are not going to cover all the MSI commands or how to configure MECM and Intune in this section, just how to access the core MSI file.

To do this, follow the steps described:

1. Download the version of Workstation Pro for which you want to access the MSI file for.

2. Copy the downloaded Workstation Pro installer into a temporary folder such as C:\temp as shown in Figure 8-3.

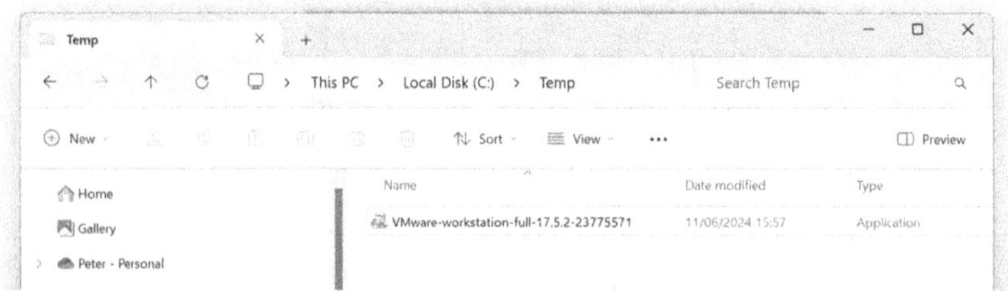

Figure 8-3. *Copying the Workstation Pro Installer into a Temp Folder*

3. Now launch the Workstation Pro installer.

4. You will see the **Welcome to the VMware Workstation Pro Setup Wizard** as shown in Figure 8-4.

Figure 8-4. *Workstation Pro Setup Wizard*

5. Do not click **Next** as we are not going to use the installer. Launching the installer is purely to access the MSI which will now have been copied to another folder as we will see in the next step.

6. Now open a Windows Explorer session.

7. Navigate to the following folder location:

   C:\Users\vonov\AppData\Local\Temp\{40EB739C-B694-40E3-8F80-631209827A5D}~setup

   In your environment, you will have a different user directory that reflects the current logged in user C:\Users\<user>\. Also, the GUID will be different. You will see that the folder with the GUID name will have been created at the same time you launched the Workstation Pro installer.

8. Open the GUID folder as shown in Figure 8-5.

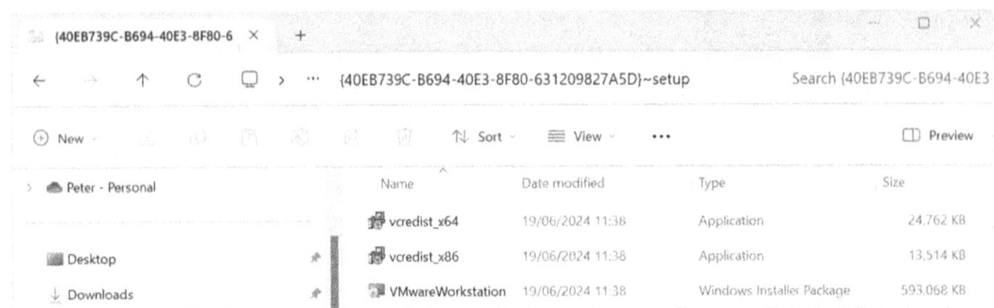

Figure 8-5. *VMwareWorkstation MSI Files*

9. Now copy the **vcredist_x86.exe** file, the **vcredist_x64.exe** file, and the **VMwareWorkstation.msi** file to a new folder, for example, C:\Install as shown in Figure 8-6.

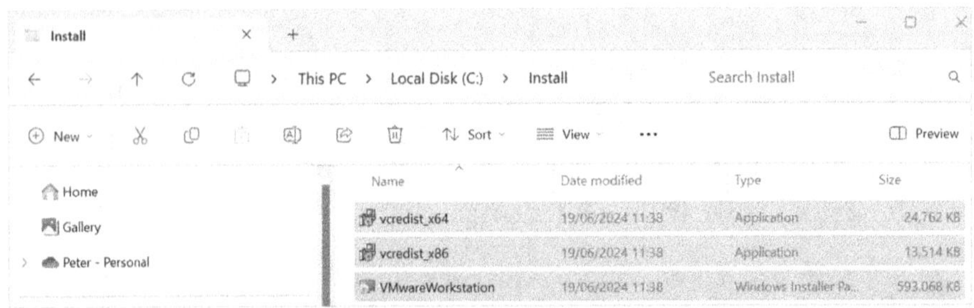

Figure 8-6. *VMwareWorkstation MSI Files Copied to Install Folder*

10. To complete the installation using the MSI installer, you will need to run the following commands:

```
vcredist_x86.exe /install /quiet /norestart

vcredist_x64.exe /install /quiet /norestart

msiexec.exe /i VMwareWorkstation.msi
```

With the latter of the commands, you can then add the command switches that we discussed in the previous section.

We have now looked at how to extract and use the MSI installer file for installing Workstation Pro.

Summary

In this chapter, we have looked at the options for installing Workstation Pro in an unattended mode, detailing all the different options that can be configured as part of that installation.

We looked at both the options using the InstallShield version of the installer and the `VMware-workstation-full-17.5.2-23775571.exe` option and the command line switches that go with it.

Next, we looked at how to extract the core MSI installer file and how to install Workstation Pro using the msiexec command along with the various command line switches.

In the next chapter, we are going to look at what's new in the latest version of WorkStation Pro since the publication of Volume 1 of this book.

CHAPTER 9

What's New

In the previous *Workstation Pro* book, Volume 1, we focused on version 17.0.1 when demonstrating the more practical steps such as installation and building virtual machines.

Since the publication of that book, several newer and updated versions of Workstation Pro have been released, and so in this final chapter, we are going to look at what has changed since the publication of Volume 1.

We will discuss each of the new releases since version 17.0.1 and what has changed in terms of features if anything has changed or if it is just a bug fix release.

VMware follows the standard software versioning process using the **X.Y.Z** format, where **X** is a major version release, **Y** is a minor version release, and **Z** is a patch release.

Workstation Pro Releases

Since Volume 1 was published, there have been a total of four updates which we will now look at in order of the version number.

P. von Oven, *Learning VMware Workstation Pro for Windows: Volume 2*,
https://doi.org/10.1007/979-8-8688-0864-7_9

Workstation Pro 17.0.2

In April 2023, Workstation Pro 17.0.2 was released with a build number of 21581411. As we highlighted above, this is just a patch release. The patch in this instance fixed two Common Vulnerabilities and Exposures (CVE): CVE-2023-20869 and CVE-2023-20870.

Another fix in this version was to resolve an issue when upgrading from 17.0.0 or 17.0.1 whereby the Workstation Pro application failed to close when the upgrade installer launched.

Workstation Pro 17.5

As a minor version release, launched in October 2023 (Build 22583795), Workstation Pro 17.5 introduced some new features:

- New security enhancements:
    - New encryption scheme using XTS instead of CBC that enables the for maximum protection without the overhead and potential reduction in performance
- Control virtual machines using the VMRUN command:
    - Power virtual machines on or off, capture snapshots, manage network adapters, run an executable program, manage files and directories, and manage processes running on the operating system, which we covered in Chapter 3 of this book
- Import and export virtual machines with vTPM device:
    - Allows you to import or export a virtual machine using the OVF Tool even with a vTPM device enabled

- Manage power operations of encrypted virtual machines using VMREST API:
    - Allows you to power on or power off, suspend, pause, resume, or retrieve the state of an encrypted virtual machine using the VMREST API service
- VMware hardware version 21:
    - Support for up to 256 NVMe devices: 4 controllers and 64 devices per controller
    - Support for NVMe 1.3 in Windows 11 and Windows Server 2022 guest operating systems

Workstation Pro 17.5.1

As a patch version release, launched in February 2024 (Build 23298084), this release just contained a fix for CVE-2024-22251.

Workstation Pro 17.5.2

Released in May 2024, Workstation Pro 17.5.2 (Build 23775571) is just a patch release that fixes CVE-2024-22267, CVE-2024-22268, CVE-2024-22269, and CVE-2024-22270.

However, there was one other significant change with this release and that is the way Workstation Pro is licensed.

Workstation Pro is now available for free for personal usage and is licensed in that way by default when you install it. The same is true for Workstation Player.

Ultimately that means that you don't need a license key if you are using Workstation Pro for personal use.

If you want to continue to use Workstation Pro in a commercial environment, i.e., for business use, then you will need a commercial subscription and associated license key. The commercial subscriptions are now offered through a single Desktop Hypervisor Pro product SKU.

To find out more about the new subscription model of licensing Workstation Pro, then click the following link to the Broadcom support website:

`https://knowledge.broadcom.com/external/article?articleNumber=315642`

The final point to discuss in this chapter, given the acquisition of VMware by Broadcom, is where do Workstation and other desktop hypervisor solutions sit.

Broadcom Ownership

One final thing to discuss is where do the Workstation Pro and Workstation Player solution fit within the Broadcom product portfolio.

The first question to answer is that although these solutions fall under the desktop category, or end-user computing, they remain within VMware Broadcom camp. They are not part of the divesture to Omnissa and so will continue to be developed and supported by Broadcom.

This is also true of the Linux versions of Workstation Pro and Workstation Player as well as Fusion (the Apple Mac version of the desktop hypervisor solution) although not covered by these books.

Summary

In this chapter, we have looked at the new versions of Workstation Pro that have been released subsequently to the publication of Volume 1 of this book.

We looked at those new versions and what each one contained, whether that be a simple patch update or a minor version that contained new features.

The biggest of those new features was in the way that Workstation Pro and the other desktop hypervisor solutions are licensed.

That now brings us to the end of this book. I hope that you found the content useful and that it will help you to plan, design, install, and manage your own Workstation Pro and Workstation Player environments.

Index

A

B

C

P. von Oven, *Learning VMware Workstation Pro for Windows: Volume 2*,
https://doi.org/10.1007/979-8-8688-0864-7

D

E

F

G

H

P

U

V

W

X, Y

Z

GPSR Compliance
The European Union's (EU) General Product Safety Regulation (GPSR) is a set of rules that requires consumer products to be safe and our obligations to ensure this.

If you have any concerns about our products, you can contact us on

ProductSafety@springernature.com

In case Publisher is established outside the EU, the EU authorized representative is:

Springer Nature Customer Service Center GmbH
Europaplatz 3
69115 Heidelberg, Germany

www.ingramcontent.com/pod-product-compliance
Lightning Source LLC
LaVergne TN
LVHW010335260326
834688LV00036B/721
* 9 7 9 8 8 6 8 8 0 8 6 3 0 *